# HANDBOOK

## TO THE

## UNIFORM MECHANICAL CODE

*An illustrative commentary*

**International Conference of Building Officials**

*Second Printing*

ISBN 1-58001-007-5

Publication Date: April 1998

COPYRIGHT © 1998
by

**INTERNATIONAL CONFERENCE OF BUILDING OFFICIALS**
5360 WORKMAN MILL ROAD
WHITTIER, CALIFORNIA 90601-2298

PRINTED IN THE U.S.A.

# *Preface*

The *Uniform Mechanical Code*™ (UMC) is designed to provide complete requirements for the installation and maintenance of heating, ventilating, cooling and refrigeration systems. This code is a publication of the International Conference of Building Officials (ICBO).

The *Uniform Mechanical Code* is one of a family of codes and related publications published by ICBO and other organizations, such as the International Fire Code Institute, which have similar goals as far as code publications are concerned. The *Uniform Mechanical Code* is designed to be compatible with the other codes, as together they make up the enforcement tools of a jurisdiction.

The code is divided into the following major subdivisions:

1.  The text of the *Uniform Mechanical Code* (sometimes referred to as "the body of the code").

2.  The appendices.

As discussed in Section 103, Appendix A is an integral part of the UMC; the provisions of Appendices B and C do not apply unless specifically included in the adoption ordinance of the jurisdiction enforcing the code.

In this handbook, wherever reference is made to "this code," "the code," "UMC" or the "*Uniform Mechanical Code,*" the reference is to the 1997 edition of the *Uniform Mechanical Code.*

The format to be followed in this handbook is to present commentary only for those portions of the code for which commentary would be useful in furthering the understanding of the provision and its intent. Commentary will not be provided for those sections of the code for which commentary would be redundant or where the intent is obvious.

The reader will note throughout the code that there are section headings that follow the section numbers and are intended to be descriptive of the material encompassed in the section that follows. The section headings are printed in the *Uniform Mechanical Code* for convenience only, and as they are outside of the actual section, they are not part of the code itself as far as the enforceable provisions of the code are concerned.

## Common Code Format and Metrication

In 1993, a task committee composed of representatives of the International Conference of Building Officials, Building Officials and Code Administrators International, Southern Building Code Congress International, American Society of Heating, Refrigerating and Air-conditioning Engineers, Inc., and the American Institute of Architects developed an outline of chapters for use by the model mechanical codes as an initial step in establishing a common code format. This was only an initial step, which facilitated the use of the model codes by architects, engineers and designers. The common chapter format assists in locating provisions dealing with a specific subject in each of the model mechanical codes. The initial effort was not directed at unifying specific requirements, but it would be logical to assume that unification would be a future effort.

The 1997 *Uniform Mechanical Code* has also been metricated as an aid to architects and engineers who are working on federally funded projects. In general, the converted value is a "soft conversion" that follows the inch-pound (IP) value in parentheses. Conversion to "hard" values will follow as the economics of metricated production may dictate. For figures, metric equivalent formulas immediately follow the English formula and are denoted by "For **SI:**" preceding the metric equivalent.

# FOREWORD

The preparation of this handbook began as a project of the International Association of Plumbing and Mechanical Officials' (IAPMO) Education Committee in 1976. Over the years, many talented individuals have worked on and contributed to its development. Among those whose contributions we gratefully acknowledge are:

Gordon Aleshire

Frank Axen

Denvert H. Boney

Steven Brandvold

Vincent Canzano

William Carroll

John Carter

Roger Davidson

Mario Fala

Roy Fetterley

Jim Finn

Glenn Gearhard

Robert Guenther

Walter Haire

Grace Harper

Sivert O. Hendrickson

Drew Johnese

John La Torra

Arthur J. Lettenmaier

Charles Lunt

George McConnell

Ray Maggard

Carl Marbery

Robert Martin

Fady Mattar

William Maynard

Kenneth O'Guinn

David Olson

Phillip H. Ribbs

Robert Ritchie

Ed Schoenfeld

Bill Schweitzer

Al Spadoni

Emil Vaccarezza

Ed Wachter

John Watts

Lloyd Weaver

Please accept my apologies if you contributed to this project and are not listed above. Let me know of any omissions, and they will be corrected in the next printing.

Gordon F. Clyde
Senior Staff Engineer
International Conference of Building Officials

# CODES AND RELATED PUBLICATIONS

The International Conference of Building Officials (ICBO) publishes a family of codes, each correlated with the *Uniform Building Code* ™ to provide jurisdictions with a complete set of building-related regulations for adoption. Some of these codes are published in affiliation with other organizations such as the International Fire Code Institute (IFCI) and the International Code Council (ICC). Reference materials and related codes also are available to improve knowledge of code enforcement and administration of building inspection programs. Publications and products are continually being added, so inquiries should be directed to Conference headquarters for a listing of available products. Many codes and references are also available on CD-ROM or floppy disk. These are denoted by (*). The following publications and products are available from ICBO:

## CODES

**\*Uniform Building Code**, Volumes 1, 2 and 3. The most widely adopted model building code in the United States, the performance-based *Uniform Building Code* is a proven document, meeting the needs of government units charged with the enforcement of building regulations. Volume 1 contains administrative, fire- and life-safety and field inspection provisions; Volume 2 contains structural engineering design provisions; and Volume 3 contains material, testing and installation standards.

**\*Uniform Mechanical Code** ™. Provides a complete set of requirements for the design, construction, installation and maintenance of heating, ventilating, cooling and refrigeration systems; incinerators and other heat-producing appliances.

**International Plumbing Code** ™. Provides consistent and technically advanced requirements that can be used across the country to provide comprehensive regulations of modern plumbing systems. Setting minimum regulations for plumbing facilities in terms of performance objectives, the IPC provides for the acceptance of new and innovative products, materials and systems.

**International Private Sewage Disposal Code** ™. Provides flexibility in the development of safety and sanitary individual sewage disposal systems and includes detailed provisions for all aspects of design, installation and inspection of private sewage disposal systems.

**International Mechanical Code** ™. Establishes minimum regulations for mechanical systems using prescriptive and performance-related provisions. It is founded on broad-based principles that make possible the use of new materials and new mechanical designs.

**Uniform Zoning Code** ™. This code is dedicated to intelligent community development and to the benefit of the public welfare by providing a means of promoting uniformity in zoning laws and enforcement.

**\*Uniform Fire Code** ™, Volumes 1 and 2. The premier model fire code in the United States, the *Uniform Fire Code* sets forth provisions necessary for fire prevention and fire protection. Published by the International Fire Code Institute, the *Uniform Fire Code* is endorsed by the Western Fire Chiefs Association, the International Association of Fire Chiefs and ICBO. Volume 1 contains code provisions compatible with the *Uniform Building Code*, and Volume 2 contains standards referenced from the code provisions.

**\*Urban-Wildland Interface Code** ™. Promulgated by IFCI, this code regulates both land use and the built environment in designated urban-wildland interface areas. This newly developed code is the only model code that bases construction requirements on the fire-hazard severity exposed to the structure. Developed under a grant from the Federal Emergency Management Agency, this code is the direct result of hazard mitigation meetings held after devastating wildfires.

**Uniform Housing Code** ™. Provides complete requirements affecting conservation and rehabilitation of housing. Its regulations are compatible with the *Uniform Building Code*.

**Uniform Code for the Abatement of Dangerous Buildings** ™. A code compatible with the *Uniform Building Code* and the *Uniform Housing Code* which provides equitable remedies consistent with other laws for the repair, vacation or demolition of dangerous buildings.

**Uniform Sign Code** ™. Dedicated to the development of better sign regulation, its requirements pertain to all signs and sign construction attached to buildings.

**Uniform Administrative Code** ™. This code covers administrative areas in connection with adoption of the *Uniform Building Code*,

*Uniform Mechanical Code* and related codes. It contains provisions which relate to site preparation, construction, alteration, moving, repair and use and occupancies of buildings or structures and building service equipment, including plumbing, electrical and mechanical regulations. The code is compatible with the administrative provisions of all codes published by the Conference.

**Uniform Building Security Code** ™. This code establishes minimum standards to make dwelling units resistant to unlawful entry. It regulates swinging doors, sliding doors, windows and hardware in connection with dwelling units of apartment houses or one- and two-family dwellings. The code gives consideration to the concerns of police, fire and building officials in establishing requirements for resistance to burglary which are compatible with fire and life safety.

**Uniform Code for Building Conservation** ™. A building conservation guideline presented in code format which will provide a community with the means to preserve its existing buildings while achieving appropriate levels of safety. It is formatted in the same manner as the *Uniform Building Code*, is compatible with other Uniform Codes, and may be adopted as a code or used as a guideline.

**Dwelling Construction under the Uniform Building Code** ™. Designed primarily for use in home building and apprentice training, this book contains requirements applicable to the construction of one- and two-story dwellings based on the requirements of the *Uniform Building Code*. Available in English or Spanish.

**Dwelling Construction under the Uniform Mechanical Code** ™. This publication is for the convenience of the homeowner or contractor interested in installing mechanical equipment in a one- or two-family dwelling in conformance with the *Uniform Mechanical Code*.

**Supplements to UBC and related codes.** Published in the years between editions, the Supplements contain all approved changes, plus an analysis of those changes.

**Uniform Building Code—1927 Edition.** A special 60th anniversary printing of the first published *Uniform Building Code*.

**One and Two Family Dwelling Code.** Promulgated by ICC, this code eliminates conflicts and duplications among the model codes to achieve national uniformity. Covers mechanical and plumbing requirements as well as construction and occupancy.

**Application and Commentary on the One and Two Family Dwelling Code.** An interpretative commentary on the *One and Two Family Dwelling Code* intended to enhance uniformity of interpretation and application of the code nationwide. Developed by the three model code organizations, this document includes numerous illustrations of code requirements and the rationale for individual provisions.

**Model Energy Code.** This code includes minimum requirements for effective use of energy in the design of new buildings and structures and additions to existing buildings. It is based on American Society of Heating, Refrigeration and Air-conditioning Engineers Standard 90A-1980 and was originally developed jointly by ICBO, BOCA, SBCCI and the National Conference of States on Building Codes and Standards under a contract funded by the United States Department of Energy. The code is now maintained by ICC and is adopted by reference in the *Uniform Building Code*.

**National Electrical Code** ®. The electrical code used throughout the United States. Published by the National Fire Protection Association, it is an indispensable aid to every electrician, contractor, architect, builder, inspector and anyone who must specify or certify electrical installations.

## TECHNICAL REFERENCES AND EDUCATIONAL MATERIALS

**Analysis of Revisions to the Uniform Codes™.** An analysis of changes between the previous and new editions of the Uniform Codes is provided. Changes between code editions are noted either at the beginning of chapters or in the margins of the code text.

***Handbook to the Uniform Building Code.*** The handbook is a completely detailed and illustrated commentary on the *Uniform Building Code,* tracing historical background and rationale of the codes through the current edition. Also included are numerous drawings and figures clarifying the application and intent of the code provisions. Also available in electronic format.

***Handbook to the Uniform Mechanical Code.*** An indispensable tool for understanding the provisions of the current UMC, the handbook traces the historical background and rationale behind the UMC provisions, includes 160 figures which clarify the intent and application of the code, and provides a chapter-by-chapter analysis of the UMC.

***Uniform Building Code Application Manual.*** This manual discusses sections of the *Uniform Building Code* with a question-and-answer format, providing a comprehensive analysis of the intent of the code sections. Most sections include illustrative examples. The manual is in loose-leaf format so that code applications published in *Building Standards* magazine may be inserted. Also available in electronic format.

***Uniform Mechanical Code Application Manual.*** As a companion document to the *Uniform Mechanical Code,* this manual provides a comprehensive analysis of the intent of a number of code sections in an easy-to-use question-and-answer format. The manual is available in a loose-leaf format and includes illustrative examples for many code sections.

***Uniform Fire Code Applications Manual.*** This newly developed manual provides questions and answers regarding UFC provisions. A comprehensive analysis of the intent of numerous code sections, the manual is in a loose-leaf format for easy insertion of code applications published in IFCI's *Fire Code Journal.*

**Quick-Reference Guide to the Occupancy Requirements of the 1997 UBC.** Code requirements are compiled in this publication by occupancy groups for quick access. These tabulations assemble requirements for each occupancy classification in the code. Provisions, such as fire-resistive ratings for occupancy separations in Table 3-B, exterior wall and opening protection requirements in Table 5-A-1, and fire-resistive ratings for types of construction in Table 6-A, are tabulated for quick reference and comparison.

**Plan Review Manual.** A practical text that will assist and guide both the field inspector and plan reviewer in applying the code requirements. This manual covers the nonstructural and basic structural aspects of plan review.

**Field Inspection Manual.** An important fundamental text for courses of study at the community college and trade or technical school level. It is an effective text for those studying building construction or architecture and includes sample forms and checklists for use in the field.

**Building Department Administration.** An excellent guide for improvement of skills in departmental management and in the enforcement and application of the Building Code and other regulations administered by a building inspection department. This textbook will also be a valuable aid to instructors, students and those in related professional fields.

**Building Department Guide to Disaster Mitigation.** This new, expanded guide is designed to assist building departments in developing or updating disaster mitigation plans. Subjects covered include guidelines for damage mitigation, disaster-response management, immediate response, mutual aid and inspections, working with the media, repair and recovery policies, and public information bulletins. This publication is a must for those involved in preparing for and responding to disaster.

**Building Official Management Manual.** This manual addresses the unique nature of code administration and the managerial duties of the building official. A supplementary insert addresses the budgetary and financial aspects of a building department. It is also an ideal resource for those preparing for the management module of the CABO Building Official Certification Examination.

**Legal Aspects of Code Administration.** A manual developed by the three model code organizations to inform the building official on the legal aspects of the profession. The text is written in a logical sequence with explanation of legal terminology. It is designed to serve as a refresher for those preparing to take the legal module of the CABO Building Official Certification Examination.

**Illustrated Guide to Conventional Construction Provisions of the UBC.** This comprehensive guide and commentary provides detailed explanations of the conventional construction provisions in the UBC, including descriptive discussions and illustrated drawings to convey the prescriptive provisions related to wood-frame construction.

**Introduction to the Uniform Building Code.** A workbook that provides an overview of the basics of the UBC.

**Uniform Building Code Update Workbook.** This manual addresses many of the changes to the administrative, fire- and life-safety, and inspection provisions appearing in the UBC.

**UMC Workbook.** Designed for independent study or use with instructor-led programs based on the *Uniform Mechanical Code,* this comprehensive study guide consists of 16 learning sessions, with the first two sessions reviewing the purpose, scope, definitions and administrative provisions and the remaining 14 sessions progressively exploring the requirements for installing, inspecting and maintaining heating, ventilating, cooling and refrigeration systems.

**UBC Field Inspection Workbook.** A comprehensive workbook for studying the provisions of the UBC. Divided into 12 sessions, this workbook focuses on the UBC combustible construction requirements for the inspection of wood-framed construction.

**Concrete Manual.** A publication for individuals seeking an understanding of the fundamentals of concrete field technology and inspection practices. Of particular interest to concrete construction inspectors, it will also benefit employees of concrete producers, contractors, testing and inspection laboratories and material suppliers.

**Reinforced Concrete Masonry Construction Inspector's Handbook.** A comprehensive information source written especially for masonry inspection covering terminology, technology, materials, quality control, inspection and standards. Published jointly by ICBO and the Masonry Institute of America.

**You Can Build It!** Sponsored by ICBO in cooperation with CABO, this booklet contains information and advice to aid "do-it-yourselfers" with building projects. Provides guidance in necessary procedures such as permit requirements, codes, plans, cost estimation, etc.

**Guidelines for Manufactured Housing Installations.** A guideline in code form implementing the *Uniform Building Code* and its companion code documents to regulate the permanent installation of a manufactured home on a privately owned, nonrental site. A commentary is included to explain specific provisions, and codes applying to each component part are defined.

**Accessibility Reference Guide.** This guide is a valuable resource for architects, interior designers, plan reviewers and others who design and enforce accessibility provisions. Features include accessibility requirements, along with detailed commentary and graphics to clarify the provisions; cross-references to other applicable sections of the UBC and the Americans with Disabilities Act Accessibility Guidelines; a checklist of UBC provisions on access and usability requirements; and many other useful references.

**Educational and Technical Reference Materials.** The Conference has been a leader in the development of texts and course material to assist in the educational process. These materials include vital information necessary for the building official and subordinates in carrying out their responsibilities and have proven to be excellent references in connection with community college curricula and higher-level courses in the field of building construction technology and inspection and in the administration of building departments. Included are plan review checklists for structural, nonstructural, mechanical and fire-safety provisions and a full line of videotapes and automated products.

# TABLE OF CONTENTS

# Chapter 1
# ADMINISTRATION

### Part I—General

In addition to title and scope, Chapter 1 covers general subjects such as the purpose of the code, applications to existing mechanical systems, performance provisions relating to alternate materials and methods of construction, modifications, and tests. The provisions in Chapter 1 are of such a general nature that they apply to the entire *Uniform Mechanical Code* (UMC).

The *Uniform Mechanical Code* generally follows the format of the *Uniform Building Code*™ (UBC) in its administrative regulations because the provisions of both codes are derived from the *Uniform Administrative Code*™ (UAC). When the UAC was first proposed, proponents envisioned that it would supplant administrative provisions in each of the technical codes, but that concept was not fully accepted because it meant that each inspector would have to carry at least two codes. The general consensus is that the advantages of having both administrative and technical requirements consolidated in a single volume outweighs the ease with which administrative provisions for all the codes could be amended at one time.

Local jurisdictions are attracted more and more by the ease and efficiency with which model codes can be adopted by reference[1] rather than by transcription. Transcription requires that the full text of an ordinance be printed two or three times—a very unwieldy and expensive process. A sample ordinance for adoption by reference is provided in both the UBC and the UMC.

## SECTION 102 — PURPOSE

The requirements of the UMC are regarded as minimum provisions to safeguard life or limb, health, property, and public welfare. The specifications for a particular project may be for a more stringent standard or for higher quality than minimum code provisions. Requirements for quality above the minimum provisions specified in the code are a matter of contractual agreement between the owner and contractor; these requirements are not imposed by the building department, but are enforceable when included on approved plans.

Care must be exercised in approving a deviation from the approved plans as the effect on the entire system must be considered even though the change may be within minimum requirements.

The statement in the second paragraph of Section 102 regarding the establishment of special groups or classes of persons to be especially "protected or benefited" by the code is self-explanatory and is included to limit the liability of the adopting jurisdiction.

A discussion of the term "public welfare" contained in Section 101.2 of the *Handbook to the Uniform Building Code* is also relevant to the UMC and is as follows:

The purpose of the code is more inclusive than most people realize. A careful [reader] will note that in addition to providing for life safety and safeguarding property, the code also intends that its provisions protect the public welfare. This latter item, "public welfare," is not so often thought of as being part of the purpose of a building code. However, in the case of the UBC, safeguarding public welfare is a part of its purpose, which is accomplished by the code, for example, by its provisions which ameliorate the conditions found in substandard or dangerous buildings. Moreover, upon the adoption of a modern building code such as the UBC, the general level of building safety and quality is raised. This in turn contributes to the public welfare by increasing the tax base and livability. Additionally, slum conditions are reduced, and the consequent reduction of insanitary conditions contributes to safeguarding the public welfare. For example, the maintenance requirements of Section 3402 apply to all buildings, both existing and new, and as a result the continued enforcement of the UBC slows the development of slum conditions. A rigorous enforcement of Section 3402 will actually reduce the conditions which contribute to slums. Thus, public welfare is enhanced by the increased benefits which inure to the general public of the jurisdiction as a result of the code provisions.

## SECTION 103 — SCOPE

The intent of this code is to regulate the design and installation of systems and equipment which directly and indirectly have an effect on the building environment. This includes virtually all equipment or systems that use any form of energy, as evidenced by the wording in the first sentence of Section 103 which includes "miscellaneous heat-producing appliances."

One area of enforcement that is often overlooked and neglected is industrial processing equipment. Even though the code does not directly address the many varieties of such equipment, it is the intent of the code and responsibility of the building official to regulate the installation and maintenance of this equipment.

---

[1]O'Bannon, Robert E. (1989). *Building Department Administration.* International Conference of Building Officials, Whittier, California, pages 414-420.

## SECTION 104 — APPLICATION TO EXISTING MECHANICAL SYSTEMS

**104.1 Additions, Alterations or Repairs.** The general rule is that existing mechanical systems may be retained in service and new additions are required to conform to the current code. That is, application of the *Uniform Mechanical Code* is not retroactive; it does not require that existing systems be upgraded each time a new edition of the code is adopted. With the approval of the building official, minor repairs, additions or alterations may be made to existing mechanical systems in accordance with the code in effect at the time the original system was installed. Alterations, additions or repairs must not cause an existing system to become unsafe, overloaded, or to create unhealthy conditions for the occupants.

Checking for unsafe conditions includes inspection for excessive pressure, temperature and improper fuel use. Spillage of flue gas could indicate a need for increased vent or flue diameter, the abnormal chilling of flue gases, or a need for a requirement for power venting. Overloading may indicate the need for larger diameter piping, larger motors, larger ducts, or electrical wiring.

A mechanical system that has been performing safely and satisfactorily may, with the approval of the building official, be repaired, altered or have minor additions made in accordance with the laws in effect at the time the original installation was made.

### Inspection Checklist

A partial checklist for additions to a gas heating system would include an evaluation of the following factors:

**Fuel Supply**

____ Shutoff valve for each appliance.

____ Correct fuel for appliance.

____ Fuel-gas supply piping has adequate capacity and is in safe condition.

____ Meter size will permit delivery of the connected demand.

____ Connector sizing is correct.

**Air Supply**

____ Combustion and ventilation air openings properly sized.

____ Location of appliance.

____ Screening of openings.

____ Location of combustion air openings.

**Appliances**

____ Clearance from combustibles.

____ Working space clearances.

____ Drainage for water and discharge from temperature and pressure-relief valve.

____ Listed for installation on combustible flooring.

____ Other appropriate listings or manufacturer's installation instructions.

____ Any required backflow protection device.

**Venting System and Vent Connectors**

____ Capacity.

____ Flue gas temperature.

____ Clearances from combustible construction.

____ Multiple appliance connections or manifolds.

____ Fastening of sections and support.

**Electrical Installation**

____ Correct voltage, amperage and phase.

____ Electrical disconnect.

____ Lighting.

____ Convenience outlet.

Similar checklists may be developed for other mechanical installations.

**104.2 Existing Installations.** The concern for mechanical systems lawfully in existence is that their use, maintenance and repair have remained in accordance with the original design and location, and that hazards to life, health and property have not been created. If it is discovered that a system has been relocated, further investigation into the code in effect at the time of the relocation will be necessary to establish the true nature of the system's nonconforming entitlement. In this connection, it may be helpful to know that the first *Uniform Mechanical Code* was published in 1967. Prior to 1967, there was an Appendix Chapter 51 in the *Uniform Building Code* entitled "Heat-producing Appliances," which was available for specific adoption. Also, the Western Plumbing Officials Association, the organization which became the International Association of Plumbing and Mechanical Officials, published the *Uniform Heating and Comfort Cooling Code* in 1959, 1961 and 1964. By agreement between IAPMO and ICBO, the *Uniform Heating and Comfort Cooling Code* was discontinued when the *Uniform Mechanical Code* became available.

**104.4 Maintenance.** This section has the effect of charging the building official with the responsibility of seeing that all buildings, both existing and new, are maintained properly. This section does not require that the building official develop a schedule for reinspection of existing buildings to determine whether or not they are being properly maintained. However, it does give the building official the authority to make a reinspection of any structure if there is reason to believe that the building has been improperly maintained. As discussed in Section 102, vigorous enforcement of this section will have the effect of reducing existing deficient or unsafe conditions.

An owner is responsible for maintenance of a building's systems in a safe and hazard-free condition. Often the owner is difficult to locate or identify. In cases of a life-safety hazard, it may become necessary for the building official to order a utility disconnected; this action may also have the secondary effect of identifying the owner or the owner's representative, but it must not be used indiscriminately. The *Uniform Code for the Abatement of Dangerous Buildings*™ is available for adoption in jurisdictions having hazardous conditions warranting abatement proceedings. The jurisdiction's legal counsel must be consulted for procedural advice when issuing a notice and order to repair a mechanical system.

**104.5 Moved Buildings.** This section takes into consideration that the movement of a building may often involve changes in use and occupancy. There is also concern for damage resulting from lifting and transportation, so testing of all systems is essential. The intent of the code is that moving a building essentially creates a new structure which is required to comply with all current requirements.

## SECTION 105 — ALTERNATE MATERIALS AND METHODS OF CONSTRUCTION

The intent of this section is to allow the use of new technologies that are not currently provided for in the code.

The building official has a number of criteria for approving the use of alternate materials and methods. Evaluation, research reports or recommendations of a professional staff or a committee of experts may be used as a guideline in issuing approvals.

Research reports cover many materials that will prove to be of assistance to personnel administering the UMC, particularly in fuel-gas piping and hydronic systems. A few large jurisdictions operate their own testing facilities, but in general, medium-sized and small jurisdictions will not enjoy this advantage. Listings by agencies that have been approved by the building official in connection with the reference standards compiled in Part III of Chapter 16 will in most instances provide the criteria needed to determine the acceptability of mechanical equipment. In discharging responsibility for approving equipment, it is well to recognize that the standards used by listing agencies may not always coincide with the requirements of the UMC. Thus, it is necessary to review reports of testing to be sure that the standard employed is consistent with code requirements.

An example is that the Underwriters Laboratories® (UL®) uses National Fire Protection Association (NFPA) 96 to evaluate commercial kitchen ventilating systems. National Fire Protection Association 96 and Part II of Chapter 5 of the UMC are not identical; hence, it is not safe to assume that a commercial kitchen hood and duct system that UL has evaluated for compliance with NFPA 96 will also comply with the requirements of the UMC and UBC. Code requirements must be checked for each appliance or device.

## SECTION 106 — MODIFICATIONS

The intent of this section is to allow a deviation from the code when compliance, usually due to physical or structural conditions, will cause a hardship.

## SECTION 107 — TESTS

This section provides the building official with discretionary authority to require tests to substantiate proof of compliance with code requirements and the intent of the code.

It is quite possible to have a good product and a substandard or inappropriate application. Inspectors can often prevent misapplication of products or equipment by discussing with an applicant the scope and the extent of the installation before any work begins. Evaluation of products by an independent agency is not normally something that can be done efficiently at a jobsite. The tests frequently require laboratory conditions and equipment that cannot be duplicated in the field.

The following is a list of generally accepted testing organizations and the product directories they provide:

- International Approval Services (IAS)

  *Directory of AGA and CGA Certified Appliances and Accessories*

- Underwriters Laboratories, Inc. (UL)

  *Gas and Oil Equipment Directory*

  *Fire Protection Equipment Directory*

  *Electrical Appliance and Utilization Equipment Directory*

  *Building Materials Directory*

  *Fire Resistance Directory*

  *Hazardous Location Electrical Equipment Directory*

- Underwriters Laboratories of Canada (Issues product directories covering many of the same equipment categories as UL in the United States.)

In addition to the above testing organizations, ICBO Evaluation Service, Inc. (ICBO ES), and IAPMO provide certification for a wide variety of testing laboratories that are usually recognized as "approved" agencies as defined in the UMC. It is important to recognize that many of these smaller testing agencies are competent in more restricted fields of testing than the larger nationally recognized agencies.

Standards-writing agencies may or may not maintain testing facilities. The following standards-promulgating agencies do not test equipment or material:

- American National Standards Institute (ANSI)
- American Society for Testing and Materials (ASTM)
- International Conference of Building Officials (ICBO)

  **NOTE:** The International Association of Plumbing and Mechanical Officials and ICBO ES evaluate reports prepared by independent testing agencies and, based on staff analysis and committee actions, compile and publish a directory of research recommendations (evaluation reports) for use by code administrators. The International Association of Plumbing and Mechanical Officials has recently announced the opening of a new test laboratory.

- American Gas Association (AGA)—A trade association. AGA's members include gas distribution, transmission, and service companies; gas appliance and equipment manufacturers; foreign affiliates; and individual members. A wholly owned subsidiary, AGA Laboratories performs testing for compliance with nationally recognized consensus standards and issued the *Directory of AGA Certified Appliances and Accessories,* which is now published by the

International Approval Services. The newly issued 1997 IAS Directory contains both designs certified by AGA or the Canadian Gas Association (CGA) or both, and is a larger publication.

- The National Sanitation Foundation (NSF)—An independent nonprofit organization that develops standards in environmental and public health areas. Much of NSF's emphasis in food-processing equipment is directed toward sanitation concerns such as cleanability, protection against contamination and durability in service.

## Part II—Organization and Enforcement

### SECTION 108 — POWERS AND DUTIES OF BUILDING OFFICIAL

**108.1 General.** This section authorizes and directs the building official to enforce the provisions of the UMC. Enforcement of the code can vary considerably among jurisdictions. Local policies are dictated by such variables as climatic conditions, flooding, freezing, snowfall, water quality or hardness, soil conditions, wind direction and intensity, type of structures, age of structures, surface topography, and altitude. Unusual conditions may prevail within certain areas or regions of a jurisdiction. Special applications of the code must be stressed in these regions to ensure satisfactory installation and operation of mechanical systems. In addition, the enforcement of codes can vary due to policies established by the building official.

**108.3 Right of Entry.** This section is compatible with United States Supreme Court decisions since the 1960s regarding acts of inspection personnel seeking entry to buildings for the purpose of making inspections. Under current case law, an inspection may not be made of property, whether it be a private residence or a business establishment, without first having secured permission from the owner or person in charge of the premises. If entry is refused by the person having control of the property, the building official must obtain an inspection warrant from a court having jurisdiction in order to secure entry. The important feature of the law regarding right of entry is that entry must be made only by permission of the person having control of the property, or lacking this permission, entry may be gained only through the use of an inspection warrant.

If entry is again refused after an inspection warrant has been obtained, the jurisdiction now has recourse through the courts to remedy this situation. One avenue is to obtain a civil injunction in which the court directs the person having control of the property to allow an inspection. Alternatively, the jurisdiction can initiate proceedings in criminal court for punishment of the person having control of the property. It cannot be repeated too strongly that criminal court proceedings should never be initiated against an

owner or other person having control of the property if an inspection warrant has not been obtained. Also, because the consequences of not following proper procedures can be so devastating to a jurisdiction if suit is brought against it, the jurisdiction's legal officer should always be consulted in these matters. For further reading on this subject, see Chapter 12 of *Building Department Administration.*[2]

**108.4 Stop Orders.** The most common reasons for the issuance of stop orders are because a permit for the work has not been issued or because of noncompliance with code requirements.

One reason for failure to obtain a permit for the installation is that no one ever intended to obtain a permit. Another reason is that someone thought that another person would secure the permit. Sometimes permits are denied due to building, zoning or licensing restrictions. Sometimes the person performing the work may not possess the required trade, business or contractor's license. In some cases, municipal or public utilities are overloaded, and new construction, building additions or alterations are suspended or postponed. This can be due to undersized or surcharged sewers, lack of water, or lack of adequate pressure. There may be inadequate gas or electric energy supplies. Town and regional planning or zoning decisions may also be a deterrent to the issuance of a permit.

A building official will seldom place a stop order for permitted work that is found defective during the first inspection. However, if the defective condition is not corrected, a stop order may be issued during a subsequent inspection, provided reasonable time has elapsed for correction of the problem noted during the first inspection.

**108.5 Authority to Disconnect Utilities in Emergencies.** Discretion must be employed in using this authority. The authority is generally used only when a building is on fire or has been severely damaged due to fire or explosion or has suffered structural damage. Action must be taken when the building official is concerned about public safety. A building official is required, when possible, to give written notification to the serving utility, as well as to the owner and occupant, of a decision to disconnect utilities.

[2]O'Bannon, Robert E. (1989). *Building Department Administration.* International Conference of Building Officials, Whittier, California.

When utilities are to be disconnected, the building official must immediately notify the owner or occupant and the utility supplier that such services have been disconnected at a certain time and date. All concerned must be cautious to avoid damage to structure, contents or equipment (including freezing or flooding in certain areas) due to the loss of energy supply. The decision to interrupt utilities is critical even when buildings are burning because shutting off fuel or electrical supplies will generally interrupt lighting, controls, fans, pumps and emergency water supplies; such equipment and services are often vital to firefighting. Emergency electrical generators may be operated with fuel gas from pipelines or liquefied petroleum gas from pressurized tanks. Some jurisdictions require that such emergency electrical generators have a separate gas piping system from the utility meter to the generator. These separate emergency generator fuel lines must be identified and care must be exercised to determine which services can be discontinued during the emergency. Depending on the type of structure, turning off utilities should be a last resort except in a small residential or commercial structure. Shutting off building services must be done at the direction of the fire officer, building official or utility supervisors so that the emergency equipment is not subverted.

**108.6 Authority to Condemn Equipment.** When equipment or a portion thereof regulated by the code has become hazardous to life, health or property, a written order to have it removed or restored to a safe and sanitary working condition is required. The written order should always contain a time limit for compliance (24, 48 or 72 hours, for example). If a time limit is not stipulated, there is a tendency to operate the system or equipment even with the written notice attached to it. Defective equipment must always be checked to ensure that it has either been repaired or removed by the expiration date of the notice. An accident resulting from the operation of defective equipment can be more than a personal tragedy; it is a failure to protect the public health and safety and it is often the beginning of lengthy litigation. The building department must be certain that unsafe equipment is not operated. The person who operates equipment may not be aware of the consequences of a violation or not anticipate the damage that may result from operation of defective equipment. Some defects, such as leaking piping, slipping belts and defective safety controls, are obvious. Many mechanical failures or suspected defects, such as spillage of flue gases at draft hoods, cracked heat exchangers, defective aquastats, defective thermostats or limit switches, or low water or high temperature and pressure indicators, remain undetected by unskilled persons but nevertheless constitute a major hazard.

The building official should determine that disconnected equipment is left in a safe condition. If fuel-gas piping is disconnected from an appliance, the piping must be securely capped or plugged. The ends of electrical wires that could be energized must be insulated and secured. Fuses must be removed and breakers must be shut off and tagged. Motors must be shut off at the circuit

breaker or motor control center and tagged (i.e., DON'T START). Pumps, piping, boilers, heaters and cooling systems must be drained to avoid corrosion or freezing. The ends of all piping systems must be plugged or capped whenever equipment is removed or disconnected. Closing shutoff valves is not adequate because valves may be opened through ignorance or vandalism. Provisions must be made to avoid the entry of foreign materials, including insects, into piping and equipment.

When the building official is aware that equipment at a premises is hazardous to life, health or property, it can be ordered removed or restored to a safe condition. The code provisions for condemnation of equipment may be applied to specific components of a mechanical system.

The second paragraph of Section 108.6 contains an important procedural provision regarding notices to owners, the serving utility and occupants when equipment or an installation is to be disconnected. Following delivery of the required notices, the building official is charged by the code with verifying that the disconnection has been accomplished. If equipment is maintained in violation of the notice to disconnect, the building official is required to prevent, restrain, correct or abate the violation. The salient point is that simply delivering or hanging the notice is not an adequate action in and of itself. The requirement is related to Section 108.9, which requires the cooperation of other officials of the jurisdiction.

**108.7 Connection after Order to Disconnect.** Reconnections to temporary sources of energy, fuel or power supply or from energy, fuel or power supply to any equipment that has been ordered disconnected is prohibited. This would usually be in the form of portable electric generators or fuel tanks, propane cylinders, or such portable or temporary fuel sources. Anyone making an illegal connection may be liable for resulting damage or injury, fires, etc., resulting from the operation of condemned equipment.

Many mechanical systems now have elaborate methods of programming, safety interlocks and automatic controls. The mechanical system must be thoroughly tested by the installers for leaks, correct rotation, alignment, vibration, electrical voltage, amperage, power phase, calorific value of fuel, pressures, types of liquids, refrigerants, lubricants, water and air supplies, to name a few.

When a mechanical system is reactivated, operating and safety controls must be thoroughly checked. Examples of these controls include stack switches, flow switches, aquastats, thermostats, high- or low-pressure switches, flow switches or low water or liquid level controls, plus temperature- and pressure-relief valves. All start-up or light-off and shut-down sequences must be checked to determine that the system will operate safely as originally designed and intended in compliance with regulations governing existing equipment. The entire system must be evaluated before a specific piece of equipment is authorized for operation.

The building official must authorize reconnection and use of equipment that has been condemned. It is advisable that a department representative be present to witness the testing and start up of equipment. Depending on the reason the equipment was condemned and the size or complexity of the equipment, it may also be advisable to have a start up scheduled with representation from the equipment manufacturer or supplier and the contractor who repaired the equipment. Further, an owner or authorized agent should also be present.

Sometimes it is advisable to include representatives from the serving utility and the insurers of the property or equipment so that everyone concerned with the operation of the equipment is satisfied or at least notified of the events relating to the condition and operation of the equipment within the system. Considerable detail has been expressed here regarding start up and recommissioning of equipment, but everything from purging and light off to the operation of safety controls must be considered. If caution is not exercised, an unsafe condition may be perpetuated rather than corrected.

**108.8 Liability.** It is the intent of the UMC that the building official shall not become personally liable for any damage that may occur to persons or property as a result of the building official's acts as long as he or she acts in good faith and without malice or fraud. However, there seems to be an increasing trend in the courts to find civil officers personally liable for careless acts. Section 108.8 requires that the jurisdiction defend the building official if a suit is brought against him or her. Furthermore, the code requires that any judgment resulting from a suit be assumed by the jurisdiction. Regardless of this language in the code, however, the jurisdiction may elect to not defend the building official on the basis, for example, that he or she acted carelessly.

The intent of the second paragraph is that the jurisdiction, by reason of its approvals authorized by the UMC, shall not assume the responsibility of the person owning or controlling the building or structure for damages to persons or property caused by any defects in the building. This provision is based on the doctrine that governmental actions of jurisdictions are not subject to liability. The courts have held that building department operations are governmental functions.

Case law regarding tort liability of building officials is in a state of flux at the current time and old doctrines may not be applicable. Therefore, the legal officer of the jurisdiction should always be consulted whenever there is a question about liability.

## SECTION 109 — UNSAFE EQUIPMENT

The provisions of Section 109 are intended to define what constitutes unsafe equipment. The *Uniform Mechanical Code* requires in the second paragraph of Section 108.6 that written notice to condemn equipment shall indicate the reason for condemnation.

The term "unsafe equipment" may refer to many parts of a system or possibly the entire assemblage. It would not be practical for the building official to list each defective part. The term "unsafe equipment" is used to indicate a generally hazardous condition. The term can be employed to prevent operation of an entire system without giving details of each specific part. When a mechanical system has been declared *unsafe,* the distinction of how unsafe or how insanitary is of no consequence. Unsafe equipment is a public nuisance and must be abated by repair, rehabilitation, replacement, demolition or removal.

The section declares that unsafe equipment is a public nuisance and requires repair or abatement. The abatement procedures are indicated to be as set forth in the *Uniform Code for the Abatement of Dangerous Buildings* or such alternate procedures that may be adopted by the jurisdiction. If the dangerous buildings code or an alternate procedure has not been adopted by the jurisdiction, Section 109 indicates that the jurisdiction may institute other appropriate action to abate the violation. The intent of this last provision is that, even though procedures have not been adopted, the jurisdiction may abate the hazard of dangerous buildings through proper legal proceedings, being particularly careful that the owners of the buildings have had the advantage of due process.[3]

## SECTION 110 — BOARD OF APPEALS

The *Uniform Mechanical Code* intends that the board of appeals has very limited authority to hear and decide appeals of orders and decisions of the building official relative to the application and interpretations of the code. Moreover, the code now specifically restricts the board to interpretation of the technical provisions of the code and does not permit waivers of the code requirements. Any broader authority to be granted to the board of appeals must be granted in the adoption ordinance by a modification of Section 110.

## Part III—Permits and Inspections

Part III of this chapter regulates issuance of permits and includes specific requirements for work requiring permits, information required to obtain a permit, fees to be charged for the permit and detailed requirements for the inspection process.

## SECTION 112 — PERMITS

**112.1 Permits Required.** The intent of this section is that the requirement to obtain a permit applies to persons, firms or corporations doing the work or causing the work

---

[3]O'Bannon, Robert E. (1989). *Building Department Administration.* International Conference of Building Officials, Whittier, California.

to be done. More than one permit may be issued when different contractors are working on different systems within the same structure. There must be no duplication of permits for the same portion of a mechanical system. The person holding the permit is responsible for the work.

**112.2 and 112.3 Exempt Work.** This section exempts certain kinds of work from the permit/inspection process, primarily because of the workload it would impose on the inspection agency and because the requirement for inspection of exempt work could be unenforceable. However, the intent is that this work must still comply with the code. (See comments on Section 103—Scope.)

The following types of equipment are exempt from permits:

1. **Portable heating, ventilating or cooling appliances or equipment, or a portable evaporative cooler.** Usually, this type of equipment is of low capacity, and the appliances are packaged units manufactured to standards not included in Part III of Chapter 16. Many portable appliances are listed; however, operating instructions and safe clearances are often indicated on the manufacturer's identification plate or label. The owner or occupant is provided with information on the safe use of portable appliances. The user of the equipment is responsible for ensuring the equipment is maintained and operated as specified by the manufacturer. Due to the portable nature of the equipment, inspection by the jurisdiction would be ineffective because conditions within the premises could change frequently.

2. **Closed systems of steam, hot or chilled water piping within heating or cooling equipment regulated by this code.** A closed system is a piping system where the same hot, warm or cooled water is contained and is circulated whenever the equipment is operated.

3. **Replacement of component parts of assemblies of an appliance that does not alter its original approval and complies with other applicable requirements of this code.** The original appliance or equipment must have been approved and installed in compliance with the code. The replacement parts must maintain the same operating safety features, temperature and pressure range and the same fuel, voltage and all other features as the original parts. Any changes that alter the original specifications or approved listing may void the equipment listing.

4. **Refrigerating equipment that is a part of a refrigeration system installed under another permit.** For example, a permit for a refrigeration compressor system includes the component parts of that system.

5. **Unit refrigeration system.** A unit refrigeration system is defined as one that is not attached to ductwork, does not exceed 3 horsepower, and has been factory assembled and tested before its installation. When repairs are made, only factory-authorized replacement parts must be used.

## SECTION 113 — APPLICATION FOR PERMIT

**113.1 Application.** In this section the UMC requires that a permit be applied for and describes the information required not only on the permit application itself, but information to be filed with the permit application. Essentially, the code requires that plans, engineering calculations and other data necessary to describe the work to be done be filed with the application for a permit. The building official is permitted to waive the requirement for the filing of plans and other data, provided the building official is assured that the work for which the permit is applied is of such a nature that plans or other data are not necessary to obtain compliance with the code.

Every application shall contain the following specific data:

1. **Identification and description of the work that will be done.** Detailed project specifications, drawings or directions are frequently not prepared for small installations and renovations. For this reason the information supplied on the permit application is the only guidance available for inspection authorities to determine the type and location of the equipment installed.

2. **The description must readily identify and definitely locate the work.** If the only description is the street address, the result can be very confusing. A complete description is essential in new residential subdivisions. An applicant, contractor or an inspector may be easily confused by multiple sites in a new subdivision. References must be made to the legal land description, including lot, block and subdivision numbers. When applicable, the description should also include the unit designator.

3. **The use or occupancy for which the proposed installation is intended.** This information enables a plan checker to determine if the application complies with zoning regulations. Some jurisdictions have zones where certain uses are restricted or prohibited due to fire, chemical or other environmental hazards. These may include the storage of certain paints, thinners, flammable or combustible liquids, chemicals, compressed gases, lumber, or furniture and cabinet manufacturing where shavings and sawdust would constitute a hazard. The requirements for approval may vary, depending on the size of the mechanical system, occupancy of the building and maximum number of persons who may occupy the building.

4. **When required, a permit application must be accompanied by plans, diagrams, computations or other data.** This requirement is amplified in Section 114.2.

5. **The application must be signed by the permittee or an authorized agent.** Some departments maintain a file of authorized signatures as a courtesy to local builders. The signature on the permit application

may be considered as acceptance of responsibility for permit and code compliance.

6. **The applicant is required to provide other data and information that is required and requested by the building official.** This might include product or material procedures data or information to assess demands on the municipal or public services such as electrical energy, fuel gas, water, sewer, sewage treatment, fire-protection hydrants, or other services in addition to information on grades, location, etc.

**113.2 Plans and Specifications.** The code requires that one or more sets of plans and specifications be submitted with each application for a permit. Most jurisdictions require a minimum of two sets—one set retained by the building department until the completion of the job and the second set maintained on the jobsite by the permit holder. Notations, tests, inspections and approvals are documented on the plans, inspection records or both. The remarks are dated and signed as inspections or alterations progress. This procedure is especially important on extensive projects where a part of the system is completed, installed, and concealed or buried before work on other sections is even commenced. A complete set of plans and specifications should be constantly marked up to indicate the inspection progress on the project. A great deal of time and effort is required for accurate records of inspection. Time spent in this documentation may prove to be extremely valuable at a later date.

The exception in this section is usually applied where simple systems are installed or altered and the inspection staff is sufficiently knowledgeable about the system to ensure code compliance.

**113.3.2 Direct-fired gas makeup and industrial air heaters.** The installer must submit plans for the proposed installation indicating the heater's location and the location of all accessory equipment that may be necessary for the proper and safe operation of the equipment.

# SECTION 114 — PERMIT ISSUANCE

**114.1 Issuance.** The permit issuance process is intended to provide records in the code enforcement agency to ensure orderly controls of the inspection process. Thus, the application for permit is intended to describe in detail the work to be done, while the plans and other data filed with the application are intended to graphically depict the work to be done. In this section the building official is directed to review the application for permit *and the plans and specifications* filed with the permit. This review of plans and specifications is not a discretionary procedure, but rather one that is mandated by the code. The building official is not at liberty to check only a portion of the plans. The drawings as well as the specifications and other data filed must be checked in order for the building official to comply with the code. In fact, if the submitted information is not reviewed by the building official, the building offi-

cial is in effect presuming the infallibility of the designer in addition to violating the code.

The code also charges the building official with the issuance of a permit if it has been determined that the information filed with the application shows compliance with the code and other laws and ordinances applicable to the building at its location in the jurisdiction. The building official may not withhold the issuance of a permit if these conditions are met. Thus, the building official would be in violation of the code to withhold the issuance of a permit because of failure of the applicant to comply with the code in an unrelated area.[4]

This section also provides for issuing partial permits. This provision is normally used on large projects to reduce the delay in beginning construction while waiting for the entire system to be designed or on a speculative building where future tenant requirements are unknown at the time of partial permit issuance. This provision should be reserved for occasions when waiting for complete drawings and specifications would be a hardship on the applicant. Usually, the final drawings for the mechanical systems cannot be completed until the architectural drawings are finalized. Delay caused by the approval of architectural and structural drawings before the commencement of design drawings for the electrical and mechanical trades may cause delays in meeting completion target dates. The code enforcement agency cannot compensate for a designer's failure to provide an adequate time schedule for a project. However, they can compensate when a delay is caused by unusual workloads internally (i.e., in the code enforcement agency).

**114.2 Retention of Plans.** The inspector should request a copy of the approved plans when making an inspection. This practice will assist in determining that the installation is in compliance with code requirements and the permit. The permit holder's approved plans should be marked and signed as the inspection progresses. It may be helpful to mark the system on the approved plans with colored pencils whenever a certain part of the system has been tested, inspected and approved.

**114.3.1 Validity of permit.** While it may be poor public relations to suspend or revoke a permit or to require corrections of the plans after they have been approved, it is clearly the intent of the code that the approval of plans or the issuance of a permit may not be done in violation of the code or of other pertinent laws or ordinances.

It is often impossible for a plan checker or building official to thoroughly check every detail of every set of plans and specifications including the location, elevation and details of public services. The workload of plan checkers is extremely heavy at some times of the year. In order to process plans, it is not always possible to employ the detailed examination needed to guarantee error-free plans. A designer of a mechanical system cannot expect to place the responsibility for accuracy and compliance with regu-

---

[4]Vogelsang, John (1974). Kay Ellis vs. the City Council of Burlingame, California. *Building Standards,* March-April, pages 18-19.

lations on the building department. Fees are primarily levied to cover the cost of inspection and plans examination.

Issuance of a permit based on plans, specifications and other data does not prevent the building official from subsequently requiring corrections of errors to plans and specifications. Even after a permit has been issued and errors are noticed, a building official is required to secure code compliance.

If the permit holder refuses to make corrections, a stop order may be issued as provided for in Section 108.4.

**114.4.1 Expiration.** The *Uniform Mechanical Code* anticipates that once a permit has been issued, construction will soon follow and proceed expeditiously until its completion. However, this ideal procedure is not always the case; therefore, the code makes provisions for those cases where work is not started or where the work in progress has been suspended for a period of time. It is assumed by the code that the code enforcement agency will have expended some effort and conducted follow-up inspections of the work, etc.; therefore, at least half of the permit fee must be obtained in order to compensate the agency for the work. However, see the discussion of fee refunds under Section 115.6.

## SECTION 115 — FEES

**115.1 General.** The *Uniform Mechanical Code* anticipates that many jurisdictions will establish their own fee schedules and, therefore, recognizes that the fees to be charged for permits and for plan review will be either as set forth in this section or as established by the jurisdiction.

It is *not* the intent of the UMC that the fees collected by the department for mechanical permits and plan review always be adequate to cover the costs to the department in these areas, since the fee schedule is fixed and does not reflect changes in the economy. It is anticipated that the method for determining the building permit fee based on valuation will compensate for shortfall or overage in mechanical permit fees. It is, therefore, the intent of the Uniform Codes that the fees collected by the department for construction permits and plan review be adequate to cover the costs to the department. For a discussion on building permit fees based on valuation, refer to the *Handbook to the Uniform Building Code* (Section 107.2, Permit Fees).

**115.5 Investigation Fees: Work without a Permit.** When work requiring a permit is started without a permit, the code directs the building official to cause an investigation to be made of the work already done. The intent of the investigation is to determine to what extent the work completed complies with the code and to describe with as much detail as possible the work that has been completed. Because it is anticipated that the investigation may require considerable time and effort, the code specifies that a fee should be paid by the person doing the work equal in amount to the permit fee that would be required. The investigation fee is to be paid in addition to the regular permit and plan check fees. Moreover, the investigation fee is to be paid whether or not a permit is later issued.

**115.6 Fee Refunds.** This section authorizes the building official to refund a portion of the permit fee, the plan check fee or both for good cause. An example would be when the permit fee is collected in error. Another reason for authorizing the refund of the fees paid would be because circumstances beyond the control of the applicant cause delays and eventual expiration of either the permit or the plan review. In these cases the code authorizes the building official to recommend refunding up to 80 percent of the fee paid, with the intent that at least 20 percent of the fee paid has been expended by the department in record keeping.

## SECTION 116 — INSPECTIONS

**116.1 General.** The inspection function of the building department is one of the most important activities of the department. A department can have the best plan checking operation possible, but if the field inspection does not require construction to be in compliance with the code, it is wasted effort. On the other hand, a strong field inspection activity can offset, to some degree, weak plan checking.

Inspections during construction are referred to as rough inspections, with the final inspection being performed when a system is complete and ready to be used. Even though the code states that mechanical systems shall not be connected to the energy fuel-supply lines until authorized by the building official, the intent is to allow connection for purposes of testing before final inspection. (See Section 117.2.)

The important consideration is that a mechanical system cannot be put in normal and continuous operation nor can the premises be occupied or open to the public without final inspection. An occupancy permit or business license should not be issued before completion of final inspections and approvals from appropriate regulatory agencies.

**116.2 Operation of Mechanical Equipment.** Mechanical systems may be operated when installations or repairs are made to existing equipment or fixtures in an occupied portion of a building, provided a request for inspection is made within 48 hours of the completion of repairs. However, no work may be permanently concealed until inspection is completed and approval is granted. This provision allows emergency maintenance functions to be performed and the system to be operated for normal service. If this provision were not included, the result could be damage to structures, systems and food spoilage and disruption of various industrial or commercial services.

**116.3 Testing of Equipment and Systems.** This section refers to the tests required to be performed on refrigeration equipment, steam and hot-water boilers and piping, and fuel-gas piping. The important consideration is that Chapter 10, regulating steam and hot-water boilers and piping, and Chapter 13, regulating fuel-gas piping, are now code requirements.

**116.4 Inspection Requests.** An inspection request must be made by the person doing the work authorized by the permit because that person knows the progress that has been made. It is desirable that the person requesting inspection be present to discuss the installation with the inspector. However, whether the permit holder is present or not, all corrections should be clearly listed in writing and a copy should be retained by the department. If the inspector only issues a rejection notice, the installer must contact the building department to determine what alterations or corrections are required, resulting in lost time for all concerned.

Requests for inspection may be in writing or by telephone. The common procedure now is by telephone and many jurisdictions have provisions for 24-hour recording of telephone messages. When a specific time for inspection is requested, the requestor is usually required to contact the inspector personally.

It is the duty of a person requesting inspections to provide access and means for proper inspection of the work. This is sometimes overlooked by persons requesting inspections. Ladders must be adequate to comply with federal or state safety requirements and must be of sufficient length so the inspector can safely climb up and reach the equipment or system being inspected. A ladder which reaches 3 feet (914 mm) below the roof so the inspector can see only the top of a flat roof is not considered adequate access to equipment on that roof. Provisions for access include lighting, walking space, and drainage of water from the adjacent areas or pathways to equipment. Inspection doors providing access for a visual inspection of a mechanical system are required.

**116.6 Reinspections.** If reinspection is necessary because work has not progressed to the point where it is ready for inspection, the code authorizes the building official to charge a reinspection fee. The reinspection fee is not mandated and normally would not be charged unless there is a pattern of inspection calls and repeated disapprovals for portions of the work that inspection was requested, failure to provide access, failure of the testing procedure, deviation from the approved plans, or using unapproved materials.

## SECTION 117 — CONNECTION APPROVAL

**117.1 Energy Connections.** When an energy source is reconnected without authorization from the building department or appliances or equipment are operated in violation of an order by the building official, the result is usually a notification by phone and confirmation in writing to the owner and to the utility provider stating that the energy source is going to be disconnected at the property line and the meter removed.

One of the most effective enforcement tools available to inspection agencies is the ability to control energy connections.

# Chapter 2
# DEFINITIONS

## SECTION 201 — GENERAL

This chapter provides definitions of terms that are applicable specifically to the code and that may not have an appropriate definition for code purposes in *Webster's Third New International Dictionary of the English Language, Unabridged,* copyright 1986. Most of these definitions are very specific and have a meaning that must be carefully considered when interpreting the intent of the code. See the definition of "absorption unit" described in this commentary for an example of the specific nature of the definitions in the UMC.

There are also definitions in Sections 502 and 507 and in several of the standards. Therefore, in order to determine whether or not a definition for a specific item is in the UMC, Chapter 2 must be examined as well as the chapter that covers the specific subject for which a definition is desired.

Many of the definitions in Chapter 2 are self-explanatory. The following commentary will discuss some of those definitions.

## SECTION 202 — ACCEPTED MEANINGS

This section requires that Webster's unabridged dictionary shall be used to provide ordinarily accepted meanings for terms that are not specifically defined in the code. Therefore, the code defines terms that have specific intents and meanings insofar as the code is concerned and leaves it up to Webster's unabridged dictionary to provide meanings for all other terms.

## SECTION 203 — A

**ABSORPTION UNIT.** This definition is an example of the specific nature and intent of code definitions. The "Recognized Standards" included in Part III of Chapter 16 are intended as guides to the design, testing and installation of equipment regulated by the UMC. Building officials look for a label on gas-fired absorption units for summer cooling specifying that the unit being inspected complies with ANSI Z21.40.1-1981 and addenda Z21.40.1a-1982. As defined in the UMC, an absorption unit is further required to be factory assembled and tested. Thus, the definition contains some elements of a regulatory requirement that might be more appropriately relocated in the text of Chapter 11. Although it is generally preferable in code writing to separate regulatory requirements from definitions, this specific definition could state merely that an absorption unit is a unit listed as complying with ANSI Z21.40.1-1981 and its 1982 addendum.

**ACCESSIBLE.** This definition was added in the 1991 edition of the UMC. The intent is that removing or opening a panel, door or similar obstruction may require no more than a key or common hand tool and does not require disassembly of component parts of the system or adjacent systems or structures. Being accessible would permit the use of portable access equipment such as a ladder. However, note the difference between merely being accessible and "readily accessible." The latter term does not permit use of portable access equipment.

**AIR, EXHAUST.** The intent of this definition is that exhaust air be conveyed to the exterior of the building in such a manner that it will not, under normal circumstances, reenter the building through doors, windows or other openings.

**AIR-MOVING SYSTEM.** This is a system designed to provide heating, cooling or ventilation in which one or more air-handling units are used to supply air to a common space or to draw air from a common plenum or space. This definition was added to the UMC in 1994 to assist building officials in applying UMC Section 608. The most frequently asked question is can I avoid the requirement for automatic shutoff of individual fans by installing multiple fans having a capacity smaller than 2,000 cubic feet per minute (cfm) (940 L/s)? The definition answers this by defining an air-moving system as consisting of one or multiple air-handling units that either draw from a common area or plenum, or supply a common space. The answer to the question is that one or multiple air handlers are one system when they supply or take returns from the same spaces and therefore, one cannot avoid the requirement for shutoff upon detection of smoke by using multiple smaller capacity air-handling units.

## SECTION 205 — C

**CENTRAL HEATING PLANT** or **HEATING PLANT.** The intent of this definition is that the equipment directly uses fuel or electrical energy to generate the heat being used. This distinction is made in the UBC definition of "central heating plant" in UBC Section 204. The reason for the distinction in the UBC is to further clarify the kind of equipment that must be enclosed by fire-resistive construction required by Section 302.5 of the UBC.

**Chimney, Residential Appliance-type.** The addition of the last sentence to this definition, added in the 1991 edition, explaining the designation of Type HT chimneys was a companion change to the addition of the definition for "closed combustion solid-fuel-burning appliance." The addition of closed combustion-type solid-fuel-burning stoves or room heaters to Table 8-B adds Footnote 1 requiring the use of HT chimneys. These code changes were made based on the determination that solid-fuel-burning appliances may produce creosote, which can accumulate in the appliance venting system and serve as fuel for an extremely destructive chimney fire.

**CONDENSING APPLIANCE.** This definition was added to the 1985 edition as a result of design improvements by manufacturers to produce more efficient appliances. With improved efficiencies, flue gas temperatures were lowered, resulting in moisture created by the combustion process condensing in the flue instead of being expelled with the flue gases as steam or water vapor. This condition requires special consideration with respect to appliance design and materials selection due to the acidity of the condensate.

## SECTION 206 — D

**DIRECT-VENT APPLIANCES.** This definition was added in 1976. These appliances were previously called "sealed combustion system appliances," which were defined as such in the 1973 UMC. This change was made to conform with the terminology used in the standards regulating the construction and testing of these appliances.

**DUCT SYSTEMS.** The 1991 edition deleted the definitions for low-, medium-, and high-pressure duct systems to conform with current industry standards that no longer classify duct systems in this manner. Duct systems and their construction requirements are now based on a wider range of "pressure classes" (refer to UMC Standard 6-1).

## SECTION 214 — L

**LISTED** and **LISTING.** This definition was changed in the 1991 edition of both the UBC and UMC to clarify that the building official has responsibility and authority for determining which standards are acceptable for purposes of listing equipment and materials.

**LOW-PRESSURE HOT-WATER-HEATING BOILER** and **LOW-PRESSURE STEAM-HEATING BOILER.** These definitions were added to the 1991 edition of the UMC.

## SECTION 216 — N

**NONCOMBUSTIBLE.** The questions that occur most frequently with respect to this definition concern the application of gypsum wallboard. The intent of the definition is that gypsum wallboard does not comply with the requirements of Item 1 of this definition and, therefore, should not be used in assemblies to reduce clearance requirements. In addition, gypsum wallboard is not intended to be used in assemblies that provide reduced clearances where temperatures reach 125°F. (See Section 601.1.3.) Gypsum wallboard is accepted by the Building Code for use in fire-resistive assemblies. See UBC Tables 7-A, 7-B, and 7-C.

## SECTION 217 — O

**OCCUPANCY.** The occupancy definitions in this section are taken directly from UBC Chapter 3 with minor editorial changes such as deletion of referenced tables and to delete material not pertinent in the UMC. It is the intent that there be no difference in interpretation of the occupancy definitions between the UMC and UBC.

## SECTION 218 — P

**PLENUM.** This definition was amended in the 1991 edition to list specific locations that are to be considered as plenums. The intent of this definition, before as well as after this change, is to include uninhabited areas that are connected by an opening to the indoor environment of a building.

# Chapter 3
# GENERAL REQUIREMENTS

## SECTION 301 — SCOPE

Chapter 3 of the UMC was entirely revised in 1997 to conform more closely with the common code format, to eliminate editorial inconsistencies and to consolidate requirements in consistent language as employed in the UBC format. For example, Section 301.2 refers to the standards set forth in full text in Part II of Chapter 16 (there is one for Chapter 3) and also to the standards listed in Chapter 16, Part III as recognized standards (there are some 138 of these). The section also calls the user's attention to the requirements of the *National Electrical Code*® (NEC®) (ANSI/NFPA 70) and also to UBC Standard 8-1, Test Method for Surface-burning Characteristics of Building Materials, which is set forth in full in UBC Volume 3.

## SECTION 302 — APPROVAL OF EQUIPMENT

This section distinguishes between listed equipment, which complies with a specific standard and which the building official has determined to be suitable for the application intended, and unlisted equipment. For example, a building official would surely not approve installation of a gas-fired toilet where natural gas or LP-gas is unavailable; nor where a sanitary sewer and running water are available. To determine suitability of a particular standard, the building official must review the content of the standard, particularly its scope and applicability.

This section brings together various 1994 provisions relating to the ways in which equipment (and appliances) may be found to be acceptable for use in mechanical systems regulated under this code.

The building official retains authority to accept unlisted equipment under the provisions of Sections 105 and 302.2. An added requirement is that unlisted equipment must be determined to be safe by actual examination. This authority will most often be exercised when an acceptable standard is unavailable because the equipment is not mass produced, but is built on an as-ordered basis. Industrial machinery and equipment frequently fall into this category. It is important that the installer as well as the inspector review the complete terms of listing as found in the manufacturer's installation instructions and not just those requirements found on the label.

Section 302.3 reinforces the building official's authority to require testing as a condition for approving mechanical equipment.

## SECTION 303 — INSTALLATION

This section is a further effort to reduce the bulk of the code and to rid it of details concerning the installation of individual appliances and equipment. It now says (once) to use the conditions of listing and manufacturer's installation instructions as a minimum requirement. Section 303.1.1 incorporates the prohibition of unvented room heaters that was previously found in Section 807 of the 1991 edition and Section 327.6 in the 1994 edition. Section 303.1.3 contains the provisions regarding elevating sources of ignition in garages previously located in Section 308 of the 1994 code.

Finally, the section now requires the building official to make a decision on whether the code or a referenced standard is the more restrictive. Additional requirements might be found in the Building Code, the Electrical Code or the Plumbing Code. Also, if the jurisdiction has its own sewer, electric and water utilities, there may be further rules in the regulations that the building official is required to enforce as a condition precedent to issuing permits. Although most jurisdictions delegate Fire Code enforcement to the fire marshal, often the building official is charged with enforcement of zoning and subdivision regulations. It is a great help to applicants for permits if the department offers one-stop service for internal coordination of all jurisdictional requirements that may be conditions on a request for a building permit. By providing one-stop service, the building official avoids much criticism and antagonism when unanticipated obstacles to permit issuance arise. Therefore, a fully detailed explanation accompanied by a checklist is often used by counter attendants to be sure that an applicant fully understands. The exceptions to Section 303.1.1 were intended to apply to portable unvented oil-burning heaters to conform the UMC with the provisions contained in Section 6106 of the UFC. However, in the code development process a mistake was made so that Section 303.1.1 became broadly applicable to all fuel-burning equipment and not just to portable oil-fired heaters. With the suspension of the UMC code change process, there remains no available route to correct the error. That is to say that the original code change text for revised Chapter 3 was erroneous. See 1994 UMC Section 327.6, which indicates the intended application. (See Code Change Number 289, *Building Standards,* Part III, November-December 1994.)

**303.1 General.** This section requires that equipment shall be installed as required by terms of its approval, manufacturer's installation instructions and the conditions of listing constitute the minimum requirements for installation. Specific requirements of the UMC and other relevant codes and regulations of the local jurisdiction are additional requirements governing installation.

**303.1.1 Prohibited installations.** Unvented and direct fired fuel-burning equipment may be used to provide heating only in occupancy Groups F, S and U.

**303.1.2 Floor furnaces.** Vented floor furnaces may be used only in slabs above grade or locations where it extends down into an underfloor crawl space. Figure 3-1 illustrates dimensional provisions for floor furnaces. Figure 3-2 illustrates the prohibited installation of a floor furnace in a slab on grade.

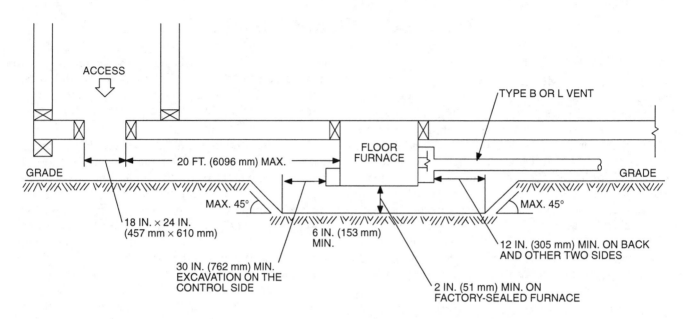

**TYPICAL FLOOR FURNACES**

**FIGURE 3-1**

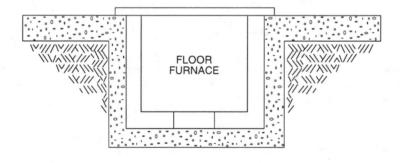

**FLOOR FURNACES IN SLAB—PROHIBITED**

**FIGURE 3-2**

**303.1.3 Elevation of ignition source.** This section addresses (1) potential physical damage to appliances and (2) location of appliances with respect to flammable vapors and also cellulose nitrate plastic.

Physical damage to appliances may be avoided by elevating appliances or by locating appliances out of the path of moving equipment; protection against physical damage may also be provided by erecting concrete or pipe stanchions or, more commonly, by installing wheel stops. The suitability of the various methods suggested would be a decision to be made by the local building official. The hazard to be considered is property damage and possible acci-

dental release of fuel from a broken fuel line if an appliance were struck by a moving vehicle.

Garage areas and warehouses are especially vulnerable to flammable vapors from fuel leaks from vehicles and leaks from stored fuels, paints and solvents. The 18-inch (457 mm) height requirement in this section applies to appliances that provide a source of ignition for flammable vapors, including standing pilots, relays, switches, starting switches inside some types of motors and similar devices.

**303.2 Conflicts.** If conflicts between this code and the conditions of listing or the manufacturer's installation instructions arise, the more restrictive provision as determined by the building official shall be followed.

## SECTION 304 — LOCATION

As a general principle, equipment should be located as required by this section.

**304.1 General.** The requirements of this section have been referred to in previous sections of this commentary (refer to the commentary on Sections 302 and 303.1). Mechanical equipment shall be located as required by this section, specific requirements elsewhere in this code, and the conditions imposed by the equipment's approval.

**304.2 Indoor Locations.** There are two reasons for the requirements of this section: (1) to provide adequate space for maintaining and servicing the equipment and (2) to prevent excessive heat build up in a confined space. Both of these conditions are considered for appliances listed for installation in closets and alcoves.

**304.3 Outdoor Locations.** When using the provisions of this section, remember that (1) the building official must approve the installation of all unlisted equipment and this section does not imply that approval will be granted and (2) the requirements of this section and Tables 3-A and 3-B apply only to unlisted equipment and are not intended to be used to provide reduced clearances for listed equipment. Equipment installed outside buildings shall be listed and labeled for outdoor installation or shall be installed within an approved weatherproof enclosure.

**304.4 Pit Locations.** Usually the method of securing an appliance, if required, is given in the manufacturer's installation instructions as a condition of its listing. Generally speaking, equipment regulated by the UMC should be securely fastened in place except that equipment defined as portable by Section 218 and residential washers, dryers and kitchen ranges. Provisions for securing water heaters were deleted from this section in the 1991 edition because installation of domestic water heaters is regulated by the Plumbing Code. Without exception, a competent engineer should evaluate methods of securing equipment in Seismic Zones 3 and 4 when the manufacturer's installation instructions do not address this subject.

Additional reasons for requiring equipment to be secured in place are to prevent damage to electrical, gas or refrigerant connections due to vibration or accidental impact.

**304.5 Prohibited Locations.** Equipment shall not be located in a hazardous location unless listed and approved for the specific installation. Fuel-burning equipment, electric resistance heating devices or electrostatic air cleaners shall not be installed in a surgical procedure or medical treatment room. Fuel-burning equipment shall not be installed in a closet, bathroom or a room readily usable as a bedroom, or in a room, compartment or alcove opening directly into any of these.

> **EXCEPTIONS:** 1. Direct vent equipment and electric heat furnaces.
>
> 2. Access to furnaces located in an attic or underfloor crawl space may be through a closet.
>
> 3. A vented appliance located in an unconfined space in accordance with the combustion air requirements of Chapter 7.
>
> 4. A fireplace may be approved for installation in a bathroom or bedroom if equipped with an approved method of obtaining combustion air from outside.
>
> 5. A warm-air furnace in an enclosed space with combustion air obtained from outside the building in conformance with Chapter 7 and having a tightfitting gasketed door with a closer may have access through a bathroom or bedroom.

Equipment burning liquefied petroleum gas (LPG) or liquid fuel shall not be located in a pit, an underfloor space, below grade or similar location where vapors or fuel might unsafely collect unless an approved method for the safe collection, removal and containment or disposal of the vapors or fuel is provided.

In areas subject to flooding, equipment that would be damaged or create hazardous conditions if subjected to inundation shall not be installed at or below grade unless suitably protected by elevation or other approved means.

Figures 3-3 and 3-4 illustrate typical requirements for this section.

*(Continued on page 17)*

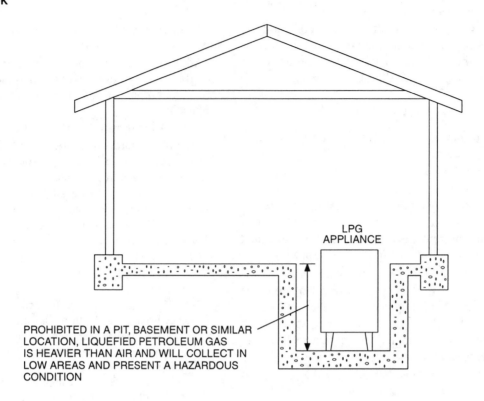

PROHIBITED IN A PIT, BASEMENT OR SIMILAR
LOCATION, LIQUEFIED PETROLEUM GAS
IS HEAVIER THAN AIR AND WILL COLLECT IN
LOW AREAS AND PRESENT A HAZARDOUS
CONDITION

LPG
APPLIANCE

**TYPICAL SECTION 304 REQUIREMENT**

**FIGURE 3-3**

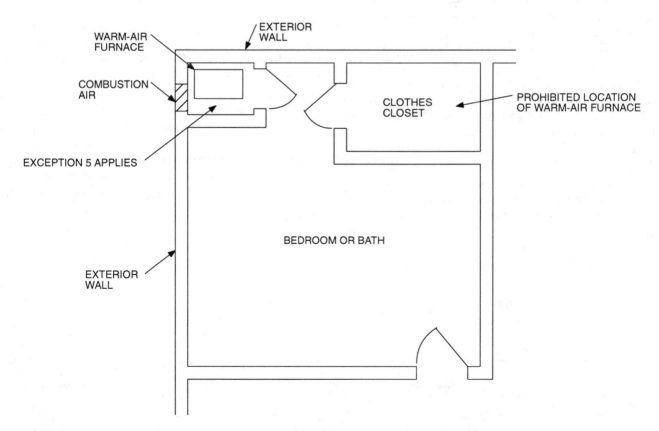

**NOTE:** Electric furnaces, electric heat pumps, electric wall furnaces and electric room heaters may be installed according to
their listing in bedrooms and bathrooms because electrical heating appliances do not deplete oxygen in closed rooms.

**FIGURE 3-4**

*(Continued from page 15)*

**304.6 Clearances to Combustible Construction.** This is a revision and simplification of the detailed appliance installation instructions formerly included in the 1994 UMC. Instead of repeating manufacturer's installation instructions for each category of equipment, the 1997 UMC now says listed heat-producing equipment shall be installed to maintain the required clearances specified in the listing. If equipment is unlisted, Table 3-A clearances shall be utilized and the clearances may be reduced by the use of one of the assemblies contained in Table 3-B. The rationale for this provision is that the manufacturers of listed equipment could have their products listed and tested with integral heat shielding, but the clearance reductions in Table 3-B are applicable to protection of combustible building construction not to an individual piece of equipment. See Figure 3-5.

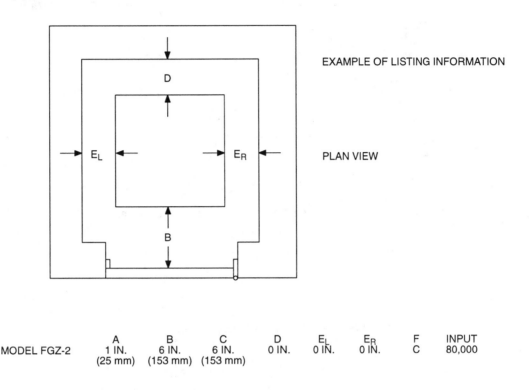

EXAMPLE OF LISTING INFORMATION

PLAN VIEW

| MODEL FGZ-2 | A<br>1 IN.<br>(25 mm) | B<br>6 IN.<br>(153 mm) | C<br>6 IN.<br>(153 mm) | D<br>0 IN. | $E_L$<br>0 IN. | $E_R$<br>0 IN. | F<br>C | INPUT<br>80,000 |
|---|---|---|---|---|---|---|---|---|

A. CLEARANCE ABOVE BONNET

C. CLEARANCE FROM FLUE OR VENT CONNECTOR IN ANY DIRECTION

F. TYPE OF FLOOR ("C" = COMBUSTIBLE; "NC" = NONCOMBUSTIBLE)

**FIGURE 3-5**

**304.7 Clearances for Maintenance and Replacement.** These provisions were previously located in Sections 304, 305 and 314.

**304.8 Clearances from Grade.** Material in this section was previously located in Section 316.

**304.9 Protection from Damage.** This material was previously located in Sections 308 and 323.

## SECTION 305 — TYPE OF FUEL AND FUEL CONNECTIONS

This material was previously located in Section 303.

## SECTION 306 — ELECTRICAL CONNECTIONS

This material was previously part of Sections 309 and 320.

## SECTION 307 — ACCESS AND SERVICE SPACE

This material was previously located in Sections 312, 314, 319, 320, 322, 323, 324, 325 and 326. Figure 3-6 illustrates access requirements for an appliance and Figure 3-7 illustrates a typical furnace compartment. See Figure 3-8 for equipment in attics. Figures 3-9 through 3-14 illustrate provisions in Sections 307.4 and 307.5.

*(Continued on page 22)*

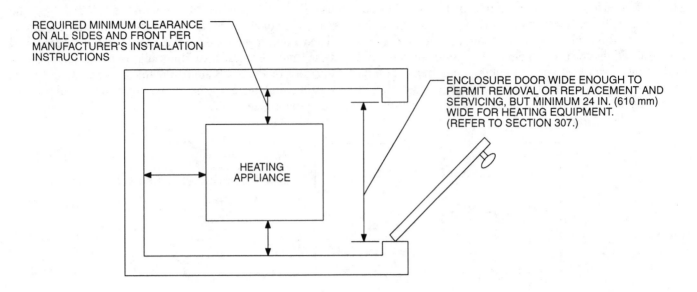

REQUIRED MINIMUM CLEARANCE ON ALL SIDES AND FRONT PER MANUFACTURER'S INSTALLATION INSTRUCTIONS

HEATING APPLIANCE

ENCLOSURE DOOR WIDE ENOUGH TO PERMIT REMOVAL OR REPLACEMENT AND SERVICING, BUT MINIMUM 24 IN. (610 mm) WIDE FOR HEATING EQUIPMENT. (REFER TO SECTION 307.)

PLAN VIEW

**ACCESS TO APPLIANCE FOR INSPECTION, SERVICE OR REPAIR**

**FIGURE 3-6**

SECTION THROUGH FURNACE COMPARTMENT AND HALL

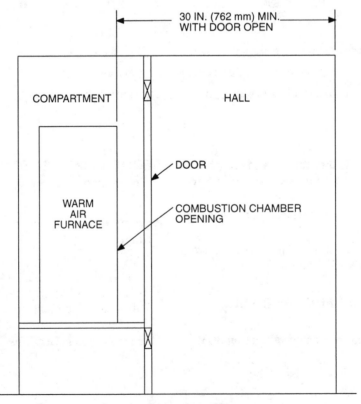

30 IN. (762 mm) MIN. WITH DOOR OPEN

COMPARTMENT

HALL

WARM AIR FURNACE

DOOR

COMBUSTION CHAMBER OPENING

**TYPICAL FURNACE COMPARTMENT**

**FIGURE 3-7**

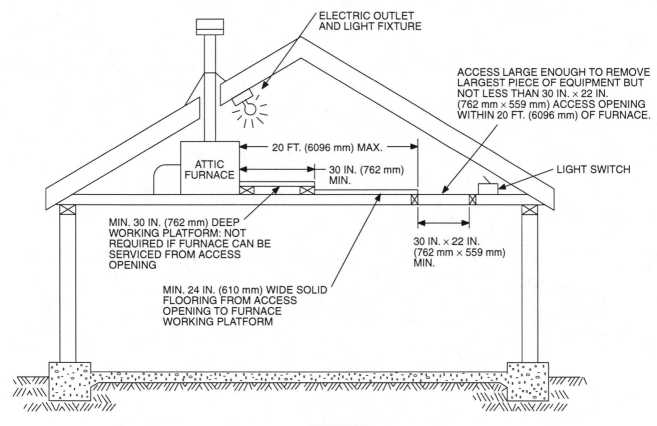

**FIGURE 3-8**

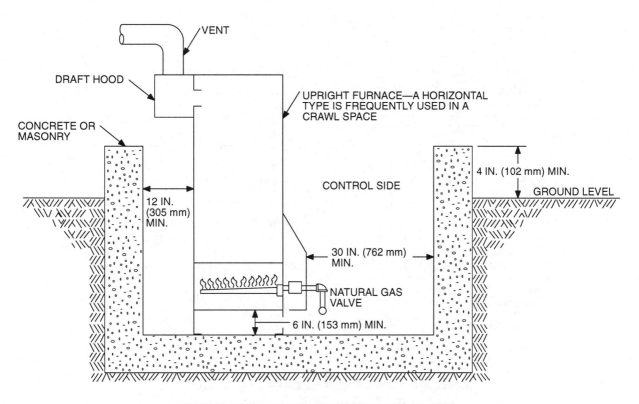

**TYPICAL CRAWL SPACE EQUIPMENT INSTALLATIONS**
(Not Permitted in Floodplain Areas)

**FIGURE 3-9**

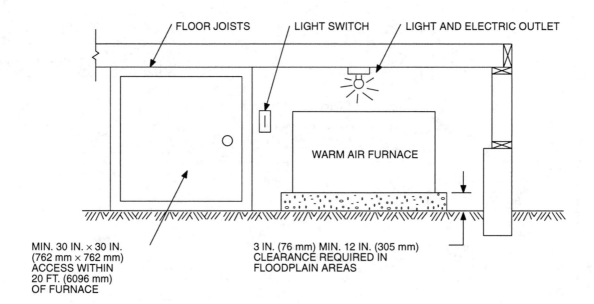

**HORIZONTAL FURNACE ON A SLAB**

**FIGURE 3-10**

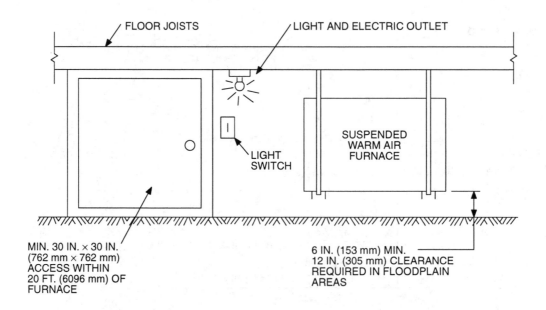

**HORIZONTAL FURNACE SUSPENDED FROM FLOOR JOISTS**

**FIGURE 3-11**

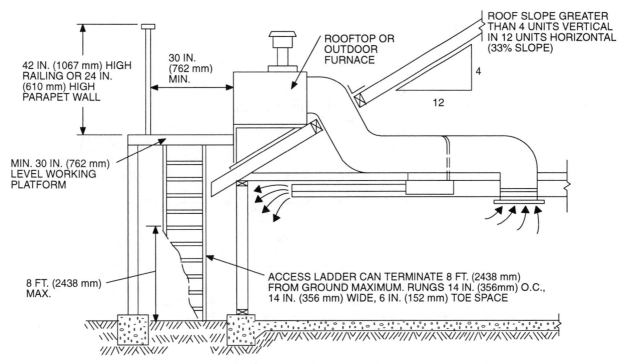

42 IN. (1067 mm) HIGH RAILING OR 24 IN. (610 mm) HIGH PARAPET WALL

30 IN. (762 mm) MIN.

ROOFTOP OR OUTDOOR FURNACE

ROOF SLOPE GREATER THAN 4 UNITS VERTICAL IN 12 UNITS HORIZONTAL (33% SLOPE)

4

12

MIN. 30 IN. (762 mm) LEVEL WORKING PLATFORM

8 FT. (2438 mm) MAX.

ACCESS LADDER CAN TERMINATE 8 FT. (2438 mm) FROM GROUND MAXIMUM. RUNGS 14 IN. (356mm) O.C., 14 IN. (356 mm) WIDE, 6 IN. (152 mm) TOE SPACE

**TYPICAL ROOFTOP INSTALLATIONS**

**FIGURE 3-12**

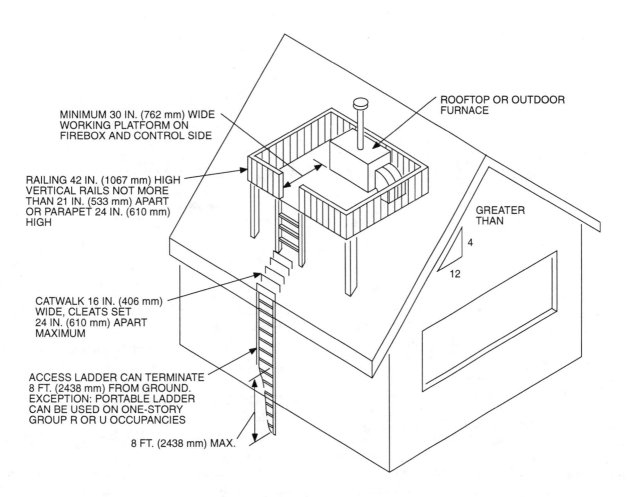

MINIMUM 30 IN. (762 mm) WIDE WORKING PLATFORM ON FIREBOX AND CONTROL SIDE

ROOFTOP OR OUTDOOR FURNACE

RAILING 42 IN. (1067 mm) HIGH VERTICAL RAILS NOT MORE THAN 21 IN. (533 mm) APART OR PARAPET 24 IN. (610 mm) HIGH

GREATER THAN

4

12

CATWALK 16 IN. (406 mm) WIDE, CLEATS SET 24 IN. (610 mm) APART MAXIMUM

ACCESS LADDER CAN TERMINATE 8 FT. (2438 mm) FROM GROUND. EXCEPTION: PORTABLE LADDER CAN BE USED ON ONE-STORY GROUP R OR U OCCUPANCIES

8 FT. (2438 mm) MAX.

**FIGURE 3-13**

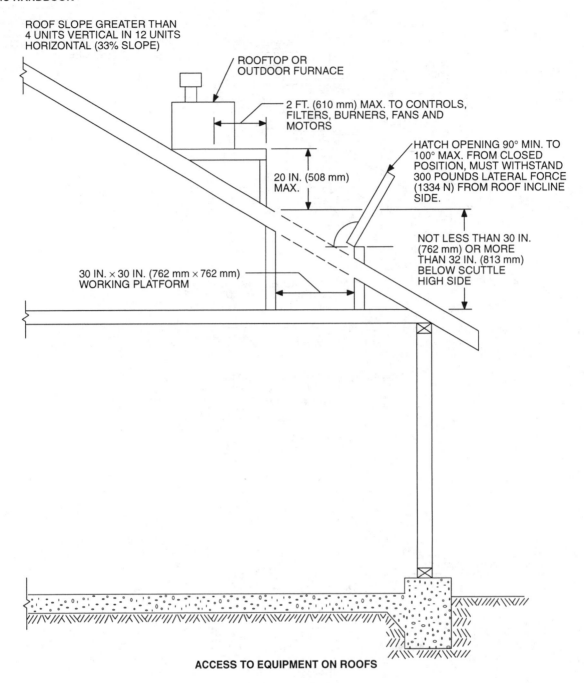

ROOF SLOPE GREATER THAN
4 UNITS VERTICAL IN 12 UNITS
HORIZONTAL (33% SLOPE)

ROOFTOP OR
OUTDOOR FURNACE

2 FT. (610 mm) MAX. TO CONTROLS,
FILTERS, BURNERS, FANS AND
MOTORS

HATCH OPENING 90° MIN. TO
100° MAX. FROM CLOSED
POSITION, MUST WITHSTAND
300 POUNDS LATERAL FORCE
(1334 N) FROM ROOF INCLINE
SIDE.

20 IN. (508 mm)
MAX.

NOT LESS THAN 30 IN.
(762 mm) OR MORE
THAN 32 IN. (813 mm)
BELOW SCUTTLE
HIGH SIDE

30 IN. × 30 IN. (762 mm × 762 mm)
WORKING PLATFORM

**ACCESS TO EQUIPMENT ON ROOFS**

**FIGURE 3-14**

*(Continued from page 17)*

**307.3 Equipment in Attics.** This section provides additional code requirements for the installation of attic furnaces, focusing primarily on servicing and replacement access. The only requirement unique to attic furnaces is the requirement that a continuous floor 24 inches (610 mm) in width be provided from the firebox side of the furnace to areas required to service "temperature-limit control, air filter, fuel-control valve, vent collar or air-handling unit." In many cases, this will require continuous flooring 24 inches (610 mm) in width on three sides of the equipment and 30 inches (762 mm) on the control side. Figure 3-8 illustrates the requirements of this section.

## SECTION 308 — EQUIPMENT SUPPORTS AND RESTRAINTS

This material was previously located in Section 304. New requirements were added.

## SECTION 309 — DISCHARGE OF BYPRODUCTS

Some of these requirements were previously located in Section 310 and Chapter 8. New requirements were added. Figure 3-15 illustrates a dry well that may be used in some jurisdictions when first approved by the building official.

This section must be reviewed in conjunction with the requirements of the IPC for indirect waste piping, wet vented systems, and special wastes. It is not the intent of the commentary to fully discuss the principles contained in Chapter 7 of the IPC. It is anticipated that plumbing inspection and mechanical inspection efforts will coordinate the enforcement of these requirements and that inspectors charged with enforcement of this section will also be familiar with all the requirements. The following list describes the basic requirements of sections that affect the installation of condensate waste piping:

**IPC Section 202. Indirect Waste Pipe.** Provides definition of term as it applies to the IPC.

**IPC Section 802. Indirect Waste Conditions.** This section requires that waste drained from equipment regulated by the UMC be drained to the building drainage system by means of indirect waste pipes. However, the intent of the UMC is to allow condensate waste to be discharged to other approved disposal areas such as a dry well in areas where soil conditions permit.

## SECTION 310 — IDENTIFICATION

This material was previously located in Sections 304 and 307 and in Chapter 11. New requirements were added. Figure 3-16 illustrates typical requirements for identification of equipment.

## SECTION 311 — CONTROLS

This material was previously located in Section 306. Figure 3-17 shows the required location of the air outlet temperature limit control device in a forced-air and gravity-type warm air furnace.

## SECTION 312 — PERSONNEL PROTECTION

This material was previously located in Section 316. New requirements were added.

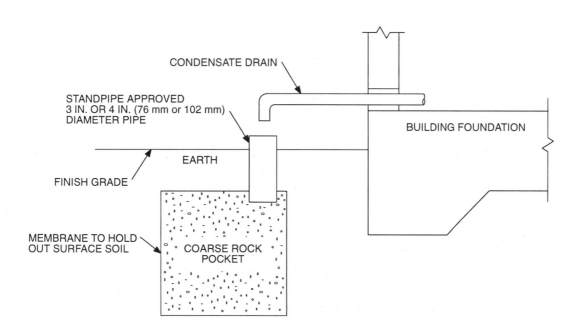

1. Condensate drains sized to comply with Section 309.

2. Condensate should drain to plumbing fixture or other approved location: dry well disposal is unsuitable for nonpermeable or expansive soil conditions.

**FIGURE 3-15**

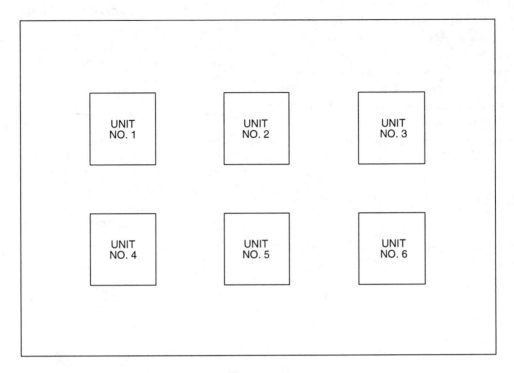

ROOF PLAN

**NOTE:** "AH" means "Air-handling Unit"

MECHANICAL ROOM

**TYPICAL REQUIREMENTS FOR IDENTIFICATION OF EQUIPMENT**

**FIGURE 3-16**

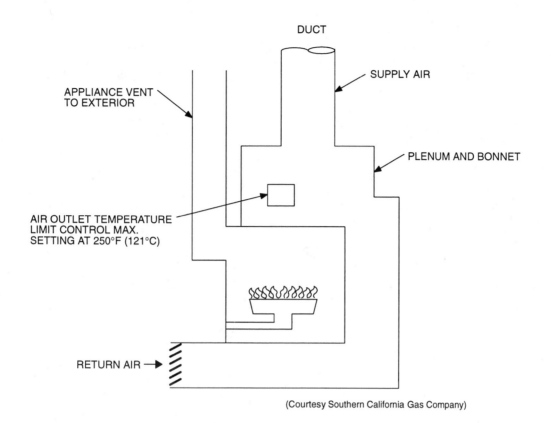

DUCT

SUPPLY AIR

APPLIANCE VENT
TO EXTERIOR

PLENUM AND BONNET

AIR OUTLET TEMPERATURE
LIMIT CONTROL MAX.
SETTING AT 250°F (121°C)

RETURN AIR →

(Courtesy Southern California Gas Company)

**AIR OUTLET LIMIT CONTROL**

**FIGURE 3-17**

# Chapter 4
# VENTILATION AIR SUPPLY

Chapter 4 was revised in its entirety in the 1997 UMC to improve format and consistency with the common code format.

## SECTION 401 — SCOPE

In the common code format, mechanical ventilation airflow quantities are specified in UBC Chapter 12, entitled "Interior Environment." In general, the minimum quantity for mechanical ventilation systems is 15 cfm (7.08 $^L/_S$) of outside air per occupant in most occupancies. Natural ventilation system exterior openings such as openable windows are also acceptable. An alternate mechanical ventilation requirement based on ANSI/ASHRAE Standard 62-89 is provided in UBC Appendix Chapter 12, which must be specifically adopted. See UBC Section 101.3. The major change in the section contains recognition of UMC Standard 4-1, Test Performance of Air Filter Units, which is identified in Part II of Chapter 16 as being UL Standard 900, bearing the same title, and is invoked in Section 402.3. In the 1994 code, this was Section 403.

## SECTION 402 — SUPPLY AIR

This section applies to mechanical ventilation systems and not to openable windows.

**402.1 General.** This is a new requirement. Supply of ventilation air shall be obtained from an approved outside air source or a return air source or both, and shall be conveyed by ducts unless the approved equipment does not require a duct connection.

**402.2 Screened Openings.** Openings, both inlet and outlet require screening.

**402.3 Filters.** In air supply systems, filters are required and shall be listed as Class I or II units. In institutional occupancies where the supply air system serves sensitive areas, additional filters having a minimum efficiency of 90 percent are required downstream of cooling coils, humidification equipment and supply fans.

**402.4 Make-up Air.** This section contains the requirement for make-up air supply systems to be electrically interlocked to their associated exhaust systems.

**402.5 Duct Size.** This is a new requirement that calls the designer's attention to the need for correct duct sizing in air supply systems to maintain a balanced pressure within the building and to avoid creation of excessively large negative pressure due to the operation of exhaust systems.

## SECTION 403 — OUTSIDE AIR

**403.1 General.** Chapter 12 and Appendix Chapter 12 of the UBC establish outside air requirements for mechanical ventilating systems. This new section of the UMC provides the designer with a cross reference to the amounts required for Building Code compliance. Section 403 establishes the appropriate location for outside air inlets to ensure that objectional odors and noxious gases are not entrained in the act of ventilating a building.

## SECTION 404 — RETURN AIR

Except in unusual circumstances, a part of the air for mechanical ventilation may be obtained from within the building itself. The locations that are itemized in Section 404.1 are those from which air should not be recirculated. It is almost self-evident that to compensate for a lack of recirculation, additional quantities of outside air will be required.

## SECTION 405 — DIRECT GAS-FIRED MAKE-UP AIR SYSTEMS

Direct gas-fired make-up air heaters are not suitable for installation, except in commercial or industrial occupancies, because of their listing. They should not be installed for heating residential occupancies. The common application is in commercial kitchens to provide tempered make-up air for employee comfort and to compensate for the heat loss due to operation of the kitchen exhaust system.

# Chapter 5
# EXHAUST SYSTEMS

### Part I—Product-conveying and Environmental Air Systems

## SECTION 501 — SCOPE OF PART I

Many industrial processes produce air contaminants in the form of dusts, fumes, smokes, mists, vapors and gases. Contaminants should be controlled at the source so they are not dispersed through the workplace or allowed to increase to flammable or toxic concentrations. Zero concentration of contaminants is not economically feasible. Absolute control of contaminants cannot be maintained, and workers can assimilate small quantities of various toxic materials without injury. Industrial hygiene science is based on the fact that most air contaminants become toxic only if their concentration exceeds a maximum allowable limit for a specified period.

Flammable gases and vapors can also be products of industrial processes. A flammable liquid's vapor pressure and volatility or rate of evaporation determines its ability to form an explosive mixture. These properties can be expressed by the flash point, which is the temperature to which combustible liquid must be heated to produce a flash when a small flame is passed across the surface of the liquid. Uniform Mechanical Code Standard 2-3 reproduced in Appendix A of the UMC is an accepted method of determining the flash point of flammable liquids. In practice, the air-vapor or air-gas mixture must be in the explosive range before it can be ignited. If the concentration is limited to a certain percentage of the lower explosive limit of the material, the resulting factor of safety allows latitude for imperfections in air distribution and variations in temperature or mixture and guards against unpredictable or unrecognized sources of ignition.

Combustible dust is another product of some industrial and food-processing operations. Many organic and some mineral dusts can produce dust explosions. Often, a primary explosion results from a small amount of dust in suspension that has been exposed to an ignition source; the pressure and vibration created can dislodge larger accumulations from dust on horizontal surfaces, creating a larger secondary explosion. Explosive dusts are potential hazards whenever uncontrolled dust escapes, dispersing in the atmosphere or settling on horizontal surfaces such as beams and ledges.

Exhaust systems should be designed to dispose of these contaminants, flammable vapors and dusts. Exhaust systems have four basic components:

1. The hood, or entry point of the system;
2. The duct system, which transfers air;
3. The air-cleaning device, which removes contaminants from the air; and
4. The air-moving device, which provides motive power for overcoming system resistance.

Chapter 5, Part I, covers the requirements for the installation of product-conveying duct systems. The provisions are meant to cover the transfer and disposal of not only solid particles, but also the transfer and disposal of contaminants, flammable vapors, fumes, dusts, smokes, spray, mists, fogs, etc.

In addition, Section 504 is included to regulate environmental air-ventilation systems that are not part of heating or cooling systems such as makeup-air and air exhaust systems, domestic range vents, domestic dryer vents, commercial dryer exhaust systems, and bathroom and laundry room exhausts. The construction of environmental air duct systems is covered in Chapter 6.

Please note that provisions for commercial hood and kitchen ventilation systems are covered separately in Chapter 5, Part II.

## SECTION 502 — DEFINITIONS

**"ENVIRONMENTAL AIR DUCT** is ducting used for conveying air at temperatures not exceeding 250°F (121°C) to or from occupied areas of any occupancy through other than heating or air-conditioning systems, such as ventilation for human usage, domestic kitchen range exhaust, bathroom exhaust ducts, and domestic-type clothes dryer exhaust ducts.

**"FLAMMABLE VAPOR OR FUMES** is the concentration of flammable constituents in air that exceeds 10 percent of its lower flammability limit (LFL).

**"PRODUCT-CONVEYING DUCT** is ducting used for conveying solid particulates, such as refuse, dust, fumes and smoke; liquid particulate matter, such as spray residue, mists and fogs; vapors, such as vapors from flammable or corrosive liquids; noxious and toxic gases; and air" heated "at temperatures exceeding 250°F (121°C)" by other than a heating system. Environmental air ducts are typically installed in structures intended for human occupancy. Product-conveying duct systems are usually installed in industrial and commercial occupancies.

## SECTION 503 — MOTORS AND FANS

**503.1 General.** Motors and fans must be sized to provide the air movement needed for efficient operation of the system. Among the factors to be considered are required volume, required velocities, duct and fitting pressure losses, and fan characteristics. The code requires that motors in areas containing flammable vapors or dusts be of types approved for use in such an environment.

A manually operated remote control switch installed in an approved location (one that is well marked and accessible) must be provided to shut down the fans and/or blowers in flammable vapor or dust-conveying systems.

Electrical equipment such as saws, grinders, buffing wheels, etc., used in industrial operations that generate explosive or flammable vapors, fumes or dusts must be electrically interlocked with the product-conveying ventilation system. This interlock prevents operation of contaminant-producing power equipment when the ventilation system is not operating. In this way, a dangerous build-up of vapor or dust may be avoided since the vapor or dust can be ignited by spark or heat from power equipment. Motors or fans used to convey flammable dust or vapors must be located outside the duct or be protected with approved shielding and dustproofing methods.

An acceptable design can be a fan within the duct, with the motor located outside and connected via a belt. See Figure 5-1. Such motors and fans must be accessible for servicing and maintenance. This is essential for reliable operation and long system life.

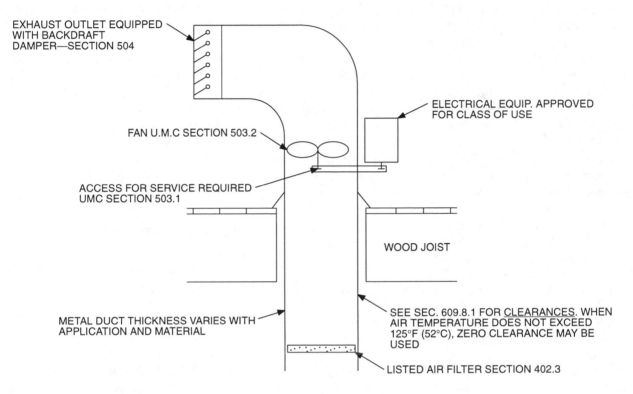

EXHAUST OUTLET EQUIPPED WITH BACKDRAFT DAMPER—SECTION 504

FAN U.M.C SECTION 503.2

ACCESS FOR SERVICE REQUIRED UMC SECTION 503.1

METAL DUCT THICKNESS VARIES WITH APPLICATION AND MATERIAL

ELECTRICAL EQUIP. APPROVED FOR CLASS OF USE

WOOD JOIST

SEE SEC. 609.8.1 FOR CLEARANCES. WHEN AIR TEMPERATURE DOES NOT EXCEED 125°F (52°C), ZERO CLEARANCE MAY BE USED

LISTED AIR FILTER SECTION 402.3

**ENVIRONMENTAL AIR DUCTS**

**FIGURE 5-1**

**503.2 Fans.** Either all parts of fans in contact with explosive or flammable vapors, fumes or dusts must be made of nonferrous or nonsparking materials or their casing must be constructed or lined with such materials. However, when the size and hardness of material passing through the fan(s) could produce a spark, both the fan and the casing must be made from nonsparking materials. When spark-resistant fans are required, their bearings must be outside the air stream carrying explosive or flammable vapors. In addition, all fan parts must be electrically grounded. These safety precautions minimize the likelihood of sparking that may ignite flammable vapors or dusts. Such special purpose fans should be listed for their intended use by an approved agency.

For the following applications, fans must be of the radial-blade or tube-axial type (see Figure 5-2):

1. To handle materials likely to clog the blades (metals, wet or heavy dusts); and
2. For buffing or woodworking systems.

**503.2.1 Equipment identification plate.** Equipment used to exhaust explosive or flammable vapors, fumes or dusts must bear an identification plate showing the ventilation in cubic feet per minute (m³/s) for which the system was designed.

**503.2.2 Corrosion-resistant fans.** Fans located in a product-conveying duct system containing corrosive vapors must be built from, or coated thoroughly with, corrosion-resistant materials. The manufacturer of the fan and the listing agency should verify that the chosen fan is acceptable for the particular corrosive vapor to be vented. Each corrosive vapor has its own properties. No single fan material possesses universal application for all types of vapors.

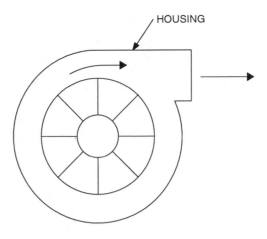

CENTRIFUGAL RADIALLY BLADED FAN

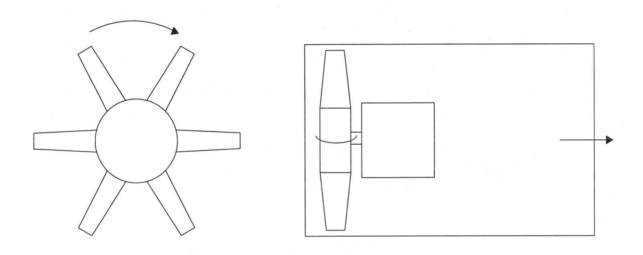

**TUBE-AXIAL FAN**
**SECTION 503.2**

**FIGURE 5-2**

## SECTION 504 — ENVIRONMENTAL AIR DUCTS

Environmental air ducts not elsewhere regulated by the UMC must comply with this section. Construction of duct systems is specified in Chapter 6. Exhaust ventilation ducts must terminate outside the building in a location complying with the Building and Mechanical codes [3 feet (914 mm) from the property line and 3 feet (914 mm) from openings into the building to minimize recirculation] and should be equipped with backdraft dampers. Ducts used as part of an approved smoke-control system do not require design as Class I product-conveying ducts.

Ducts used for domestic kitchen range ventilation and domestic clothes dryers must be of metal and have a smooth interior surface. An exception to Section 504.2 permits ducts serving downdraft grill ranges to be of Schedule 40 PVC if buried under a concrete slab.

**504.3 Domestic Dryer Vent.** Domestic dryer exhaust can be ducted by a flexible duct connector, not more than 6 feet (1829 mm) in length, as long as no part of the connector is concealed within construction. Section 504.3.2 contains a length limitation on domestic dryer moisture-exhaust ducts, while Section 908 specifies the minimum size of domestic clothes dryer moisture-exhaust ducts and also contains a minimum makeup-air opening for dryers installed in compartments. The minimum makeup-air requirement arises because a clothes dryer is, in effect, an air pump removing air from the compartment in which it is installed. For length limitations and additional information, refer to Section 908.

Bathroom and laundry exhaust ducts may be flexible, nonmetallic, corrugated or gypsum wall board subject to the temperature and moisture limitations of Section 601.1.

Exhaust ducts for commercial dryers, laundries, dry cleaning and other commercial establishments must be installed in accordance with their listing.

**504.3.1 Moisture-exhaust ducts.** Moisture-exhaust ducts must terminate outside of the building and be equipped with a back-draft damper. Screens are not allowed at the duct termination. It should be noted that a moisture-exhaust duct should not be terminated in an attic, even if it is well ventilated, because the moisture vapor may condense on the roof sheathing, rafters or insulation, particularly in cold climates. Exhaust ducts for clothes dryers must not be connected with metal screws or fastening devices that may extend inside the duct. This is to prevent the accumulation of lint, which may create a fire hazard. The best fasteners for use in this application would be blind pop rivets. To avoid the hazards of cross connections, clothes dryer exhaust ducts may not extend into or through ducts or plenums. Figures 5-3 and 5-4 show typical domestic clothes dryer installation.

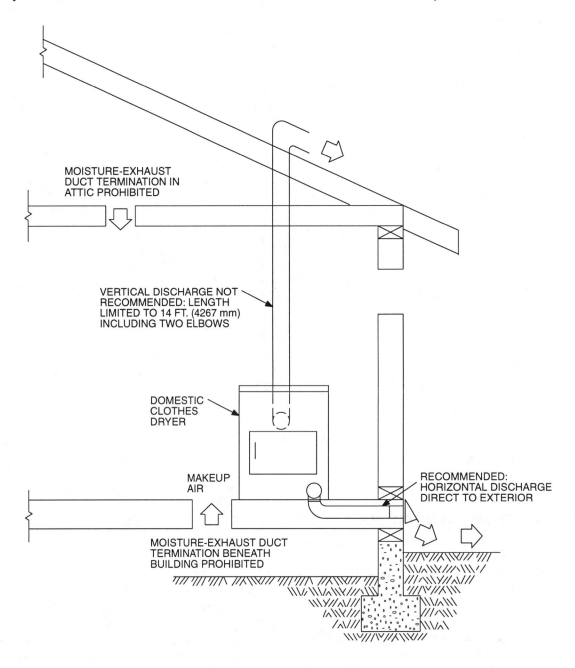

MOISTURE-EXHAUST DUCT TERMINATION IN ATTIC PROHIBITED

VERTICAL DISCHARGE NOT RECOMMENDED: LENGTH LIMITED TO 14 FT. (4267 mm) INCLUDING TWO ELBOWS

DOMESTIC CLOTHES DRYER

MAKEUP AIR

RECOMMENDED: HORIZONTAL DISCHARGE DIRECT TO EXTERIOR

MOISTURE-EXHAUST DUCT TERMINATION BENEATH BUILDING PROHIBITED

**TYPICAL DOMESTIC CLOTHES DRYER AND MOISTURE-EXHAUST DUCT**

**FIGURE 5-3**

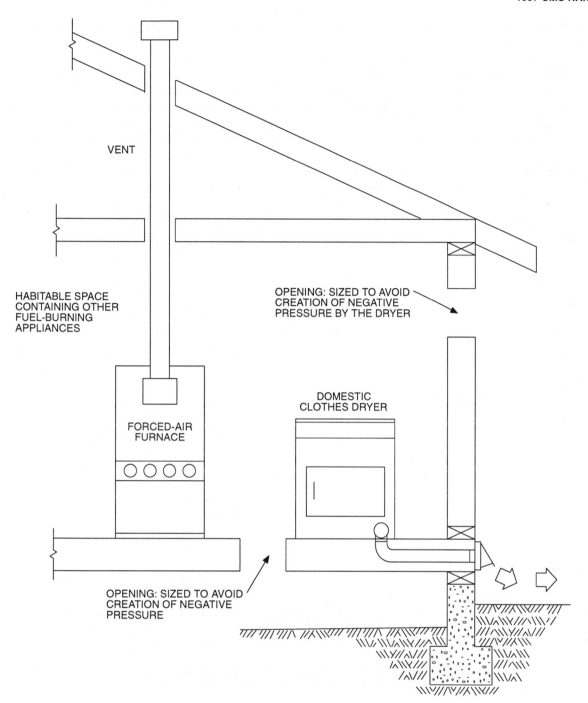

VENT

HABITABLE SPACE
CONTAINING OTHER
FUEL-BURNING
APPLIANCES

OPENING: SIZED TO AVOID
CREATION OF NEGATIVE
PRESSURE BY THE DRYER

DOMESTIC
CLOTHES DRYER

FORCED-AIR
FURNACE

OPENING: SIZED TO AVOID
CREATION OF NEGATIVE
PRESSURE

**CLOTHES DRYER AND FORCED-AIR FURNACE**

**FIGURE 5-4**

**504.3.2 Length limitation.** Unless otherwise permitted or required by the listing of the device, and approved by the building official, domestic clothes dryer moisture-exhaust ducts are not to exceed a total combined vertical and horizontal length of 14 feet (4267 mm), including two 90-degree elbows. Two feet (610 mm) is to be deducted from the total allowed length for each 90-degree elbow in excess of two. Although this section allows longer lengths if permitted by the listing of the clothes dryer, it is prudent for the building official to use discretion since the dryers are not usually installed at the time of final inspection and the homeowner/occupant may switch the appliance later.

## SECTION 505 — PRODUCT-CONVEYING SYSTEMS

**505.1 General.** When product use or handling generates emissions that must be removed, as required by the Building or Fire codes, or poses a hazard to life and property, a mechanical ventilation or exhaust system must be installed to control, capture and transport these emissions.

The product-conveying system must be designed such that emissions are confined to the area where they are generated and are removed by the duct system to an approved location or treated to remove the contaminants by acceptable means. Ducts that convey explosives or flammable vapors, fumes or dusts must extend from the source and area of first containment directly to the building exterior without entering or passing through other spaces. See Figure 5-5.

> **EXCEPTION:** Ducts conveying products at less than 25 percent of their LFL may pass through other spaces.

In addition, exhaust ducts may not extend into or through ducts or plenums because of the potential for cross contamination.

Separate and distinct systems must be provided for incompatible materials. Mixing incompatible materials could cause explosion, chemical reaction, precipitation of solids or liquids in the duct system or could reduce the system's life. Contaminated air must not be circulated to occupied areas. The designer can show that contaminants have been removed. Obviously, recirculation of air contaminated with explosive or flammable vapors, fumes or dusts; flammable or toxic gases; or radioactive material must not be allowed, regardless of the level of removal that can be achieved.

Note that under UMC Section 609.5 ducts conveying explosive dust must have explosion vents located outside the building.

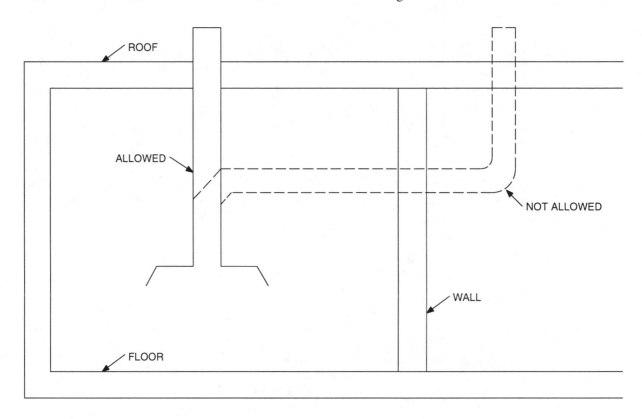

**VENTILATION DUCT DIRECTLY TO EXTERIOR WHEN HANDLING
FLAMMABLE VAPORS. DUSTS OR EXPLOSIVE MIXTURES
SECTION 505.1**

**FIGURE 5-5**

**505.4 Minimum Velocities and Circulation.** In conveying solid particulates, vapors, or noxious, corrosive, flammable or explosive gases, adequate velocity must be maintained throughout the system. Otherwise, many contaminants will tend to precipitate, condense or separate from the air stream; if this occurs, the deposit may obstruct the duct system. Mixtures within the work area must be diluted below 25 percent of their LFL with air that does not contain other contaminants. Minimum velocities are set forth in Table 5-A of the UMC for various common industrial materials.

The entire work area ventilation system must be designed and constructed so that contaminants are captured by an air stream at the area of generation (typically a single workstation), and conveyed directly into the product-conveying duct system.

Systems for the removal of vapors, gases and smoke must be designed using the constant velocity or equal friction methods. Systems for particulate matter are to be designed using the constant velocity method. Systems conveying explosive or radioactive materials are to be prebalanced through duct sizing. Other systems may be designed with balancing devices such as dampers, provided that minimum-position blocking devices are installed to prevent restricting flow below the minimum required volume or velocity.

While the duct system can be designed and installed with predictable results, humidities and temperatures within the industrial plant can be difficult to control or predict. Large openings such as windows, doors or vents can drastically alter the environment. Similarly, subsequent remodeling of the structure or the heating, ventilating and air-conditioning (HVAC) system may affect the product-conveying system and is difficult to predict. Care should be taken when reviewing proposed remodeling or alterations to these installations so that the existing exhaust systems are not adversely affected.

A common question posed by those who design product-conveying duct systems is whether a small cyclone-type dust collector or self-contained or portable mechanical dust-collection system can be used to collect flammable dusts in bags or containers at each piece of woodworking equipment, in lieu of the central system required by UBC Section 306.8. Since storage of wood residues should be in exterior noncombustible containers or in other approved locations as specified in UBC Section 306.8, a central product-conveying duct system that will transport hazardous dusts to the outside of the building is required.

**505.6 Makeup Air.** In order to maintain a balanced-pressure environment, makeup air must be provided to replenish the air exhausted by the ventilation system. The makeup air intakes or outside air sources must be located to avoid recirculation of contaminated air within enclosures.

**505.7 Hoods and Enclosures.** When air contaminants are produced in a concentrated area, hoods and enclosures must be used to capture these contaminants. A concentrated source area is typical of many industrial processes that generate product contaminants. The hood or enclosure design must be such that the air currents created by the exhaust system will capture the contaminants and transport them directly to the exhaust duct. This is usually achieved by creating a partial vacuum within the hood or a slight positive pressure around the hood. The volume of air must be great enough to dilute explosive or flammable vapors, fumes or dusts to below 25 percent of the lower explosive or flammability limit of the contaminant. The lower flammability limit is unique to each material to be exhausted and is also a function of temperature, humidity

and other factors. Research in mines, refineries, chemical and other industrial plants, and in farm environments of all types, has led to the current body of scientific knowledge and field experience in what constitutes a "safe lower limit." Much of this knowledge has been acquired the hard way, through fires, explosions, property damage, injury and loss of life.

Hoods must be made of steel and must have a base metal thickness as follows:

Class 1 and Class 5
  Duct Systems            22 gage (0.027 inch) (0.69 mm)
Class 2
  Duct Systems            20 gage (0.033 inch) (0.84 mm)
Class 3
  Duct Systems            18 gage (0.044 inch) (1.12 mm)
Class 4
  Duct Systems            14 gage (0.068 inch) (1.73 mm)

Class 5 corrosive systems may use approved nonmetallic hoods only when the corrosive mixture is nonflammable. Metal hoods used in such installations must be protected with corrosion-resistant material.

Hood edges must be rounded to avoid the risk of personal injury. The clearance of hood to combustible construction must not be less than that required for the exhaust duct.

## SECTION 506 — PRODUCT-CONVEYING DUCT SYSTEMS

**506.1 Classification.** This section identifies five classes of product-conveying ducts according to their use:

**Class 1.** Ducts conveying nonabrasives, such as smoke, spray, mists, fogs, noncorrosive fumes and gases, light fine dusts or powders.

**Class 2.** Ducts conveying moderately abrasive particulate in light concentrations, such as sawdust and grain dust, buffing and polishing dust.

**Class 3.** Ducts conveying Class 2 materials in high concentrations and highly abrasive materials in low concentrations, such as manganese, steel chips and coke.

**Class 4.** Ducts conveying highly abrasive material in high concentrations.

**Class 5.** Ducts conveying corrosives, such as acid vapors.

## Part II—Commercial Kitchens

## SECTION 507 — COMMERCIAL KITCHEN HOODS AND KITCHEN VENTILATION SYSTEMS

**507.2 Definitions.** For the purpose of Chapter 5, Part II, the following definitions apply:

**COMMERCIAL FOOD HEAT-PROCESSING EQUIPMENT** is equipment used in a food establishment for heat-processing food or utensils and which produces grease vapors, steam, fumes, smoke or odors which are re-

quired to be removed through a local exhaust ventilation system.

**COMPENSATING HOOD** is a hood that has an outside air supply with air delivered below or within the hood. When makeup air is diffused directly into the exhaust within the hood cavity, it becomes a short-circuit hood.

**GREASE FILTER** is a device used to capture by entrapment, impingement, adhesion or similar means, grease and similar contaminants before they enter a duct system.

**HOOD** is an air-intake device connected to a mechanical exhaust system for collecting and removing grease, vapors, fumes, smoke, steam, heat or odors from commercial food heat-processing equipment.

**Type I Hood** is a kitchen hood for collecting and removing grease and smoke.

Figure 5-6 illustrates the concepts of both conventional and compensating Type I hoods.

**Type II Hood** is a general kitchen hood for collecting and removing steam, vapor, heat or odors.

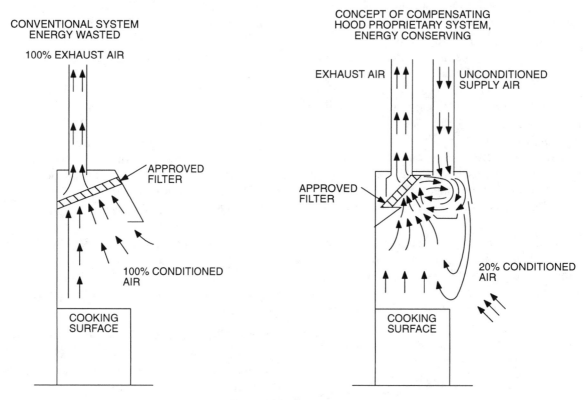

**COMMERCIAL KITCHEN GREASE HOODS**

**FIGURE 5-6**

**507.3 Grease Duct Materials.** At least No. 16 manufacturer's standard gage steel or No. 18 gage stainless steel is required for grease ducts and plenums serving a Type I hood for removing grease-laden vapors and smoke.

**507.3.1 Fan casing.** Exhaust fan housing serving a Type I hood must be constructed of steel.

> **EXCEPTION:** Fans listed as "power roof ventilators for restaurant cooking appliances."

**507.3.2 Joints and seams of grease ducts.** All joints and seams must be made with a continuous liquid-tight weld or braze on the external surface of the duct system. A vibration isolation connector may be used, provided it consists of noncombustible packing in a metal sleeve joint of approved design. The section of the duct between a Type I hood and the ceiling above is not considered as part of the hood and must comply with the thickness requirement for ducts; its joints and seams must be welded if no vibration isolation connector is installed. Note that even the connection between a grease duct and the hood's collar must be made with a continuous liquid-tight weld or

braze. Also, the plenum area downstream of the filters and hood collar should be considered as part of the grease duct system.

**507.3.3 Grease duct supports.** Duct bracing and supports must be of noncombustible material securely attached to the structure and designed to carry gravity and lateral loads within the stress limitations specified in the Building Code. Bolts, screws, rivets and other mechanical fasteners must not penetrate duct walls.

**507.3.4 Nongrease ducts.** Ducts and plenums serving Type II hoods (for removing steam, vapor, heat or odors) must be constructed of rigid metallic materials for ductwork and must be braced and supported as required in Chapter 6. Pressurized ducts must be adequately sealed.

**507.3.5 Corrosion protection.** Ducts and plenums exposed to outside atmosphere or subject to a corrosive environment must be protected against corrosion. Methods of protection include, but are not limited to, galvanization of metal parts, protection with noncorrosive paints and waterproof insulation.

**507.4 Prevention of Grease Accumulation.** Duct systems serving a Type I hood must be constructed in such a manner that grease cannot be pocketed or deposited in any portion of the duct system. The horizontal portions of the duct system must slope at least $1/4$ inch per lineal foot ($1/4$ unit vertical in 12 units horizontal) (2% slope) toward the hood or toward an approved grease reservoir. When horizontal ducts exceed 75 feet (22 860 mm) in length, they must slope at least 1 inch per lineal foot (1 unit vertical in 12 units horizontal) (8% slope).

When a centrifugal fan is used, it must be positioned so that the discharge outlet is either vertical or in a bottom horizontal position. A typical centrifugal fan installation on a roof is shown in Figure 5-7. The air must be directed so that impingement on the roof and other equipment or parts of the structure is avoided. Vertical discharge fans must include an approved drain outlet at the bottom of the housing to allow grease to be drained to an approved collection device. In addition, vertical discharge fans (upblast) should be listed specifically as suitable for application in restaurant exhaust systems. Note that the difference between an ordinary exhaust fan and those listed for grease exhaust systems is that the latter category is tested for a maximum operating temperature of 300°F (149°C). An approved grease-collection device is a device approved by the building official for capturing grease, such as a trough draining by gravity to a reservoir that could be washed in the dishwasher or in the pot-scrub sink. It could also mean provisions for a washdown with a hot detergent solution or steam, either manually controlled or automatically controlled by a timer.

SCHEMATIC DIAGRAM—DO NOT USE FOR CONSTRUCTION

FOR DUCTS SERVING TYPE II HOODS, SEE UMC TABLES 6-A AND 6-B AND SECTION 507.3.4

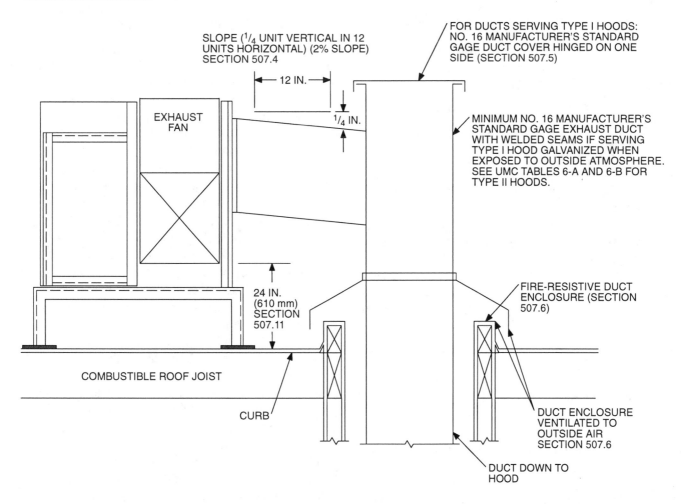

**TYPICAL DETAILS—KITCHEN EXHAUST SYSTEMS**

**FIGURE 5-7**

**507.4.1 Grease diverter.** When a centrifugal fan with bottom horizontal discharge is installed outside the building, a duct or fitting that directs the discharge upward may be connected to the fan outlet when the following conditions are met:

1. The duct or fitting must be constructed of metal as specified in Tables 6-A and 6-B or in UMC Standard 6-1.

2. The maximum total developed length of the duct or fitting measured along the center line cannot exceed three times the vertical dimension of the fan outlet.

3. The duct or fittings must have openings to permit drainage of grease to an approved collection device.

**507.5 Cleanouts and Other Openings.** Grease duct systems cannot have openings except those that are necessary for the proper operation and maintenance of the system. A portion of a duct system that is inaccessible from the duct entry at the hood or from the discharge at the fan must be provided with cleanout openings. The entire interior of the duct system must be accessible for cleaning. Cleanout openings must be equipped with tightfitting doors constructed of a gage of steel at least as thick as that required for the duct. The doors must be equipped with a substantial latching method that is strong enough to hold the doors tightly closed and designed so the doors can be opened without the use of a tool.

**507.6 Duct Enclosure.** Figure 5-8 illustrates a number of Mechanical Code requirements applicable to a commercial kitchen exhaust system. A grease duct serving a Type I hood that penetrates a ceiling, wall or floor must be enclosed in a duct enclosure from point of penetration to the outside air. A duct may only penetrate exterior walls at locations where unprotected openings are permitted by the Building Code. A grease duct enclosure is constructed like a shaft enclosure as covered by the Building Code; however, all requirements are included in the UMC. UBC Section 711 requirements are not applicable to grease duct enclosures. Duct enclosures must be of at least one-hour fire-resistive construction in all buildings and of two-hour fire-resistive construction in Types I and II fire-resistive buildings.

The duct enclosure must be sealed at the point of penetration of the ceiling, wall or floor and vented to the exterior through weather-protected openings. The duct enclosure must be separated from the duct by at least 3 inches (76 mm) and not more than 12 inches (305 mm), and it must serve only a single grease exhaust duct system. The *Uniform Mechanical Code* does not require that a makeup air duct required by Section 402.4 be enclosed in a duct enclosure. However, some designs of factory-built compensating hoods have the makeup air duct located so close to the grease exhaust duct that it is impossible to separate the ducts with a duct enclosure; in fact, at least one listed compensating hood has the makeup air duct entirely surrounding the grease exhaust duct. In those instances, both ducts should be fabricated of 16 gage steel and installed in the same enclosure.

When a Type I hood penetrates a ceiling, wall or furred space, Section 508.4 requires that that portion be enclosed in an enclosure as required by Section 507.6. If a compensating hood makeup air duct penetrates the grease duct enclosure, it should be either enclosed in a rated enclosure or it should be equipped with a fire damper.

One frequently asked question is whether the special provisions of UBC Section 711 mean that a grease duct enclosure is not required in two- and three-story buildings. *Uniform Building Code* Section 711 deals with shaft enclosures protecting openings in floors. A grease duct enclosure required by Section 507.6 may run horizontally as well as vertically, but its principal purpose is to prevent the duct, which may be red hot when grease is burning in its interior, from acting as a source of ignition for combustible materials exposed to its radiant energy. By enclosing every portion of a concealed grease duct within at least one-hour fire-resistive construction, even in a one-story building, the radiation is contained, and until the duct enclosure fails, other parts of the structure will be unaffected.

The intent of the reference to the Building Code here is to ensure that a grease duct is enclosed by a construction having a full one-hour or two-hour fire-resistive rating as indicated in UBC Table 7-B. The reference to the Building Code should not be construed to permit the installation of concealed grease ducts without being enclosed in a rated grease duct enclosure.

The intent of the requirement that the duct enclosure be separated from the grease duct by at least 3 inches (76 mm) and not more than 12 inches (305 mm) is to create an air space surrounding the duct that is sealed at its lower end and vented to the exterior above the roof. The purpose of that air space or annulus is to provide warning to fire service personnel on the roof of the building when the grease duct has been penetrated by fire. In the scenario explaining the sequence of the fire development, it was theorized that during the earliest stages of a grease duct fire, flames would be confined within the duct itself and appear only at the exhaust termination above the roof. As the fire progresses, the grease duct will be burned through and flames will then appear both at the exhaust termination and at the vent at the top of the grease duct enclosure. Because of the limited fire resistance of a grease duct enclosure, the fire service personnel would be warned that structural integrity of the roof was being threatened and that it would be prudent to evacuate the roof top.

The required maximum separation of 12 inches (305 mm) was imposed to discourage other uses of the annular space, such as for electrical wiring and piping, and to facilitate cleaning the duct through openings in the duct enclosure.

SCHEMATIC DIAGRAM—DO NOT USE FOR CONSTRUCTION

PROTECT OUTDOOR DUCTS AGAINST CORROSION. SECTION 507.3.5

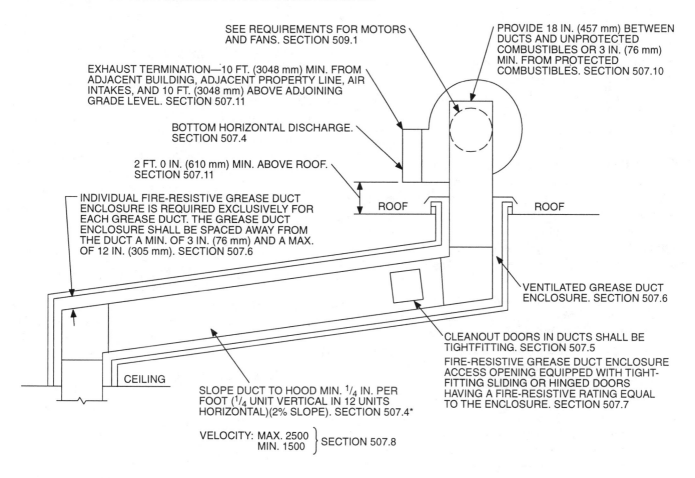

SEE REQUIREMENTS FOR MOTORS AND FANS. SECTION 509.1

PROVIDE 18 IN. (457 mm) BETWEEN DUCTS AND UNPROTECTED COMBUSTIBLES OR 3 IN. (76 mm) MIN. FROM PROTECTED COMBUSTIBLES. SECTION 507.10

EXHAUST TERMINATION—10 FT. (3048 mm) MIN. FROM ADJACENT BUILDING, ADJACENT PROPERTY LINE, AIR INTAKES, AND 10 FT. (3048 mm) ABOVE ADJOINING GRADE LEVEL. SECTION 507.11

BOTTOM HORIZONTAL DISCHARGE. SECTION 507.4

2 FT. 0 IN. (610 mm) MIN. ABOVE ROOF. SECTION 507.11

INDIVIDUAL FIRE-RESISTIVE GREASE DUCT ENCLOSURE IS REQUIRED EXCLUSIVELY FOR EACH GREASE DUCT. THE GREASE DUCT ENCLOSURE SHALL BE SPACED AWAY FROM THE DUCT A MIN. OF 3 IN. (76 mm) AND A MAX. OF 12 IN. (305 mm). SECTION 507.6

ROOF

ROOF

VENTILATED GREASE DUCT ENCLOSURE. SECTION 507.6

CEILING

CLEANOUT DOORS IN DUCTS SHALL BE TIGHTFITTING. SECTION 507.5

FIRE-RESISTIVE GREASE DUCT ENCLOSURE ACCESS OPENING EQUIPPED WITH TIGHT-FITTING SLIDING OR HINGED DOORS HAVING A FIRE-RESISTIVE RATING EQUAL TO THE ENCLOSURE. SECTION 507.7

SLOPE DUCT TO HOOD MIN. $1/4$ IN. PER FOOT ($1/4$ UNIT VERTICAL IN 12 UNITS HORIZONTAL)(2% SLOPE). SECTION 507.4*

VELOCITY: MAX. 2500 MIN. 1500 } SECTION 507.8

* WHEN DUCT LENGTH EXCEEDS 75 FEET (22 860 mm), SLOPE 1 INCH PER FOOT (1 UNIT VERTICAL IN 12 UNITS HORIZONTAL)(8% SLOPE). SECTION 507.4

**GENERAL**
1. Design of vibration isolation connectors shall be approved by the building official. Section 507.3.2.
2. Provide adequate cleanout openings for thorough cleaning of duct system. Section 507.5.
3. Provide adequate makeup air for proper operation. Section 402.4.
4. Provide a separate duct system for each hood. See Section 507.9 for an exception.
5. Thickness of ducts shall be at least 0.055-inch (1.40 mm) (No. 16 manufacturer's standard gage) steel or No. 18 manufacturer's standard gage stainless steel. Section 507.3.
6. Weld or brace all duct joints and seams on the external surface. Section 507.3.
7. Sections of duct shall not contain grease pockets. Section 507.4.

**FIGURE 5-8**

**507.7 Fire-resistive Access Opening.** When cleanouts are located on ducts inside a fire-resistive grease duct enclosure, access openings must be provided in the enclosure at each cleanout point. These access openings must be equipped with tightfitting sliding or hinged doors equal in fire-resistive protection to that required for the grease duct enclosure.

**507.8 Air Velocity.** A grease duct system serving a Type I hood must be designed, installed and adjusted so that it provides an air velocity within the duct system of at least 1,500 feet per minute (7.5 m/s) but not more than 2,500 feet per minute (12.7 m/s). The maximum velocity specification is a noise-control measurement.

It is important to maintain the minimum velocity of 1,500 feet per minute (7.5 m/s) since lower velocities may allow airborne grease and oils to condense and deposit within the ducts, creating a high fire hazard.

It should be noted that a commercial kitchen ventilation system is not required to exhaust air continuously, but only when the cooking equipment is in use. There is no requirement for duct velocity to be maintained when food is not being prepared.

**507.9 Separation of Grease Duct System.** A separate duct system must be provided for each Type I hood, except that a single duct system may serve more than one hood if located in the same story of the building, provided that all hoods served by the system are located in the same or adjoining rooms. No portions of the interconnected ducts can pass through construction that would require the opening to be fire protected as specified in the Building Code.

**507.10 Clearances.** Exposed grease duct systems serving a Type I hood must have a clearance from unprotected combustible construction of at least 18 inches (457 mm). This clearance may be reduced to 3 inches (76 mm) if the combustible construction is protected with material required for one-hour fire-resistive construction.

**507.11 Exhaust Outlets.** Unless approved by the building official, exhaust outlets for grease ducts serving commercial food heat-processing equipment must extend through the roof. The exhaust outlet must extend at least 2 feet (610 mm) vertically above the roof surface. It must also be at least 10 feet (3048 mm) away from parts of the same or contiguous buildings, property lines or air intake openings into a building and must be at least 10 feet (3048 mm) above the adjoining grade level. There are two exceptions:

1. If the air from the exhaust outlet is discharged away from such locations, the exhaust outlet may terminate 5 feet (1524 mm) from an adjacent building or contiguous building, property line or air intake opening. Note that this exception can be directly applied to a vertical upblast discharge exhaust fan.

2. If approved by the building official, the exhaust may terminate in a properly engineered air recovery system for recirculation into the room where the hood is located. It is recommended that such a system also be listed for this purpose by an approved agency.

**507.12 Fuel-burning Appliances.** Vented fuel-burning appliances located in the same space or room as a commercial kitchen hood must be arranged so as to prevent the commercial equipment hood system from interfering with the normal operation of the fuel-burning appliance venting system. The primary concern is that makeup air must be supplied so that the room containing the hood will not depressurize below atmospheric pressure, which could result in reversal of flow in the appliance venting system and, if severe enough, could affect burner performance by causing flame lifting and affect complete combustion of fuel.

## SECTION 508 — COMMERCIAL KITCHEN HOODS

**508.1 Where Hoods Are Required.** Type I or II hoods must be installed at or above the following equipment:

1. Commercial-type deep fat fryers, broilers, fry grills, steam-jacketed kettles, hot-top ranges, ovens, barbecues, rotisseries and dishwashing machines.

2. Similar equipment producing comparable amounts of steam, smoke, grease or heat in a food-processing establishment.

A "food-processing establishment" includes a building or portion thereof used for the processing of food except a dwelling unit or its kitchen.

In general, a Type I hood should be required over grease- or smoke-producing commercial-type cooking equipment, such as deep fat fryers, broilers, fry grills, hot-top ranges, ovens, barbecues, rotisseries, etc., installed in commercial businesses.

Type II hoods should be required over other cooking equipment producing steam, heat, vapors or odors, such as bakery ovens, steam tables, coffee urns, dishwashers, etc.

When a residential-type cooking range is installed in locations that are not commercial businesses, such as day-care centers, churches, social hall kitchens, lounges of office complexes, fire stations, etc., a Type II hood may be allowed with prior approval from the building official. However, when commercial-type cooking equipment is installed in these types of occupancies, the issue is not quite so clear cut, since these occupancies are not usually considered "businesses engaged in processing food." Some building officials infer from the installation of commercial cooking equipment that the use may become a business at some future time and thus have adopted a local policy that a Type I hood and fire-suppression system must be installed when commercial cooking equipment is specified. Such policy may be legally questionable, but arises from the concern that the use could become more intensive without the jurisdiction's knowledge and without fire-protection and -suppression systems.

When commercial-type kitchen ranges are proposed to be installed in individual residences, great care must be taken to investigate the installation thoroughly. Although the code does not require a Type I hood and duct system in a dwelling, when a commercial range or oven is indicated on the plans, several precautions should be observed.

A copy of the manufacturer's installation instructions should be obtained since most commercial equipment requires greater clearances at sides, rear and above than do ordinary domestic appliances. Some are not listed for installation adjacent to combustible walls or on combustible floors, and some are not suitable for installation in alcoves or with cabinets and cupboards surrounding the installation. Some are even listed for commercial installations only.

The cabinets and cupboards may have to be of noncombustible construction when close to commercial equipment, and even then they may become too hot for comfortable use or may expose combustibles within the cabinet. Similarly, clearances to combustible ceilings and cabinets above the equipment must be examined. Often, commercial burners are adjusted to produce long flames when a burner cover is removed.

Finally, if the proposal is to entirely omit a hood, the building official should consider how the heat from the range top is going to be dissipated. Many hot-top range sections have inputs exceeding 70,000 Btu/h (2051 W). A Type II hood system, either gravity or mechanically exhausted, may be needed to rid the kitchen of the heat. If the duct must pass through concealed space above the ceiling, it should be enclosed in a ventilation shaft constructed as required in Section 907 for an open-top broiler unit.

Note that Section 508.1 requires that Type II hoods be installed over all commercial dishwashing machines, regardless of rinsing temperature. The rationale underlying the requirement is to avoid release of excessive amounts of water vapor into the atmosphere in kitchen or scullery areas. The amount of water vapor released by a tray of drying dishes is exactly the same whether they have been processed in a high- or low-temperature dishwasher. The factors determining the amount of water that must be evaporated are the surface area and texture of the dishes. It makes no difference whether the moisture is evaporated slowly from a low-temperature rinse or more rapidly from a conventional high-temperature rinse. The total amount of moisture released to the air will be the same for the same wetted area of the dishes. When the dishes are hot, the water vapor is more readily seen; at a lower temperature, it is not so readily seen, but is nonetheless being released into the air. Excessive moisture in kitchens is unsanitary because it tends to condense on cool surfaces and drip onto food being prepared. This can be a particularly serious problem during severely cold weather because walls, partitions, ceilings and floors are often at temperatures below the dew point, which encourages condensation.

**508.2 Materials and Installation.** Types I and II hoods must be constructed of galvanized steel, stainless steel, copper or other materials approved by the building official for the intended use.

Type I hoods made from galvanized steel must be at least 0.030-inch (0.762 mm) (No. 22 gage) steel.

Type II hoods must be constructed of not less than 0.024-inch (0.610 mm) (No. 24 gage) steel.

Copper hoods must be made from copper sheets weighing at least 24 ounces per square foot (0.0624 kg/m$^2$).

Stainless steel hoods must be at least 0.030 inch (0.762 mm) thick.

All hoods must be securely fastened by noncombustible supports. Joints and seams must be substantially tight. Solder is not to be used except for sealing a joint or seam.

**508.3 Cleaning and Grease Gutters.** All hoods must be designed so that the entire hood can be thoroughly cleaned when installed. If provided, grease gutters must slope and drain to a collecting receptacle fabricated, designed and installed to be accessible for cleaning.

**508.4 Clearances for Type I Hood.** All portions of a Type I hood must have clearance from combustible construction of at least 18 inches (457 mm). This clearance may be reduced to 3 inches (76 mm), provided that the combustible material is protected with materials as specified for one-hour fire-resistive construction on the side facing the hood. Hoods that are less than 12 inches (305 mm) from the ceiling or the wall must be flashed solidly with materials as required for hoods described in Section 508.2, or materials conforming to one-hour fire-resistive construction.

Type I hoods or portions thereof penetrating a ceiling or furred space must conform to the grease duct enclosure requirements as described in Section 507.6.

**508.5 Grease Filters.** Type I hoods must be equipped with approved grease filters that are designed and sized for the specific purpose. Grease collecting equipment must be accessible for cleaning. The lowest edge of a grease filter above the cooking surface must be at least the height specified in Table 5-D.

Filters must be of a size, type and arrangement that will permit the required quantity of air to pass through the units at rates not exceeding those for which the filter or unit was designed or approved. Filter units must be installed in frames or holders with handles by which they may be readily removed without the use of tools, unless designed and installed to be cleaned in place and the system is equipped for such cleaning in place. They must be sized and made removable so they may be passed through a dishwashing machine or cleaned in a pot sink and arranged in place or provided with drip-intercepting devices to avoid grease or other condensate from dripping onto food or food preparation surfaces.

Grease filters must be installed at an angle greater than 45 degrees from horizontal and equipped with a drip tray beneath the lower edge of the filters to catch grease.

**508.6 Canopy Size and Location.** The inside edge of canopy-type commercial cooking hoods must overhang or extend at least 6 inches (153 mm) horizontally beyond the outer edge of the cooking surface on all open sides. The vertical distance between the lip of the hood and the cooking surface cannot exceed 4 feet (1219 mm). Figure 5-9 illustrates the difference between a canopy and a noncanopy hood. Section 508.8 prescribes a different airflow requirement for a noncanopy hood. The airflow requirement for noncanopy hoods is based on the front length in lineal feet (meters) of cooking equipment installed under the hood; i.e., Q = 300 L. If the equipment were 10 feet (3048 mm) long, Q = (300)(10) = 3,000 cfm (1.42 m$^3$/s).

Figures 5-10 and 5-11 cover typical installation details for canopy-style hoods.

**EXCEPTION:** Listed exhaust hoods may be installed in accordance with their listing and manufacturer's installation instructions.

*(Continued on page 45)*

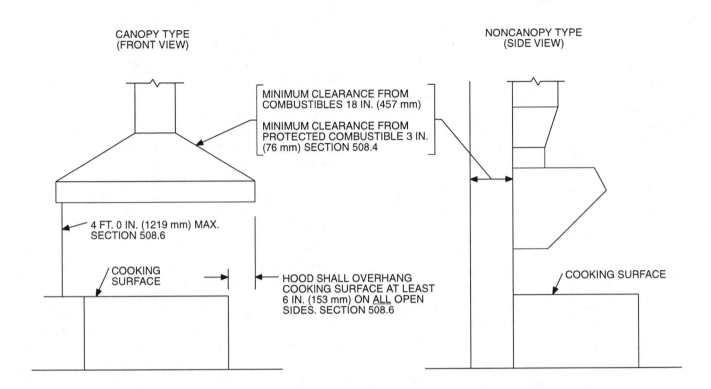

CANOPY TYPE
(FRONT VIEW)

NONCANOPY TYPE
(SIDE VIEW)

MINIMUM CLEARANCE FROM
COMBUSTIBLES 18 IN. (457 mm)

MINIMUM CLEARANCE FROM
PROTECTED COMBUSTIBLE 3 IN.
(76 mm) SECTION 508.4

4 FT. 0 IN. (1219 mm) MAX.
SECTION 508.6

COOKING
SURFACE

HOOD SHALL OVERHANG
COOKING SURFACE AT LEAST
6 IN. (153 mm) ON ALL OPEN
SIDES. SECTION 508.6

COOKING SURFACE

| GENERAL—FOR ALL HOODS | NONCANOPY TYPE |
|---|---|
| IF GUTTERS ARE PROVIDED THEY SHALL DRAIN TO AN ACCESSIBLE RECEPTACLE.<br><br>SEE TABLE 5-A FOR MINIMUM DISTANCE BETWEEN LOWER EDGE OF GREASE FILTER AND THE COOKING OR HEATING SURFACE.<br><br>GREASE FILTERS SHALL BE INSTALLED IN FRAMES OR HOLDERS WITH HANDLES AND BE READILY REMOVABLE FOR CLEANING.<br><br>ALL JOINTS AND SEAMS SHALL BE GREASE TIGHT—USE SOLDER ONLY FOR SEALING JOINTS AND SEAMS.<br><br>HOODS SHALL BE SECURELY FASTENED IN PLACE BY NONCOMBUSTIBLE SUPPORTS.<br><br>TYPE I HOODS ALSO REQUIRE APPROVED FIRE-EXTINGUISHING SYSTEMS FOR DUCTS, GREASE REMOVAL DEVICES, HOODS AND COOKING EQUIPMENT. | MINIMUM VOLUME OF AIR EXHAUSTED: SECTION 508.8<br><br>$Q$ = 300 $L$<br><br>$L$ = FEET (meters) [FRONT LINEAL FEET (meters) OF COOKING EQUIPMENT]<br><br>$Q$ = CUBIC FEET PER MINUTE ($m^3/s$) |

**FIGURE 5-9**

SCHEMATIC DIAGRAM—DO NOT USE FOR CONSTRUCTION

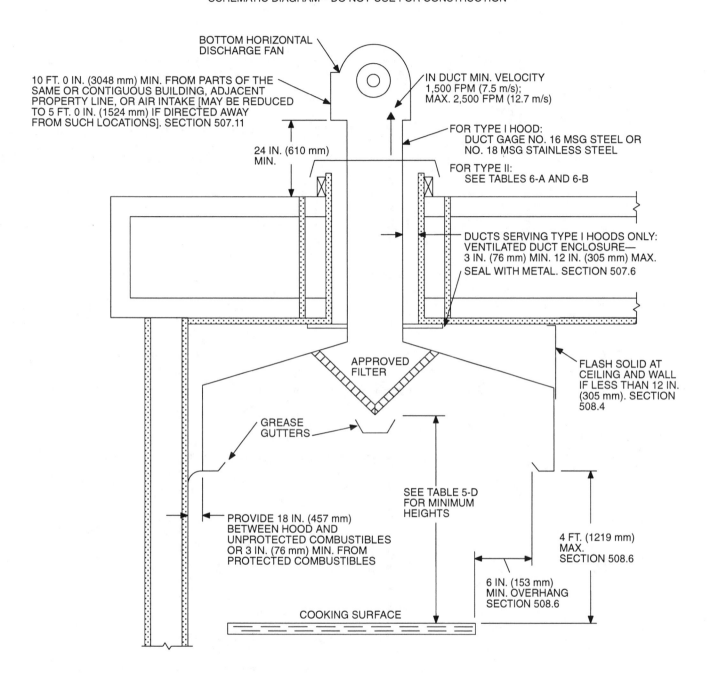

BOTTOM HORIZONTAL
DISCHARGE FAN

10 FT. 0 IN. (3048 mm) MIN. FROM PARTS OF THE
SAME OR CONTIGUOUS BUILDING, ADJACENT
PROPERTY LINE, OR AIR INTAKE [MAY BE REDUCED
TO 5 FT. 0 IN. (1524 mm) IF DIRECTED AWAY
FROM SUCH LOCATIONS]. SECTION 507.11

IN DUCT MIN. VELOCITY
1,500 FPM (7.5 m/s);
MAX. 2,500 FPM (12.7 m/s)

24 IN. (610 mm)
MIN.

FOR TYPE I HOOD:
  DUCT GAGE NO. 16 MSG STEEL OR
  NO. 18 MSG STAINLESS STEEL

FOR TYPE II:
  SEE TABLES 6-A AND 6-B

DUCTS SERVING TYPE I HOODS ONLY:
VENTILATED DUCT ENCLOSURE—
3 IN. (76 mm) MIN. 12 IN. (305 mm) MAX.
SEAL WITH METAL. SECTION 507.6

APPROVED
FILTER

FLASH SOLID AT
CEILING AND WALL
IF LESS THAN 12 IN.
(305 mm). SECTION
508.4

GREASE
GUTTERS

SEE TABLE 5-D
FOR MINIMUM
HEIGHTS

PROVIDE 18 IN. (457 mm)
BETWEEN HOOD AND
UNPROTECTED COMBUSTIBLES
OR 3 IN. (76 mm) MIN. FROM
PROTECTED COMBUSTIBLES

4 FT. (1219 mm)
MAX.
SECTION 508.6

6 IN. (153 mm)
MIN. OVERHANG
SECTION 508.6

COOKING SURFACE

TYPE I HOOD: KITCHEN GREASE HOOD
  GALVANIZED STEEL—NO. 22 MSG
  STAINLESS STEEL—0.030 IN. (0.762 mm)
  COPPER—24 OZ. PER FT.$^2$ (0.0624 kg/m$^2$)

TYPE II HOOD: GENERAL KITCHEN HOOD
  GALVANIZED STEEL—NO. 24 MSG
  STAINLESS STEEL—0.030 IN. (0.762 mm)
  COPPER—24 OZ. PER FT.$^2$ (0.0624 kg/m$^2$)

AIR CAPACITY OF CANOPY HOODS GOVERNED BY COOKING EQUIPMENT. SEE SECTION 508.7

**FIGURE 5-10**

SCHEMATIC DIAGRAM—DO NOT USE FOR CONSTRUCTION

TYPE I HOOD AND DUCT CLEARANCE REQUIREMENTS FROM
THE CEILING AND SHAFT (SECTIONS 507.10 AND 508.4)

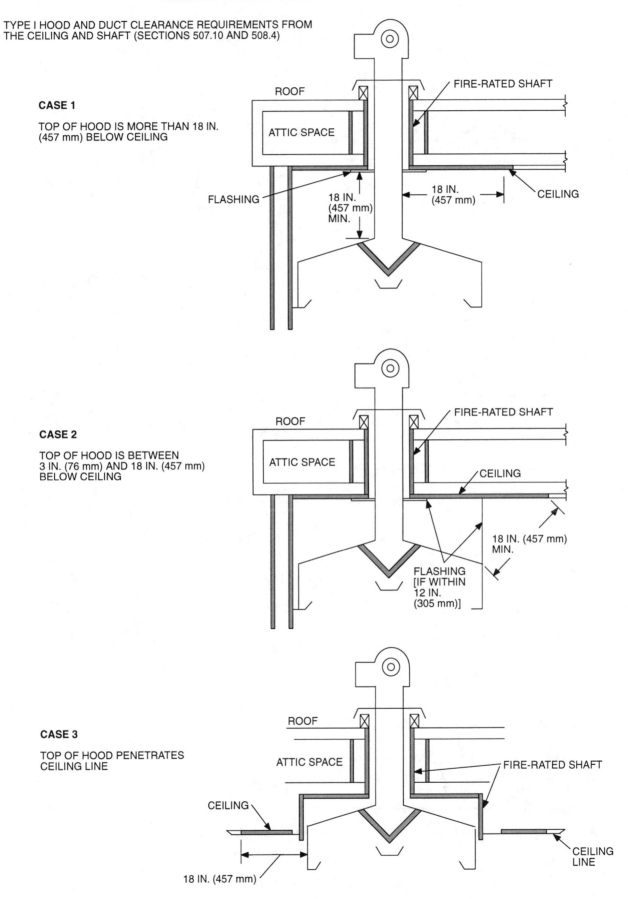

**CASE 1**

TOP OF HOOD IS MORE THAN 18 IN.
(457 mm) BELOW CEILING

**CASE 2**

TOP OF HOOD IS BETWEEN
3 IN. (76 mm) AND 18 IN. (457 mm)
BELOW CEILING

**CASE 3**

TOP OF HOOD PENETRATES
CEILING LINE

**FIGURE 5-11**

*(Continued from page 41)*

**508.7 Capacity of Hoods.** The minimum quantity of air which must be exhausted through canopy-type commercial cooking hoods by the ventilation systems is determined by application of formulas based on the following variables:

$A$ = the horizontal surface area of the hood, in square feet (m$^2$).

$D$ = distance in feet (m) between the lower lip of the hood and the cooking surface.

$P$ = that part of the perimeter of the hood that is open, in feet (m).

$Q$ = quantity of air, in cfm (m$^3$/s).

The formulas under the "For **SI:**" are for metric conversion (Système Internationale application). (See Preface on page iii.) When back-to-back cooking equipment is covered by a common island-type hood, the required airflow may be determined using the formula for three sides exposed. Type II hood airflow requirements must be in accordance with the requirements for low-temperature appliance hoods.

**508.7.1 Solid fuel.** Type I hoods for use over solid-fuel cooking equipment must be provided with separate exhaust systems. Undefined cooking equipment other than solid-fuel cooking equipment may be installed under a common hood. The minimum airflow for solid-fuel cooking equipment, grease-burning charbroilers and undefined equipment must be as follows:

| Number of Exposed Sides | Formula |
| --- | --- |
| Four (island or central hood) | $Q = 300A$ |
| Three or less | $Q = 200A$ |
| Alternate formula | $Q = 100PD$ |

The term "grease-burning charbroiler" is used to describe a broiler in which droppings from the product being cooked generally fall onto the fuel bed, onto heated lava rocks or onto heated ceramic or metallic grids. In all these arrangements, the equipment is designed so that the grease and the droppings will be vaporized to flame and smoke to impart added flavor to the product being cooked.

When the heat source is located at the sides of the product being cooked or above it, the broiler is not considered to be grease burning. The location of the heat source relative to the product being cooked is the key to classifying a broiler as a grease-burning charbroiler. The fuel or energy source producing the heat is not relevant to the classification; that is, electrically heated, gas-fired as well as charcoal or mesquite wood-burning charbroilers are all considered to be grease-burning charbroilers when the product is located above the heat source.

**508.7.2 High temperature.** Type I hoods where cooking equipment includes high-temperature appliances such as deep fat fryers:

| Number of Exposed Sides | Formula |
| --- | --- |
| Four (island or central hood) | $Q = 150A$ |
| Three or less | $Q = 100A$ |
| Alternate formula | $Q = 100PD$ |

**EXCEPTION:** Listed exhaust hoods may be installed in accordance with their terms of listing and the manufacturer's installation instructions.

**508.7.3 Medium temperature.** Type I hoods where the cooking equipment includes medium-temperature appliances such as rotisseries, grills and ranges:

| Number of Exposed Sides | Formula |
| --- | --- |
| Four (island or central hood) | $Q = 100A$ |
| Three or less | $Q = 75A$ |
| Alternate formula | $Q = 50PD$ |

**EXCEPTION:** Listed exhaust hoods may be installed in accordance with their terms of listing and the manufacturer's installation instructions.

**508.7.4 Low temperature.** Type I hoods where the cooking equipment includes low-temperature appliances such as medium- to low-temperature ranges, roasters, roasting ovens, pastry ovens and equipment approved for use under a Type II hood, such as pizza ovens:

| Number of Exposed Sides | Formula |
| --- | --- |
| Four (island or central hood) | $Q = 75A$ |
| Three or less | $Q = 50A$ |
| Alternate formula | $Q = 50PD$ |

**EXCEPTION:** Listed exhaust hoods may be installed in accordance with their terms of listing and the manufacturer's installation instructions.

The title and content of UL Standard 710 was changed in December 1990 from "Grease Extractors for Exhaust Ducts" to "Exhaust Hoods for Commercial Cooking Equipment" and previously listed grease extractors were required to be retested for conformance with the revised standard. The new listings appear in the UL *Fire Protection Equipment Directory* as "Ventilating Equipment for Commercial Cooking Appliances Category YXLT."

This information is in response to the frequently asked question: can the reduced airflow rates (less than specified in the code) be accepted for (UL) listed commercial kitchen exhaust hoods? The answer is that the building department must be consulted because the hoods are marked for the *minimum* exhaust airflow and *maximum* supply airflow rates. Greater exhaust and lesser supply airflow may be required in each specific installation to obtain complete vapor and smoke removal. Thus, the building official is likely to require testing and balancing in each installation prior to acceptance of an airflow rate lower than that specified by this code. When mixed appliances are stipulated, the building official should base airflow calculations on the appliance requiring the greatest airflow.

**508.8 Capacity for Noncanopy Hoods.** In addition to the other requirements for hoods specified in this section, the minimum volume of air to be exhausted through a noncanopy-type hood to the duct system must be at least 300 cfm per lineal foot (0.46 m$^3$/(s•m) of cooking equipment. Listed noncanopy hoods and grease filters are to be sized and installed in accordance with the terms of their listing and the manufacturer's installation instructions.

A noncanopy hood is one that does not meet the canopy size requirements specified in Section 508.6, that is, a hood that does not extend horizontally a minimum of 6 inches (152 mm) beyond the cooking surface on all open sides.

**508.9 Exhaust Outlet.** Exhaust outlets within the hood must be located to optimize the capture of particulate matter. Each outlet cannot serve more than a 12-foot (3658 mm) section of the hood.

> **EXCEPTION:** Listed hoods may be installed in accordance with their terms of listing and the manufacturer's installation instructions.

**508.10 Performance Test.** Upon completion and before final approval of the installation of a commercial kitchen ventilation system serving commercial food heat-processing equipment, a performance test may be required to verify the rate of airflow and proper performance as specified in this chapter. It should also be recalled that performance of listed hoods are evaluated under draft-free laboratory conditions. Greater amounts of exhaust or reduced supply airflow may be required in specific installations to obtain complete capture and removal of vapors and smoke by listed hoods. The permittee must furnish the necessary test equipment and devices required to perform the tests. The permissive requirement for performance testing was added to the UMC at the time compensating styles of hoods were recognized because testimony regarding the performance of such hoods was sparse and not well substantiated. A building official should use this provision if he or she has doubts about the performance of a particular hood.

## SECTION 509 — FANS, MOTORS AND SAFETY DEVICES

**509.1 General.** Motors and fans must be of sufficient capacity to provide the required air movement as specified in this chapter. Electrical equipment must be approved for the class of use as provided in the Electrical Code. Motors and fans must be accessible for servicing and maintenance. Motors must not be installed within ducts or under hoods.

The vertical descending lines formed by the letter "F" in the margin adjoining Sections 509.2 through 509.7 indicate that the IFCI Code Development Committee maintains the provisions so identified.

**509.2 Where Required.** Approved fire-extinguishing systems must be provided for the protection of commercial food heat-processing equipment.

> **EXCEPTION:** The requirement for protection does not include steam kettles and steam tables or equipment which do not create grease-laden vapors when used.

**509.3 Type of System.** The system used for protection of commercial cooking equipment must be either a system listed for application with such equipment or an automatic fixed-pipe system specifically designed for such application. Other systems must be of an approved design and must be one of the following types:

1. Automatic sprinkler system.
2. Dry-chemical extinguishing system.
3. Carbon dioxide extinguishing system.
4. Wet-chemical extinguishing system.

**509.4 Extent of Protection.** The fire-extinguishing system used to protect ventilating hoods and ducts and cooking appliances must be installed to include cooking surfaces, deep-fat fryers, griddles, upright broilers, charbroilers, grease-burning charbroilers, range tops and grills. Protection must also be provided for the enclosed plenum space within the hood above the filters and in exhaust ducts serving the hood.

That portion of the fire-extinguishing system required for protection of the plenum space within the hood beyond the filter and within the exhaust duct serving the hood may be omitted when approved listed exhaust hoods with dampers are installed. This provision recognizes that listed hoods with dampers of UL category YXZR are designed to prevent the exhaust duct gas temperatures from exceeding 375°F (190°C) and the passage of flame into the exhaust duct under conditions simulating a fire in the cooking area under the hood.

Exhaust hoods without exhaust dampers (UL category YYCW) do not offer the protection from flame and heated gases entering the grease duct. Thus, the provisions of Section 509.4.1 regarding the extent of protection in grease ducts serving listed exhaust hoods without dampers should be taken literally to require protection of grease ducts by approved automatic fire-extinguishing systems. Automatically or manually operated cleaning and washing systems are *not* tested for their suitability as fire-extinguishing systems for grease-removal devices and hoods.

**509.4.1 General.** An automatic fire-extinguishing system is required to protect cooking surfaces, deep fat fryers, griddles, upright broilers, charbroilers, range tops and grills. The enclosed plenum space above the filters in commercial kitchen hoods also requires protection. Protection is not required for urns, steam kettles or dishwashers.

Grease ducts serving unlisted commercial kitchen hoods require automatic fire-extinguishing systems as do listed exhaust hoods without dampers. A listed exhaust hood with dampers *does not* require an automatic fire-extinguishing system in the grease duct.

**509.4.2 Carbon dioxide systems.** When carbon dioxide systems are used, dampers must be arranged to operate automatically in the event that the extinguishing system operates. When the damper is installed at the top of the duct, the top nozzle must be immediately below the damper. Additional nozzles symmetrically arranged to give equal distribution must be installed within vertical ducts exceeding 20 feet (6096 mm) and horizontal ducts exceeding 50 feet (15 240 mm). The quantity of the carbon dioxide in the system must be sufficient to protect all hazards venting into the grease duct simultaneously. The minimum charge must be at least equivalent to the volume of the interior of the grease duct.

**509.5.1 General.** Fire-extinguishing systems must be interconnected to the fuel or electrical energy supply so that the fuel or electric current is automatically shut off to all equipment under the hood when the system is actuated.

Shutoffs, valves or switches must be of the type that requires manual operation to reset.

**509.5.2 Carbon dioxide system.** In addition, carbon dioxide systems must be interconnected to shut off the ventilation system when the supression system is activated.

**509.6 Special Provisions for Automatic Sprinkler Systems.** Commercial cooking equipment protected by automatic sprinkler systems must be controlled by a separate, readily accessible, indicating-type control valve that is identified. When sprinklers are used to protect deep fat fryers, each fryer must be protected with a sprinkler listed for that application and installed in accordance with the manufacturer's installation instructions.

**509.7 Manual System Operation.** A readily accessible manual activating device installed at an approved location must be provided for dry chemical, carbon dioxide and wet chemical systems. The actuation device may be either mechanically or electrically operated. If electrical power is used, the system must be connected to a standby power system and a visual means must be provided to show that the extinguishing system is energized.

Instructions for manually operating the fire-extinguishing system must be posted at a conspicuous location within the kitchen.

**509.8 Fire Dampers.** Fire dampers must not be installed in duct systems unless they are listed for such use or are part of a listed hood with dampers, a fire-extinguishing system or an approved fan bypass.

The following are specific differences between Type I and Type II commercial hoods used for kitchen ventilation systems. This list is not inclusive, but does specify the major differences between the two types:

| | TYPE I HOOD | TYPE II HOOD |
|---|---|---|
| 1. | A kitchen hood for collecting and removing grease and smoke. <br><br> Section 507.2 | A general kitchen hood for collecting and removing steam, vapor, heat or odors. <br> Section 507.2 |
| 2. | Grease ducts and plenums must be constructed of not less than 0.055-inch-thick (1.40 mm) (No. 16 manufacturer's standard gage) steel or stainless steel at least 0.044 inch (1.12 mm) in thickness. <br> Section 507.3 | Ducts and plenums must be constructed of rigid metallic materials as set forth in Chapter 6, Tables 6-A and 6-B. <br><br> Section 507.3.4 |
| 3. | Joints and seams of ducts must be made with a continuous liquid-tight weld or braze made on the external surface of the duct system. <br> Section 507.3.2 | Joints and seams of duct must be made substantially airtight by using tapes, gasketing or other means. <br> Sections 504 and 601.6 |
| 4. | A grease duct that penetrates a ceiling, wall or floor must be enclosed in a duct enclosure from the point of penetration to the outside air. <br> Section 507.6 | No requirement. |
| 5. | Air velocity within the duct system must be at least 1,500 feet per minute (7.5 m/s) and not more than 2,500 feet per minute (12.7 m/s). <br> Section 507.8 | No requirement. |
| 6. | (a) Centrifugal exhaust fan outlet (bottom horizontal) must be a minimum of 2 feet (610 mm) above the roof. <br><br> (b) Vertical discharge (upblast) exhaust fan must have its grease outlet 2 feet (610 mm) above the roof. <br><br> Section 507.11 | (a) No requirement. <br><br> (b) No requirement. <br><br><br> (c) In-line fans are allowed. |
| 7. | Exhaust outlet must be at least 10 feet (3048 mm) horizontally from parts of the same building, adjacent property line, or air intake opening into any building [may be reduced to 5 feet (1524 mm) if the discharge is directed away from such location] and must be located at least 10 feet (3048 mm) above the adjoining grade level. <br> Section 507.11 | No requirement. |
| 8. | Any type of fan, which is UL listed for use in grease exhaust systems and is installed in accordance with the terms of its listing and the manufacturer's installation instructions. | No requirement. |
| 9. | Hood must be constructed of: <br> (a) Galvanized steel not less than 0.03-inch (0.76 mm) (No. 22 gage) steel. <br><br> (b) Copper sheets weighing not less than 24 ounces per square foot (0.0624 kg/m$^2$). <br><br> (c) Stainless steel having a minimum thickness of 0.030-inch (0.762 mm). <br> Section 508.2 | (a) Galvanized steel not less than 0.024-inch (0.610 mm) (No. 24 gage) steel. <br><br> (b) Same as Type I. <br><br><br> (c) Stainless steel not less than 0.030 inch (0.762 mm). |

*(Continued on page 48)*

*(Continued from page 47)*

| TYPE I HOOD | TYPE II HOOD |
|---|---|
| 10. Ceilings within 18 inches (457 mm) measured from the top of the hood must be constructed with materials conforming to one-hour fire-resistive construction on the hood side.<br>Section 508.4 | No requirement. |
| 11. Hoods less than 12 inches (305 mm) from the ceiling or wall must be flashed solidly with materials of the thickness specified in Section 508.2 or materials conforming to one-hour fire-resistive construction.<br>Section 508.4 | No requirement. |
| 12. Hoods recessed into the ceiling must be enclosed in a rated grease duct enclosure. Ceiling must be constructed with materials conforming to one-hour fire-resistive construction, on the hood side, to a distance of 18 inches (457 mm) measured from the hood at the ceiling line.<br>Section 508.4 | No requirement. |
| 13. Approved grease filters designed for the specific purpose are required.<br>Section 508.5 | No requirement. |
| 14. Capacity of exhaust fan is the appropriate formula shown in Sections 508.7 and 508.8. | Capacity of exhaust fan is determined by applying the formula shown in Section 508.7.4. |
| 15. Fire-extinguishing system is required.<br>Section 509.2 | No requirement. |

# Chapter 6
# DUCT SYSTEMS

## SECTION 601 — SCOPE

Chapter 6 regulates the installation of duct systems (as defined in Section 206) that are used to convey indoor environmental air that has been heated or cooled for purposes of occupant comfort.

**601.1 Material.** Return air and supply air for heating and cooling systems are required to be conducted through duct systems made from the following materials:

1. Metal ducts complying with Tables 6-A, 6-B and 6-C.

2. Metal ducts complying with UMC Standard 6-1 with prior approval.

3. Factory-made air ducts complying with UL 181.

Tables 6-A, 6-B and 6-C describe limitations placed on duct systems made from the following traditional sheet metals: carbon sheet steel, galvanized steel with thickness measured in Manufacturers Standard Gage or Galvanized Sheet Gage, aluminum with thickness measured in Brown and Sharp (B.&S.) Gage and cold-rolled copper measured in ounces per square foot. Needless to say, copper duct systems are seldom seen now.

Table 6-A covers rectangular sheet metal ducts for systems where static air pressure does not exceed 2-inch water column (0.49 kPa). Table 6-A may be used for pressures in excess of 2-inch water column (0.49 kPa) provided that duct thickness is specified to be two gages heavier than set forth in the table, but caution should be exercised in using the rule. It would be preferable to consult UMC Standard 6-2 when pressures exceed 2-inch water column (0.49 kPa).

Table 6-B covers round and flat oval ducts for systems up to 10-inch wc pressure (2.45 kPa).

Table 6-C covers required gages of sheet metal ducts and plenums in single-family units. In these three tables, duct dimensions, permissible girth joints and longitudinal seams are described together with the appropriate sheet metal gage or weight.

Another acceptable method for the design and installation of metal ducts is to utilize UMC Standard 6-1, "Standard for Metal Ducts," with prior approval of the jurisdiction.

This standard is a revised compilation of two standards published by the Sheet Metal and Air-Conditioning Contractors National Association (SMACNA) and takes more of an "engineered systems approach" than is found in Tables 6-A, 6-B and 6-C. Trade-offs are apparent between reinforcing and selected gage. Hangers, trapeze angle loads, joint reinforcement (both transverse and intermediate), transverse deflection, and allowable stress are considered in great detail. The standard is also well illustrated.

When use of UMC Standard 6-1 is approved, shop drawings of the duct design should be submitted to the building department to permit the plans examiner to verify the options chosen by the fabricator.

An inspector should become familiar with sheet metal gages. Since field marking of sheet metal gage is uncommon, the inspector should have a tablet of samples, a gage wheel, a ball-end micrometer or other means to verify that the minimum required weight of material is being installed. When in doubt, the burden of proof should be placed on the contractor or installer. Sheet metal gage should be checked in the early stages of the job before metal ducts are installed. Note that carbon sheet steel and galvanized sheet have minimum recommended thicknesses specified in Appendix D. The footnotes should also be read carefully.

Refer to Section 601.5 for factory-made air duct requirements.

Nonmetallic duct materials are required when ducts are installed in the ground (see UMC Section 601.1) and may be used in a concrete slab, provided the joints are tightly sealed to prevent the entry of liquids prior to hardening of the concrete. Ducts are required to "be made substantially airtight" in Section 601.6; however, this requirement is primarily intended to prevent moisture from the ground from entering the duct system.

Figure 6-1 illustrates a typical detail for embedded ducts.

Corridors may not be used as a part of an air distribution system when required by Section 1004.3.4 of the Building Code to be of fire-resistive construction. This requirement is to assist in maintaining a smoke-free environment in the exit passageway in the early stages of a fire.

Concealed building spaces may be used as ducts or plenums, which include spaces within fire-rated assemblies, provided the penetrations into these spaces are protected by approved membrane-penetration fire stops as required by UBC Section 709.7 or combination fire and smoke dampers as required in UBC Sections 713.10 and 713.11.

Figure 6-2 illustrates a panned joist space that could be used for return air in a dwelling.

The required flame-spread index and smoke-developed index stipulated in Section 601.4 would preclude this construction in other than dwellings. See Exception 1.

Gypsum products exposed in ducts and plenums such as plaster and drywall (gypsum wallboard) require special attention. Since these materials are adversely affected by high humidity and dampness as well as temperature extremes, their use is restricted to installations where temperature and humidity are controlled. (See Section 601.1.3.)

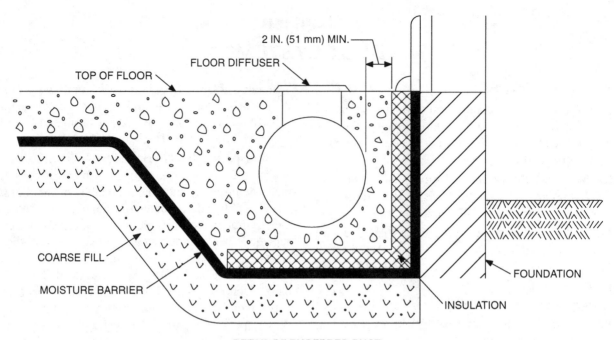

2 IN. (51 mm) MIN.

FLOOR DIFFUSER

TOP OF FLOOR

COARSE FILL

MOISTURE BARRIER

INSULATION

FOUNDATION

**DETAIL OF EMBEDDED DUCT**

**FIGURE 6-1**

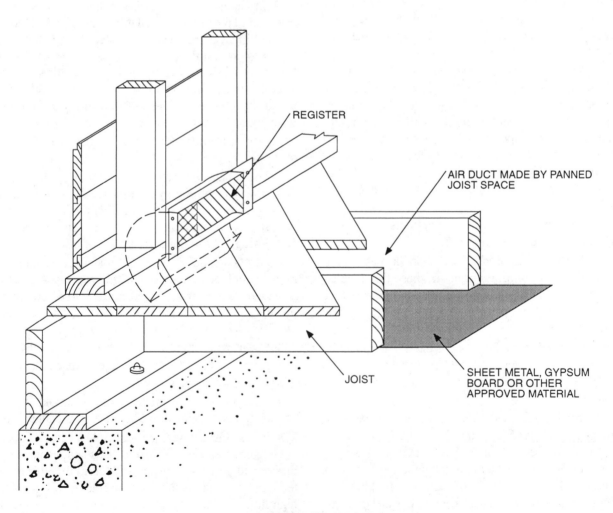

REGISTER

AIR DUCT MADE BY PANNED JOIST SPACE

JOIST

SHEET METAL, GYPSUM BOARD OR OTHER APPROVED MATERIAL

**DETAIL OF PANNED JOIST SPACE**

**FIGURE 6-2**

**601.3 Contamination Prevention.** Exhaust ducts are not permitted to extend into or through ducts or plenums, because most duct system joints and seams exhibit some degree of leakage that could contaminate the air flowing in another duct or plenum.

**601.4 Combustibles within Ducts or Plenums.** This section requires that materials exposed to the airstream in ducts and plenums exhibit specified surface-burning characteristics except for certain locations and products as indicated. The purpose of the requirement is to limit propagation of flames through the duct system or plenum and to limit the quantity of smoke resulting from involvement of insulating and acoustic materials. The method of testing to determine surface-burning characteristics of materials is covered by UBC Standard 8-1 and also commonly referred to as the Steiner Tunnel Test, ASTM E 84, and UL 724. A UL label merely indicates that the material would be suitable based on its flame-spread index and smoke-

developed index; the listing cautions that thermal conductivity, vapor resistance and other properties of the material have not been investigated. Uniform Building Code Standard 8-1 is found in the *Uniform Building Code,* Volume 3. Figure 6-3 shows a typical label that is required to be attached to tested materials that comply with the flame-spread index and smoke-developed index required in this section.

Electrical wiring and nonmetallic fire sprinkler piping in ducts or plenums are required to be tested in accordance with UMC Standard 6-2 and to exhibit "a peak optical density of 0.5 or less" and "exhibit flame travel of 5 feet (1524 mm) or less." This requirement is not in addition to the requirements of UBC Standard 8-1. The 1991 edition of the UMC was amended to allow nonmetallic fire sprinkler piping to be used if it complies with the same fire and smoke characteristics required for electrical wiring.

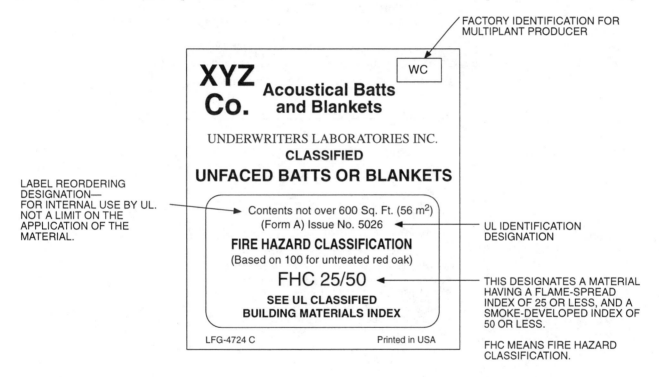

**TYPICAL LABEL FOR COMBUSTIBLE MATERIALS WITHIN DUCTS AND PLENUMS**

**FIGURE 6-3**

**601.5 Factory-made Air Ducts.** Factory-made air ducts must be approved by the jurisdiction for the intended use and must comply with the requirements of UL 181, "Factory-made Air Ducts." The broad range of products covered under this standard is often of proprietary design. They typically come in flexible or rigid lengths, or in sheets or boards for field assembly into rigid duct. Their composition is nominally metal and/or mineral materials. Nonmetallic or organic materials may only be used as "binders, adhesives, sealants, or finishes." Unbonded asbestos fiber materials are not permitted.

The manufacturer must mark every portion of a factory-made air duct system to show compliance with the standard. The contractor must install the system in accordance with the terms of its listing and the installation instructions shipped with the duct material. Uniform Mechanical Code Standard 6-3, "Standard for Installation of Factory-made Air Ducts," should be consulted. It is found in UMC Appendix A.

One of the most critical areas of field inspection of factory-made air ducts is to determine that proper methods and materials have been used for joining and splicing. Section 601.2.2.5 requires the manufacturer to provide directions and information for attaining proper and safe installation of the product. These instructions should include a complete and detailed description of the methods and materials to be used for joining and splicing in flexible air ducts as contained in UL 181 B. UMC Standard 6-3 contains joinery for rigid air duct systems. The materials used for this purpose are to be tested for flame resistance, corrosion and resistance to mold growth and humidity as required in UL 181. Not all duct tapes or sheet metal are approved materials for joining and splicing ducts—the materials and methods must conform with their listing, the manufacturer's installation instructions and approved standards.

Figure 6-4 illustrates two examples of UL labels for factory-made air ducts.

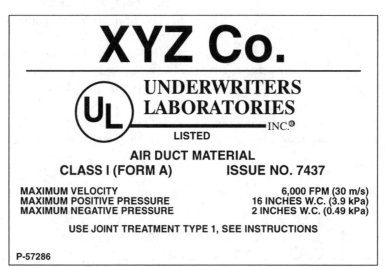

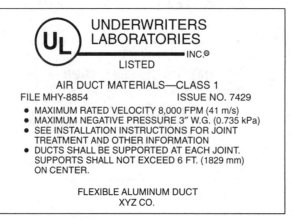

**TYPICAL LABELS FOR FACTORY-MADE AIR DUCTS**

**FIGURE 6-4**

**601.6 Joints and Seams of Ducts.** Airtightness is critical in duct systems to maintain overall energy and operating efficiency. Therefore, the installer must make all joints substantially airtight with tapes, mastics, gasketing or other means. Note that allowable air loss is not defined so this becomes a judgment call regarding sound installation practices.

Figure 6-5 illustrates acceptable methods for connecting residential round ducts.

Permissible girth joints and longitudinal seams are listed in UMC Table 6-A and are illustrated in Figure 6-6. Figure 6-7 illustrates several other types of joints and seams. The building official should be consulted if use of the joints illustrated in Figure 6-7 is contemplated.

**601.7 Metal.** This section currently does not refer to ducts complying with UMC Standard 6-1 that are acceptable with prior approval (Section 601.1), but does require prior approval to use UMC Standard 6-1.

*(Continued on page 56)*

SHEET METAL DUCT

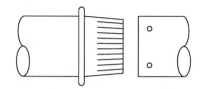

CRIMP OR LAP JOINT WITH OPTIONAL
BEAD: JOINT IS SECURED WITH THREE
EQUALLY SPACED SCREWS

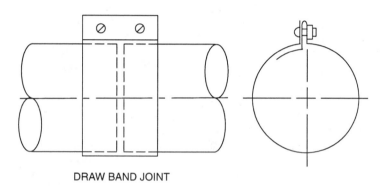

DRAW BAND JOINT

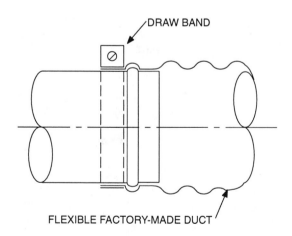

FLEXIBLE FACTORY-MADE DUCT

**RESIDENTIAL ROUND DUCT CONNECTIONS**

**FIGURE 6-5**

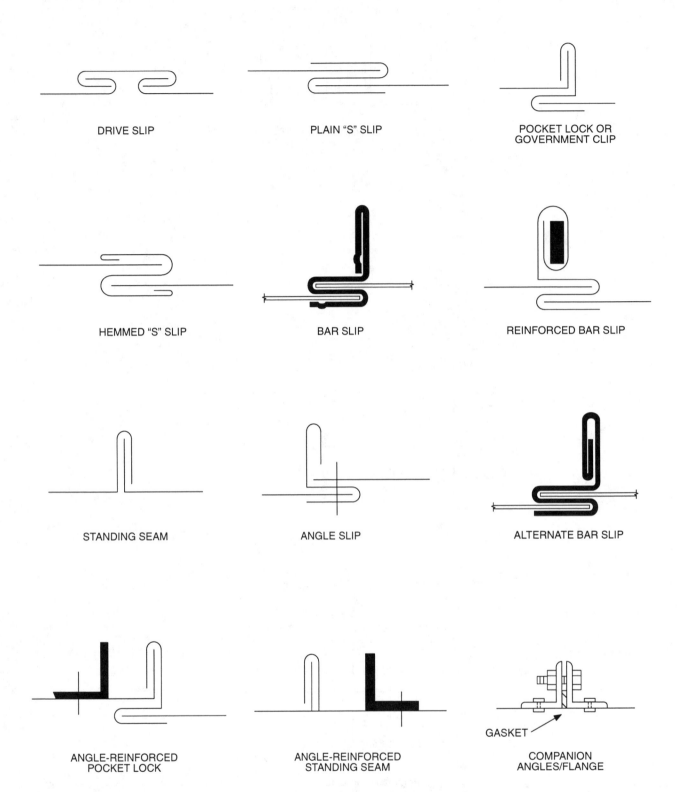

DRIVE SLIP

PLAIN "S" SLIP

POCKET LOCK OR
GOVERNMENT CLIP

HEMMED "S" SLIP

BAR SLIP

REINFORCED BAR SLIP

STANDING SEAM

ANGLE SLIP

ALTERNATE BAR SLIP

ANGLE-REINFORCED
POCKET LOCK

ANGLE-REINFORCED
STANDING SEAM

GASKET

COMPANION
ANGLES/FLANGE

**JOINTS AND SEAMS REFERENCED IN UMC TABLE 6-A**

**FIGURE 6-6**

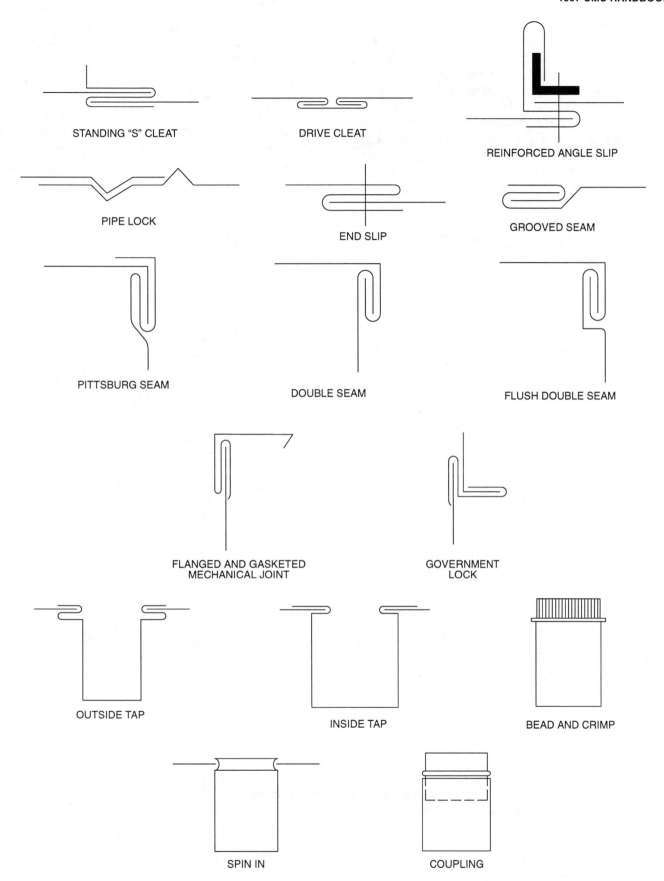

STANDING "S" CLEAT

DRIVE CLEAT

REINFORCED ANGLE SLIP

PIPE LOCK

END SLIP

GROOVED SEAM

PITTSBURG SEAM

DOUBLE SEAM

FLUSH DOUBLE SEAM

FLANGED AND GASKETED
MECHANICAL JOINT

GOVERNMENT
LOCK

OUTSIDE TAP

INSIDE TAP

BEAD AND CRIMP

SPIN IN

COUPLING

**JOINTS AND CONNECTIONS**

**FIGURE 6-7**

**601.8 Tinned Steel.** Existing tin plated ducts were common in structures built just before and during World War II for heating system ducts. Such ducts were fabricated from scrap generated during the manufacture of the tin cans for the food industry. Actually, the product was sheet steel coated on one side with tin and sold as "waster-waster" tin. These ducts may be used when cooling coils are added to an existing system, provided that the installation complies with this section. The reason for the need to replace the initial 10 feet (3048 mm) of supply duct is that tin ducts do not provide adequate protection from corrosion at this location due to the possibility of condensate from the cooling coil being entrained in the air stream. The provision is an anachronism recognizing

shortages and practices arising just prior to and during World War II materials shortages and should have been deleted from the UMC.

**601.9 Vibration Isolators.** Vibration isolators minimize noise and vibration from mechanical equipment. Without them, excessive operating noise and premature weakening of joints and supports could result. Vibration isolators must be made of approved materials and are usually provided by mechanical equipment suppliers. Canvas, Neoprene and rubber are the common materials for this purpose.

Figure 6-8 illustrates typical isolator details and points of installation within a system.

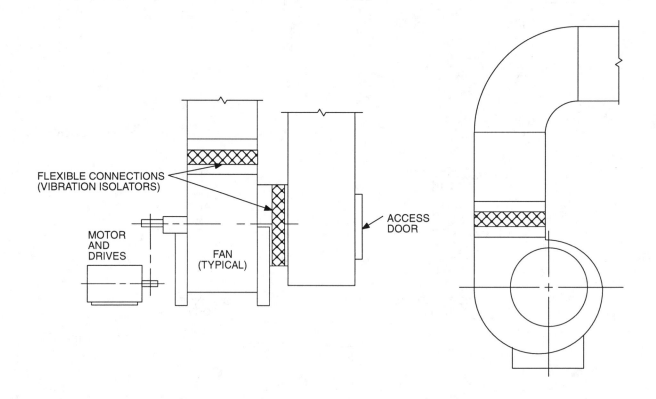

MECHANICAL EQUIPMENT: FAN OUTLET

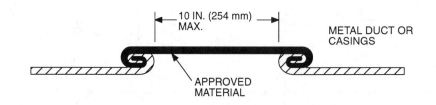

**TYPICAL VIBRATION ISOLATOR DETAILS**

**FIGURE 6-8**

## SECTION 602 — QUALITY OF MATERIAL

Lock-forming quality implies that the zinc coating will not crack when sheet steel is formed into the various configurations required to fabricate joints and seams. The inspector can require the supplier and installer of the material to provide an acceptable, recent independent laboratory report certifying compliance with UMC Standard 2-2.

## SECTION 603 — INSTALLATION OF DUCTS

**603.1 Metal Ducts.** This section addresses the support of metal ducts. Vertical and horizontal ducts are covered, as well as horizontal ducts with trapeze supports for both rectangular and round shapes.

Horizontal sheet metal ducts are required to "be braced and guyed to prevent lateral or horizontal swing." Local jurisdictions in Seismic Zones 0 and 1 sometimes amend the UMC to delete this requirement.

**603.2 Factory-made Air Ducts.** The installation of factory-made air ducts is regulated by this section. UL 81, "Factory-made Air Ducts," is cited in Section 601.1 as an acceptable material for air ducts. The class of materials required in this section is Class 0 or Class 1.

Factory-made air ducts are composed of metal and/or mineral materials, although nonmetallic or organic materials are allowed for binders, adhesives, sealants or finishes. They are typically either flexible or rigid preformed lengths of duct, or sheets or boards designed for field fabrication into lengths of rigid duct.

**603.4 Support of Ducts.** Support spacing and methods referred to as being in UMC Standard 6-3 are in Part B of the standard and are relatively minimal. Flexible duct supports are specified by the manufacturer's installation instructions.

## SECTION 604 — INSULATION OF DUCTS

Along with UMC Table 6-D, this section describes the specific required installation and performance characteristics of duct-insulating materials. Table 6-D provides insulation requirements by duct location and heating zone (obtainable from the local United States Weather Service office) for both cooling-only and heating-only modes. Three insulation types are described: mineral fiber blankets, mineral fiber blanket duct liners and mineral fiber boards. Vapor barrier and weatherproof barrier requirements are also specified.

This section requires that duct-insulating materials meet the following test requirements:

1. Insulating materials installed inside ducts shall have a mold-, humidity- and erosion-resistant face that meets the requirements of Section 604.2.

2. Insulating materials installed on the exterior of ducts (inside buildings) are required to have a specific flame-spread index of 25 and a smoke-developed index of 50 in Section 604.3. In addition, "faced" insulation "shall be legibly printed with the name of the manufacturer, nominal thickness of insulation and the flame-spread and smoke-developed ratings of the composite material."

**604.4 Identification.** In most cases, these provisions will require that duct-insulating materials and the methods of installation be listed by an approved agency, as this is the only practical way that an inspector will have assurance that test requirements are met.

## SECTION 605 — DAMPERS IN DUCT SYSTEMS

This section of the UMC was completely revised in the 1994 edition for correlation with changes made in the UBC. In earlier editions, the UBC relied heavily on UBC Standards 43-7 and 43-12 for the construction, installation, testing and marking of dampers in ducts. The deletion of damper standards from the 1994 codes in favor of identifying recognized standards UL 555, "Fire Dampers"; UL 555C, "Ceiling Dampers" and UL 555S, "Leakage Rated Dampers for Use in Smoke Control Systems," in Chapter 35 of the UBC and Chapter 16 of the UMC generated a number of related code changes in UBC Section 713. *Uniform Building Code* Sections 711 and 713 establish locations where smoke and fire dampers are required. The 1997 codes rely on the listing, label and manufacturer's installation instructions to regulate this aspect of fire and life safety. The introduction of smoke dampers (leakage-rated dampers) is related to the addition of Section 905, Smoke Control, to the UBC.

**605.2 Fire Dampers.** The requirement "that collapse of the ductwork will not dislodge the damper" was added in the 1991 edition with the intent that a fire damper will remain in place during a fire even if the duct system collapses. This can only occur if the duct is attached to the damper with a plain S slip joint as illustrated in Figure 6-6 so that the duct will break away or separate from the damper before excessive forces are transmitted to the damper during a fire or collapse of the ductwork.

**605.5 Access and Identification.** This section provides the requirements for access openings to fire dampers. Figure 6-9 illustrates a typical fire damper access panel.

**605.7 Temperature Classification of Operating Elements.** Fusible links are devices that are made to move, separate or melt at preset air temperatures, triggering the closing action of the fire damper. Their testing is described in detail in UL 33, "Heat Responsive Links for Fire Protection Service," which also includes the temperature rating classification ranges.

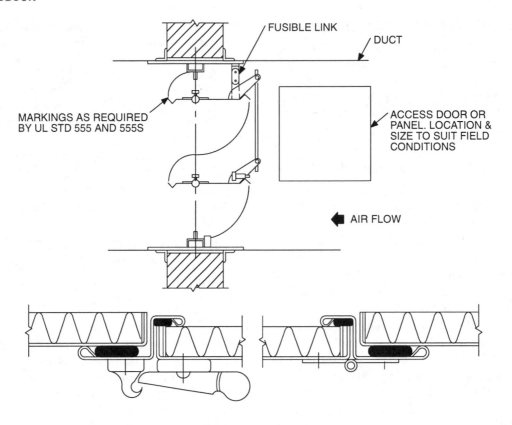

MARKINGS AS REQUIRED
BY UL STD 555 AND 555S

FUSIBLE LINK

DUCT

ACCESS DOOR OR
PANEL. LOCATION &
SIZE TO SUIT FIELD
CONDITIONS

◀ AIR FLOW

**TYPICAL ACCESS PANEL DETAILS**

**FIGURE 6-9**

## SECTION 606 — VENTILATING CEILINGS

This section regulates the installation of ventilating ceilings as defined in Section 224 of the UMC. In addition to the requirements of this section, the space above a ventilating ceiling must comply with the definition of a plenum as defined in Section 218 and, therefore, must also comply with the applicable requirements of Sections 601.1, 601.3 and 601.4.

- Exhaust ducts under positive pressure and venting systems shall not extend into or pass through ducts or plenums. (See Section 601.3).
- Materials exposed within ducts or plenums shall have a flame-spread index of not more than 25 and a smoke-developed index of not more than 50. (See Section 601.4).

Figure 6-10 illustrates the requirements for installation of a ventilating ceiling.

## SECTION 607 — UNDER-FLOOR SPACE USED AS PLENUMS

This section regulates the use of under-floor space as an HVAC supply plenum in single-family residences. The requirements for supplying heated air to under-floor space limits air temperature in contact with exposed wood construction and, at the same time, limits the volume of under-floor air to be heated each time the circulating fan is turned on.

Item 2 of this section requires special consideration because of a potential conflict with UBC Section 2306.7, which requires foundation ventilation for under-floor areas. Compliance with this section would be possible with approval by the building official to omit the ventilation openings based on the rationale that operation of the HVAC system would remove moisture that migrated into the crawl space. The original intent of the UMC, as evidenced by Item 2, was to allow these spaces to be used as plenums without ventilation. Moisture could be prevented from entering the under-floor space by compliance with Item 12 of this section.

Figure 6-11 illustrates the requirements of this section.

## SECTION 608 — SHUTOFF FOR SMOKE CONTROL

This section specifies when and where smoke detectors are to be installed. The "when" is in air-moving systems supplying air at a rate exceeding 2,000 cfm (940 L/s) except in Group R, Division 3 and Group U Occupancies. (See definition for air-moving system in Section 203.)

Smoke detectors are required in the main air-supply duct. Figure 6-12 illustrates the code-required location of smoke detectors in the main air-supply duct.

*(Continued on page 60)*

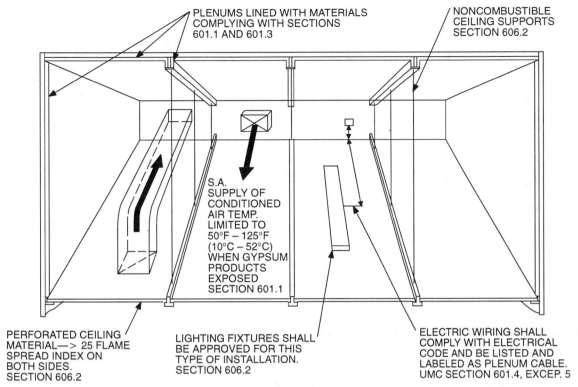

PLENUMS LINED WITH MATERIALS COMPLYING WITH SECTIONS 601.1 AND 601.3

NONCOMBUSTIBLE CEILING SUPPORTS SECTION 606.2

S.A. SUPPLY OF CONDITIONED AIR TEMP. LIMITED TO 50°F – 125°F (10°C – 52°C) WHEN GYPSUM PRODUCTS EXPOSED SECTION 601.1

PERFORATED CEILING MATERIAL—> 25 FLAME SPREAD INDEX ON BOTH SIDES. SECTION 606.2

LIGHTING FIXTURES SHALL BE APPROVED FOR THIS TYPE OF INSTALLATION. SECTION 606.2

ELECTRIC WIRING SHALL COMPLY WITH ELECTRICAL CODE AND BE LISTED AND LABELED AS PLENUM CABLE. UMC SECTION 601.4, EXCEP. 5

**VENTILATING CEILING REQUIREMENTS**

**FIGURE 6-10**

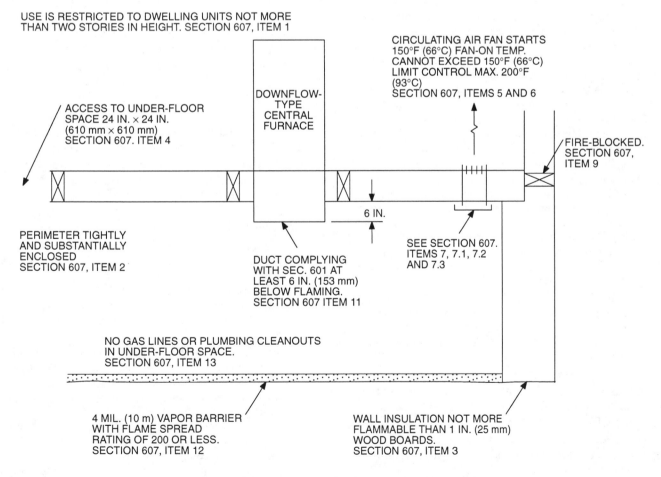

USE IS RESTRICTED TO DWELLING UNITS NOT MORE THAN TWO STORIES IN HEIGHT. SECTION 607, ITEM 1

CIRCULATING AIR FAN STARTS 150°F (66°C) FAN-ON TEMP. CANNOT EXCEED 150°F (66°C) LIMIT CONTROL MAX. 200°F (93°C) SECTION 607, ITEMS 5 AND 6

ACCESS TO UNDER-FLOOR SPACE 24 IN. × 24 IN. (610 mm × 610 mm) SECTION 607. ITEM 4

DOWNFLOW-TYPE CENTRAL FURNACE

FIRE-BLOCKED. SECTION 607, ITEM 9

PERIMETER TIGHTLY AND SUBSTANTIALLY ENCLOSED SECTION 607, ITEM 2

6 IN.

DUCT COMPLYING WITH SEC. 601 AT LEAST 6 IN. (153 mm) BELOW FLAMING. SECTION 607 ITEM 11

SEE SECTION 607. ITEMS 7, 7.1, 7.2 AND 7.3

NO GAS LINES OR PLUMBING CLEANOUTS IN UNDER-FLOOR SPACE. SECTION 607, ITEM 13

4 MIL. (10 m) VAPOR BARRIER WITH FLAME SPREAD RATING OF 200 OR LESS. SECTION 607, ITEM 12

WALL INSULATION NOT MORE FLAMMABLE THAN 1 IN. (25 mm) WOOD BOARDS. SECTION 607, ITEM 3

**TYPICAL USE OF UNDER-FLOOR SPACE AS AN AIR-SUPPLY PLENUM**

**FIGURE 6-11**

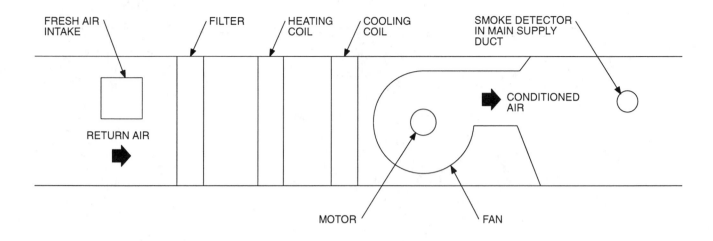

**FIGURE 6-12**

*(Continued from page 58)*

## SECTION 609 — PRODUCT-CONVEYING DUCT SYSTEMS

**609.1 Materials.** Materials used in product-conveying duct systems must be of metal and must be suitable for the intended use.

> **EXCEPTIONS:** 1. Asbestos-cement, concrete, clay or ceramic materials may be used if it can be shown that their performance will be equivalent to that of metal ducts. These materials are most commonly used for plumbing, sewer and water system supply piping. They may sometimes provide appropriate and long-lasting service as product-conveying ducts, especially if burial is necessary. The manufacturer must be consulted for instructions on suitability of such materials as ducts for the specific product to be conveyed.
>
> 2. Ducts serving Class 5 systems, conveying corrosives such as acid vapors, may be constructed of approved nonmetallic materials, but only when the material to be conveyed is determined to be nonflammable and a metal system is not suitable. Approved nonmetallic material must either be a listed product having a flame-spread index of 25 and a smoke-developed index of 50 or less, on both inside and outside surfaces, without evidence of continued progressive combustion, or must have a flame-spread index of 25 or less and be installed with an automatic fire sprinkler system inside the duct.
>
> 3. In dwelling units, ducts used in central vacuum cleaning systems may be of PVC pipe or tubing. Note that vacuum cleaner tubing has a different exterior diameter so that it cannot be inadvertently coupled to a sanitary drainage system.

Penetration of fire walls or floor-ceiling or roof-ceiling assemblies must comply with UBC Sections 709.6 and 710. Copper tube or galvanized or black steel pipes or conduits extending from within the separation between the garage and the dwelling unit to the central vacuum cleaning unit may be used and should be regarded as through penetrations.

**609.1.1 Aluminum.** Aluminum ducts must not be used where flammable or explosive dusts, vapors, or fumes are to be conveyed or in Class 2, 3 or 4 systems. Installation of aluminum ducts is limited to Class 1 systems conveying nonabrasive and noncorrosive contaminants. Aluminum ducts as well as galvanized steel ducts must not be used where the temperature of the material to be conveyed exceeds 400°F (204°C). Aluminum and zinc have been found to constitute a hazard in high-temperature conveying operations.

Metal ducts used in Class 5 systems that are not resistant to the corrosiveness of the conveyed product must be protected with a corrosion-resistant material. The ducts should be coated or lined with a nonpermeable, corrosion-resistant material as recommended by the manufacturer for the type of product being conveyed.

**609.2 Construction.** Product-conveying ducts must be of substantially airtight construction. They must not have any openings except as required for system operation and maintenance. Steel ducts must comply with Table 5-B or 5-C of the UMC for round and rectangular ducts, respectively. These tables specify required thickness, negative internal pressure and reinforcement spacing.

> **EXCEPTIONS:** 1. Class 1 product-conveying ducts that operate at less than 4 inches water column (995 Pa) negative pressure and convey noncorrosive, nonflammable and nonexplosive materials at temperatures not exceeding 250°F (121°C) may be constructed in accordance with Table 6-A, 6-B, 6-E or, with prior approval, UMC Standard 6-1.
>
> 2. Ducts used in central vacuuming systems within a dwelling unit may be of [PVC pipe or tubing]. Penetrations of fire-resistive walls, floor-ceiling or roof-ceiling assemblies [must] comply with Sections 709 and 710 of the Building Code. [Copper tubing or galvanized steel or black steel pipes] or conduit extending from within the separation between a garage and dwelling unit to the central vacuum unit [must] be used.

Use of rectangular product-conveying ducts is subject to approval by the building official. The deposit or collection of the conveyed product in the corners of the rectangular ducts is a concern. The designer should consider the adhesiveness and likelihood of buildup of the conveyed product within the duct system.

Aluminum ducts are limited for service as Class 1 ducts conveying nonabrasives only. In addition to this limitation, the thickness of an aluminum duct must be at least two B.&S. gages thicker than the gages required for steel ducts as set forth in Tables 5-B and 5-C of the UMC.

**609.3 Fittings.** In Class 2, Class 3 and Class 4 duct systems, the fittings must be not less than two gages thicker than the thickness required for straight runs.

Expansion joints are required when wide temperature variations are encountered in a product-conveying duct system, such as one carrying heated gases.

Duct branches must connect to main ducts (or plenums) at the large end of the transitions at an angle not exceeding 45 degrees with the axis of the main. The purpose is to avoid excessive turbulence and deposition of the material being conveyed.

**609.4 Cleanouts.** Accessible cleanouts are required at 10-foot (3048 mm) intervals for product-conveying ducts, except for those conveying noncorrosive vapors with no particulates. Access openings are also required to fire sprinklers and to other equipment requiring servicing within the duct.

**609.5 Explosion Venting.** Duct systems that carry explosive dusts require mechanical devices on the duct system to act as a relief in the event of an explosion. These devices include explosion vents, openings protected by antiflashback swing valves and rupture diaphragms. Openings to relieve explosive forces must always be located outside the building. When relief devices cannot provide sufficient pressure relief, the product-conveying duct system must be designed to withstand a positive internal pressure of not less than 100 pounds per square inch (psi) (689 kPa).

Provisions for excessive vacuum should also be considered although this is not required by the code. If fans are operating and the hoods, dampers or intake ducts suddenly become blocked or covered, considerable negative pressure can result, collapsing all or part of the duct system. Weighted pivot doors and spring-loaded disks similar to poppet check valves are solutions recommended by SMACNA.

**609.6 Supports.** Support spacing cannot exceed 12 feet for 8-inch (3658 mm for 203 mm) ducts or 20 feet (6096 mm) for larger ducts, unless justified by the system's design. In the design of supports, the designer must assume that at least 50 percent of the duct is full of the particulate to be conveyed.

**609.7 Fire Protection.** When ducts carrying flammable vapors or fumes have a cross-sectional dimension exceeding 10 inches (254 mm), sprinklers or other fire sprinkler devices must be installed. In horizontal ducts, sprinklers must be installed at 12-foot (3658 mm) intervals and at changes in direction. In vertical runs, sprinklers are required at the top and at alternate floor levels.

**609.8 Clearances.** Ducts that convey flammable or explosive vapors, fumes or dusts must have clearance from combustibles of not less than 18 inches (457 mm). This required clearance can be reduced only when the combustible construction is protected in accordance with Table 3-B of the UMC.

**609.8.1 Elevated temperatures.** For ducts conveying products at temperatures exceeding 125°F (52°C), the clearances must not be less than the following:

> 125°F to 250°F (52°C to 121°C)—1 inch (25 mm); 251°F to 600°F (122°C to 316°C)—8 inches (203 mm). For temperatures in excess of 600°F (316°C), the clearances must not be less than those required for chimneys in Table 8-D of the UMC.

**609.9 Protection from Physical Damage.** Where ducts are subject to physical damage, they must be protected by suitable guards.

# Chapter 7
# COMBUSTION AIR

This chapter contains the requirements for providing combustion air to fuel-burning appliances. It is important to review the definition of combustion air contained in Section 205: combustion air is the total amount of air provided to the space which contains fuel-burning equipment; it includes air for fuel combustion, for draft hood dilution and for ventilation of the equipment enclosure. An erroneous assumption could be that combustion air is only that air required to sustain the combustion of the fuel; as defined by the UMC, this is not true. All sections of this chapter, except the last sentence of Section 707.1 and 707.2, deal specifically with providing adequate combustion air to fuel-burning equipment by means of differential air pressure caused by the burning of fuel.

The burning of fuel causes pressure differentials in two ways: the use of oxygen ($O_2$) during the combustion process results in a pressure reduction in the combustion chamber; heating of the air surrounding the appliance causes expansion of the air in the appliance compartment, resulting in increased air temperature, decreased air density and increased pressure. How these pressure, temperature and density changes interrelate to cause the flow of air is sometimes difficult to visualize, but results in what is referred to as gravity flow. This process in a typical gas-fired furnace is as follows. As fuel burns, a drop in pressure occurs at the burner as a result of the consumption of oxygen ($O_2$) inducing a flow of air to the burner; the combustion products rise through the heat exchanger of the furnace and arrive at the draft hood at atmospheric or a slightly lower pressure than atmospheric. At this point, air enters the draft hood and rises, mixing with the warmer combustion products, expanding (increasing pressure and lowering density) and reaching the vent outlet at atmospheric pressure. The action in the venting system that causes the dilute flue gases to rise is characterized as buoyancy, which means that the slightly less dense flue products mixture tends to rise in air.

Therefore, the main consideration of this chapter is to ensure availability of air to the appliance for complete combustion of the fuel through unobstructed openings by means of gravity flow.

## SECTION 701 — GENERAL

**701.1 Air Supply.** Fuel gas is a mixture of hydrocarbon compounds having the chemical formula $C_nH_m$, the principal constituent being methane ($CH_4$). Minor amounts of ethane, propane and butane are frequently present, as are nitrogen and hydrogen sulphide; hydrogen found in eastern natural gases tends to raise the heating value of the fuel. In burning natural gas, oxygen from the atmosphere combines with the methane to release heat energy as follows:

$$CH_4 + 2\,O_2 \rightarrow CO_2 + 2\,H_2O + heat \qquad (1)$$

Equation (1) indicates that two volumes of oxygen are needed to burn one volume of methane.

Because atmospheric air contains approximately 20 percent oxygen and 80 percent nitrogen by volume, Equation (1) also shows that theoretically 10 cubic feet (283 L) of air will be needed to completely burn 1 cubic foot (28.3 L) of gas. The 8 cubic feet (226 L) of nitrogen in the air does not enter into the reaction to any significant extent, although a very small amount of nitrogen reacts with oxygen to produce nitric oxide (NO) and nitrogen dioxide ($NO_2$), known collectively as $NO_x$. The amount of $NO_x$ in the flue gases from a well-adjusted atmospheric burner is measured in parts per million (ppm) and varies from 10 to 100 ppm. $NO_x$ emissions are primarily of interest because of their role in smog formation.

Engineers and chemists refer to the theoretical amounts of each constituent reacted as the stoichiometric amounts. Because one cannot be sure that every molecule of fuel will be in exactly the right place to react with the oxygen, it is customary to provide about 40 percent excess air to a burner to ensure that complete combustion occurs.

Products of combustion resulting from complete combustion of a fuel are carbon dioxide ($CO_2$), water vapor ($H_2O$), heat and, if sulphur is present, sulphur dioxide ($SO_2$). Along with these products of combustion is the nitrogen ($N_2$) brought in with the air and the oxygen in the excess air.

Products of incomplete combustion are carbon monoxide (CO), aldehydes ($CH_3CHO$), heat, water vapor ($H_2O$) and carbon dioxide ($CO_2$).

Gas burners used in domestic appliances are generally of the nonluminous flame or Bunsen type. Part of the air required for combustion is inspirated as primary air into the burner mixing tube where it mixes with the fuel gas and then takes part in combustion at the burner ports. The amount of primary air is generally not enough to achieve complete combustion; therefore, secondary or excess air is required to be supplied at the burner port to achieve complete combustion. This secondary air is drawn toward the burner area by the force of the issuing mixture of gas and primary air and by the draft created by the heat of the flames. Blue flames indicate complete combustion, while yellow flames indicate insufficient primary air and possible incomplete combustion.

The air-to-gas ratio has a decided effect on how the flame spreads or propagates. The gas-air mixture must flow out of the burner ports at a rate sufficient to prevent flash back or cause it to burn in the burner head. On the other hand, the velocity of the primary air and gas mixture must not be so high that the flame will be blown from the ports. Contemporary types of burners have a wide range of adjustments. Gas supplies are generally uniform, and if appliances are properly adjusted and maintained, they should provide trouble-free operation.

In addition to air for fuel combustion, an appliance having a draft hood requires air to dilute the flue gases at the draft hood. One important function of the draft hood is the prevention of excessive negative pressure in the venting system (i.e., pressure below atmospheric), resulting in excessive draft at the burner adversely affecting efficient combustion in the appliance. In addition, by bleeding in air at room temperature through the draft hood, excessive flue gas temperatures are avoided, the stack action of the venting system is reduced and the flue gases rise through the venting system because of their buoyancy (i.e., density difference from outside air resulting from expansion of the flue gases that are heated above atmospheric ambient temperature).

When an appliance is installed in an enclosure, heat escaping through the appliance casing tends to heat the surrounding enclosure walls and may overheat adjacent combustible construction unless provision is made for ventilating the enclosure. The air required and used for ventilating a furnace enclosure is also defined by the *Uniform Mechanical Code* as one of the components of combustion air.

As illustrated in Figure 7-1, the total combustion air requirement to burn 1 cubic foot (28 L) of gas is estimated to be 29 cubic feet (821 L) consisting of the following:

Air for fuel combustion      14   (10 stoichiometric +
                                            4 excess)

Air for draft hood dilution     $\underline{15}$
                                         29

plus the requirement for ventilation of the enclosure. Estimating the ventilation requirement to be 21 cubic feet (595 L) or applying a safety factor of 1.72 to the 29 cubic feet (821 L), the total demand for combustion air becomes:

$$29 \times 1.72 = 50 \text{ cubic feet (1416 L)} \qquad (2)$$

Note that a number of uncertainties are involved in trying to arrive at an actual figure for combustion air, such as:

- Varying composition of fuel gases,
- Heating value per cubic foot (L),
- Altitude of appliance installation (which affects density of air and quantity of oxygen),
- Amount of heat leakage through appliance casing,
- Height of vent stack, and
- Wind velocity and direction at vent termination.

Therefore, the amount of combustion air required is estimated on a conservative basis to reduce the probability of oxygen-deficient combustion. Oxygen-deficient combustion is potentially dangerous because instead of all of the carbon being oxidized to carbon dioxide some carbon may be converted to carbon monoxide. Avoiding combustion that generates carbon monoxide is one reason for burning the fuel with excess air present in the combustion chamber.

$$2 \text{ vol. of CO} + 1 \text{ vol. of } O_2 \rightarrow 2 CO_2 + \text{heat} \qquad (3)$$

Equation (3) shows how the presence of available oxygen (excess air) enables partial combustion of the carbon to proceed to completion.

Having established the rationale for the amount of combustion air required to burn 1 cubic foot (28 L) of gas, it is a relatively simple matter to relate the requirement to the rule for combustion air as set forth in Sections 701.1, 701.2 and 701.3. If a room or space contains 50 cubic feet per 1,000 Btu/h (4.831 L/W) of appliance input rating, it becomes clear that combustion air obtained from that space must be replaced once per hour by infiltration.

Infiltration is the uncontrolled inward air passage through cracks and interstices in a building and around windows and doors. Such air can satisfy the combustion process when there is sufficient volume. Infiltration is assumed in any building; however, the rate of predictable air change per hour (ACH) will vary depending on the construction practices employed. Energy conservation measures, especially in cold climates, may result in inadequate infiltration to provide combustion air. Unusually tight construction as defined in Section 223 occurs when exposed walls and ceilings have continuous vapor retarders and gasketed or sealed openings, weatherstripped doors and windows and caulking applied to window joints, door frames, sole plates, and the utility penetrations are sealed or caulked. Under these conditions, infiltration should not be relied on to supply adequate combustion air, and combustion air should be obtained from outdoors.

The requirement that in buildings of unusually tight construction combustion air is to be obtained from the outside was added to the 1988 edition primarily due to improved construction practices implemented for energy conservation. The requirement was further amended in the 1991 edition to remove the requirement of prior approval to use infiltration for combustion air. This requirement was removed because of inability to enforce the provision in existing construction, as the building official's records might not be adequate to categorize a structure as being of unusually tight construction without testing to determine the infiltration rate.

Most jurisdictions enforcing an energy conservation code assume that new buildings are of very tight construction and, thus, routinely require admission of combustion air from outside.

COMBUSTION AIR

BURNING FUEL GAS—THE DERIVATION OF THE NEED
FOR 50 CUBIC FEET (1415 L) OF SPACE PER 1,000 BTU/H
(4.831 L/W) OF APPLIANCE INPUT RATING

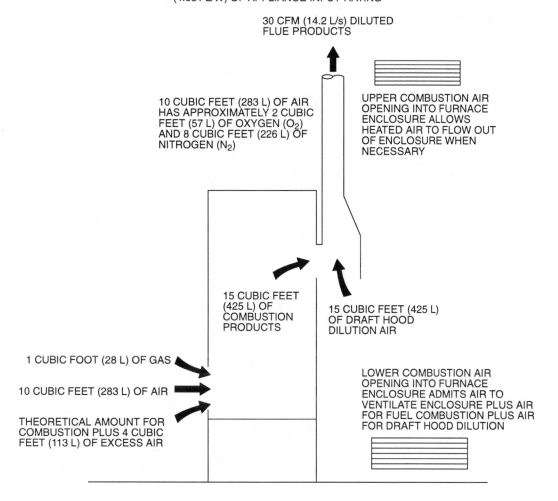

30 CFM (14.2 L/s) DILUTED
FLUE PRODUCTS

10 CUBIC FEET (283 L) OF AIR
HAS APPROXIMATELY 2 CUBIC
FEET (57 L) OF OXYGEN ($O_2$)
AND 8 CUBIC FEET (226 L) OF
NITROGEN ($N_2$)

UPPER COMBUSTION AIR
OPENING INTO FURNACE
ENCLOSURE ALLOWS
HEATED AIR TO FLOW OUT
OF ENCLOSURE WHEN
NECESSARY

15 CUBIC FEET
(425 L) OF
COMBUSTION
PRODUCTS

15 CUBIC FEET (425 L)
OF DRAFT HOOD
DILUTION AIR

1 CUBIC FOOT (28 L) OF GAS

10 CUBIC FEET (283 L) OF AIR

THEORETICAL AMOUNT FOR
COMBUSTION PLUS 4 CUBIC
FEET (113 L) OF EXCESS AIR

LOWER COMBUSTION AIR
OPENING INTO FURNACE
ENCLOSURE ADMITS AIR TO
VENTILATE ENCLOSURE PLUS AIR
FOR FUEL COMBUSTION PLUS AIR
FOR DRAFT HOOD DILUTION

**FIGURE 7-1**

## SECTION 702 — COMBUSTION-AIR OPENINGS

**702.1 Location.** When appliance enclosures are provided with openings or ducts for the purpose of providing combustion air, two openings into the enclosure are required. It is important to recognize that the upper combustion air duct must extend either upwards or horizontally as required in Section 703.1, Item 2. (See Figure 7-1 and the commentary on Section 703.1, Item 2.)

In the 1997 UMC and based on research conducted at the Gas Research Institute, the exception to Section 702.1 and Table 7-A (Column II, Item 5) was added, which permits use of a single, high combustion-air opening when all combustion air is taken from the outdoors. This system relies on alternate in and out flow of combustion air to the furnace compartment.

**702.2 Dampers Prohibited.** This section prohibits the use of fire dampers in combustion air ducts and, therefore, requires that when combustion air ducts pass through fire-rated construction, they must be enclosed in a fire-rated shaft equivalent to that required in Section 711.1 of the UBC. In addition, openings into or from combustion air ducts would not be permitted when such openings must be protected as required by Section 503.2.1 of the UBC. The requirements of this section exist because it is not immediately evident that a fire damper is accidentally closed or that it has malfunctioned, which could result in a hazardous condition, namely, an impediment to the flow of combustion air. Figure 7-2 shows an acceptable method for providing combustion air where fire-resistive construction is involved.

**702.3 Louvers, Grilles and Screens.** The $^1/_4$-inch (6.4 mm) mesh size is a specific code requirement—the mesh should not be smaller or larger in size. Smaller sizes tend to become blocked by debris and larger sizes might admit unwanted rodents and pests.

## SECTION 703 — SOURCES OF COMBUSTION AIR

**703.1 Air from Outside.** Item 1. This section allows combustion air to be provided through permanent openings to the outside of the building as illustrated in Figure 7-3.

**NOTE:** Shaft surrounding vent may be used as upper combustion air duct, provided it is of the proper area.

FIRE DAMPERS ARE NOT PERMITTED IN COMBUSTION AIR OPENING

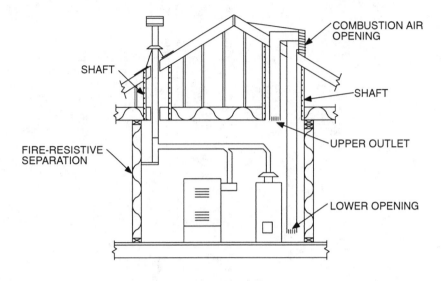

**FIGURE 7-2**

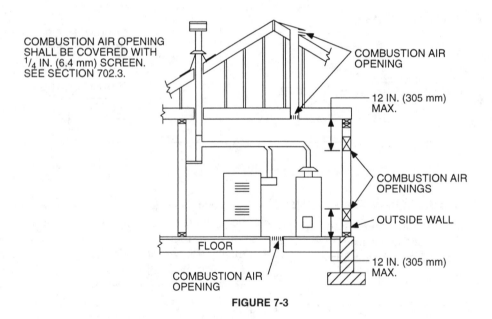

**FIGURE 7-3**

Item 2. The reason for the requirement that the upper combustion air duct shall extend horizontally or upwards to the outside is that this duct is required to ventilate the heat buildup from the appliance enclosure. As the air surrounding the equipment is heated, it rises to the top of the enclosure and is at a slightly higher pressure than atmospheric. Unless this pressure is relieved, it will continue to build and can prevent inward flow of combustion air at the bottom opening. Theoretically, the increased pressure can be maintained at a level in the appliance enclosure equal to the lowest point of the upper combustion air duct; therefore, the duct is required to be horizontal or to slope upward.

The 30-inch (762 mm) minimum height requirement in attics is to allow access for inspection and to ensure that obstructions will not prevent the free flow of combustion air, but it does not prevent the use of a duct to the outside in such spaces if the height is less. This requirement correlates with UBC Section 1505.3.

The provisions of Section 703.1 also allow combustion air to be provided through ducts extending to the exterior of the building and from attic spaces as illustrated in Figures 7-4, 7-5 and 7-6.

*(Continued on page 68)*

COMBUSTION AIR OPENINGS SHALL BE COVERED WITH $\frac{1}{4}$ IN. (6.4 mm) SCREEN. SEE SECTION 702.3.

EXTEND COMBUSTION AIR SEPARATION TO OUTSIDE OF BUILDING

COMBUSTION AIR OPENING SCREENED

UPPER OPENING

**NOTE:** The same duct shall not serve both the upper and lower combustion air openings.

LOWER OPENING

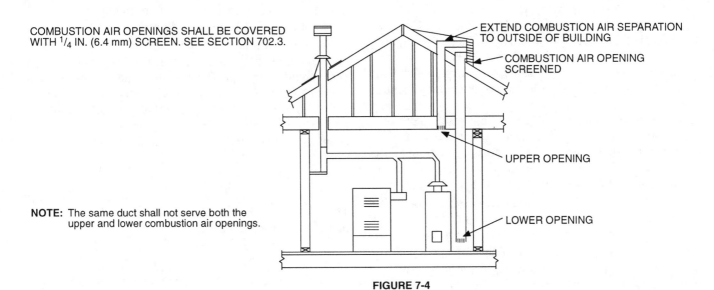

**FIGURE 7-4**

COMBUSTION AIR OPENINGS SHALL BE COVERED WITH $\frac{1}{4}$ IN. (6.4 mm) SCREEN. SEE SECTION 702.3.

DUCTS TO OUTSIDE AIR

UPPER OPENING

$\frac{1}{4}$ IN. (6.4 mm) SCREENED OPENINGS

ADJACENT ROOM

**NOTE:** The same duct shall not serve both the upper and lower combustion air openings.

LOWER OPENING

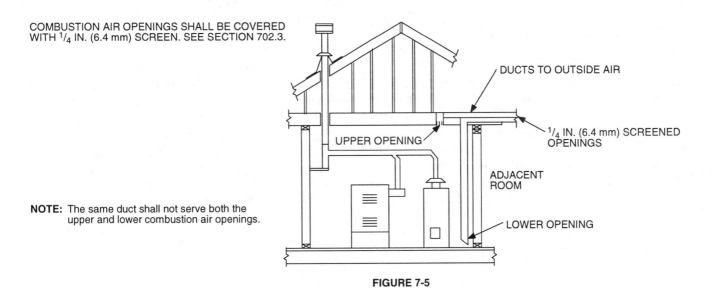

**FIGURE 7-5**

30 IN. (762 mm) MIN.

VENTILATION LOUVERS

OPENINGS NOT SCREENED. SEE SECTION 704.3.

NO. 26 GAGE GALVANIZED STEEL, 6 IN. (153 mm) ABOVE CEILING JOISTS AND INSULATION.

12 IN. (305 mm) MAX.

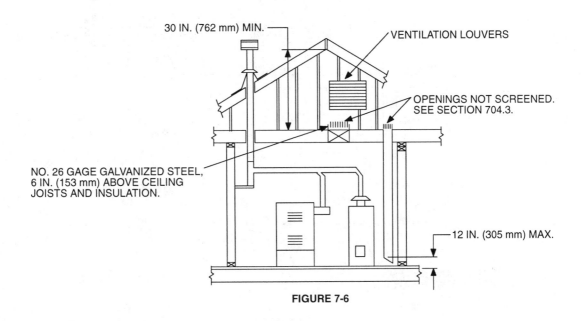

**FIGURE 7-6**

*(Continued from page 66)*

**703.2 Under-floor Supply.** The enforcement of this section requires coordination with the Building Code requirements for under-floor ventilation. Since the requirements of UBC Sections 2306.3 and 2306.4 allow construction with zero under-floor space, the minimum height of under-floor space and required combustion air opening size must be coordinated during plan check at the time permits are issued. In addition, the requirements of UBC Section 2306.7 allowing mechanical ventilation of under-floor spaces would prevent the use of an under-floor space as a source of combustion air if it is ventilated by mechanical means. (See commentary on UMC Section 703.3.)

The provisions of this section allow combustion air to be provided from under-floor areas as illustrated in Figure 7-7.

**703.3 Prohibited Sources.** Combustion air should not be taken from areas subject to negative pressure. Any potential source of negative pressure should be carefully considered to avoid unsatisfactory operation of gas appliances.

Negative pressure resulting from the operation of an exhaust fan or air-moving device affects the operation of the venting action and the combustion process. In severe cases, negative pressure may cause vent products to be drawn down the appliance vent and spill from the draft diverter, thus allowing products of combustion from an appliance to enter the occupied space and create a hazard.

Spaces ventilated by means of mechanical ventilation such as under-floor spaces and attics should not be used to provide combustion air (also see Section 706).

**703.4 Interior Spaces.** The provisions of this section determine when combustion air may be taken from interior spaces or is required to be taken from outside the building in buildings of ordinary tightness.

Figure 7-8 represents a space within a structure of ordinary tightness that could be a basement or a portion of an above-grade structure containing one or more fuel-burning appliances. The room contains 6,000 cubic feet (25′ × 30′ × 8′) [170 m³ (7.62 m × 9.14 m × 2.44 m)]. To be able to rely solely on infiltration for combustion air, the room or space should have a minimum volume of

$$\frac{100,000}{20} = 5,000 \text{ cubic feet (142 m}^3\text{) based on}$$
$$\text{Section 701.3.}$$

The one-twentieth rule can be stated in another way that is mathematically equivalent:

$$\frac{1}{20}\frac{\text{Ft.}^3}{\text{Btu/h}}\left(\frac{\text{L}}{\text{W}}\right) = \frac{50}{1,000}\frac{\text{Ft.}^3}{\text{Btu/h}}\left(\frac{\text{L}}{\text{W}}\right)$$

(numerator and denominator both multiplied by 50)

In this form, the rule requires 50 cubic feet of space for each 1,000 Btu/h of appliance input rating. You may use the form that is easiest for you to remember. The 1997 UMC uses the 50 cubic feet for each 1,000 Btu/h (4.831 L/W) form.

Figure 7-9 illustrates providing combustion air from "freely communicating interior spaces" in a building of ordinary tightness when the space containing the appliance has insufficient volume.

Figure 7-10 illustrates that in buildings of "ordinary tightness," combustion air openings to the outside are not required when the interior volume from which fuel-burning appliances can obtain combustion air is equal to or greater than 50 cubic feet per 1,000 Btu/h (4.831 L/W) in-

*(Continued on page 71)*

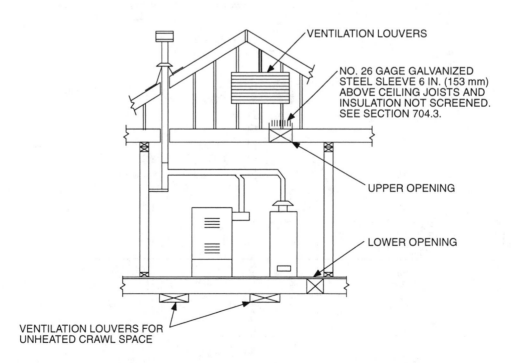

VENTILATION LOUVERS

NO. 26 GAGE GALVANIZED STEEL SLEEVE 6 IN. (153 mm) ABOVE CEILING JOISTS AND INSULATION NOT SCREENED. SEE SECTION 704.3.

UPPER OPENING

LOWER OPENING

VENTILATION LOUVERS FOR UNHEATED CRAWL SPACE

**FIGURE 7-7**

ADEQUATE VOLUME

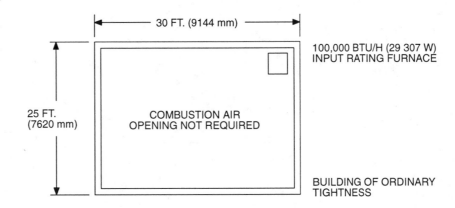

100,000 BTU/H (29 307 W)
INPUT RATING FURNACE

COMBUSTION AIR
OPENING NOT REQUIRED

BUILDING OF ORDINARY
TIGHTNESS

25 FT. × 30 FT. × 8 FT. = 6,000 CU. FT. (170 m³), THEREFORE, ROOM HAS VOLUME REQUIRED BY SECTION 703.4.1

[For **SI:** 9.14 m × 7.6 m × 2.44 m = 170 m³]

$$50 \times \frac{100,000}{1,000} \text{BTU/H} = 50 \times 100 = 5,000 \text{ FT.}^3 \ (142 \text{ m}^3)$$

[For **SI:** 29 307 L × 4.831 L/w = 141 582 L or 142 m³]

**RULE:** 50 FT.³/1,000 BTU/H (4.831 L/W) INPUT

**FIGURE 7-8**

INSUFFICIENT VOLUME
GAS- AND LIQUID-FIRED APPLIANCES

**RULE:** IF VOLUME OF ENCLOSURE IS LESS THAN 50 FT.³ PER 1,000 BTU/H (4.831 L/W) INPUT, SUPPLY THE DEFICIENCY OF COMBUSTION AIR FROM SOURCES OUTSIDE THE ENCLOSURE.

BUILDING OF ORDINARY TIGHTNESS

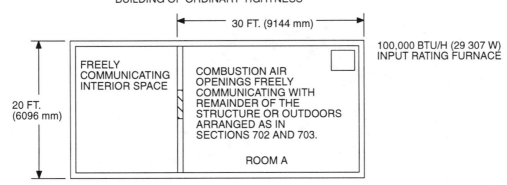

VOLUME OF ROOM A = 20 FT. × 30 FT. × 8 FT. = 4,800 FT.³ (136 m³)

100 × 50 = 5,00 FT.³ (142 m³)  VOLUME OF ROOM A IS INADEQUATE: THEREFORE, AN OPENING TO OTHER AREAS OR AN OPENING TO THE OUTSIDE IS REQUIRED. THE SIZE OF THE OPENING IS DETERMINED FROM TABLE 7-A. SINCE THIS IS A BUILDING OF ORDINARY TIGHTNESS, SECTION 703.4 WOULD PERMIT RELIANCE ON INFILTRATION FOR COMBUSTION AIR. IN THIS EXAMPLE THE VOLUME OF THE FREELY COMMUNICATING INTERIOR SPACE WOULD HAVE TO BE AT LEAST 200 CUBIC FEET (5.66 L) (5,000 minus 4,800), AND THE OPENINGS WOULD NOT BE LESS THAN 100 SQUARE INCHES (0.0645 m²) HIGH AND 100 SQUARE INCHES (0.0645 m²) LOW.

**FIGURE 7-9**

ADEQUATE VOLUME

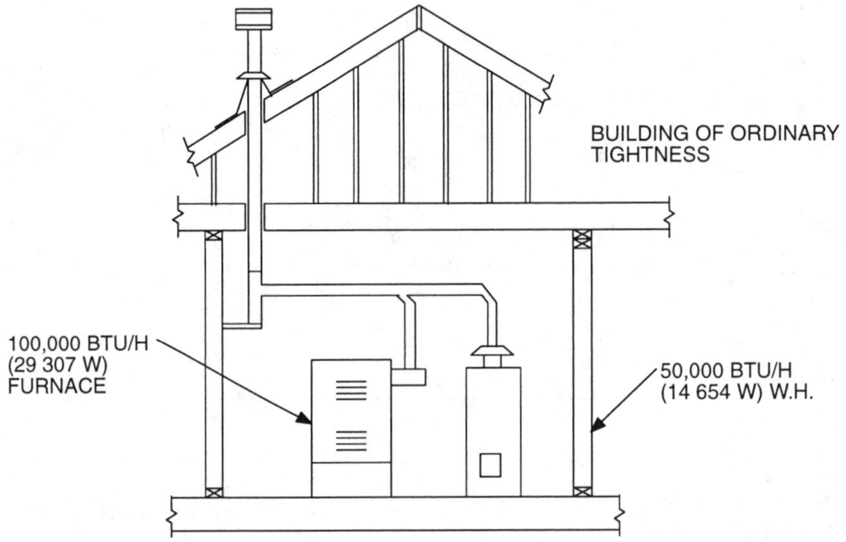

BUILDING OF ORDINARY
TIGHTNESS

100,000 BTU/H
(29 307 W)
FURNACE

50,000 BTU/H
(14 654 W) W.H.

EXAMPLE:  DIMENSIONS OF SPACE USED
LENGTH      31 FT. 3 IN. (9525 mm)
WIDTH       30 FT. 0 IN. (9144 mm)
HEIGHT       8 FT. 0 IN. (2438 mm)

TOTAL CUBIC FT. AVAILABLE 7,500 (212 m³)

TOTAL CUBIC FT. SHALL EQUAL OR EXCEED
50 FT.³/1,000 OF TOTAL BTU/H [4.831 (L/W)] INPUT
RATING OF APPLIANCES INSTALLED IN SPACE.

$$\frac{150,000}{1,000} \times 50 = 7,500 \text{ FT.}^3 \text{ (212 m}^3\text{) REQUIRED}$$

**FIGURE 7-10**

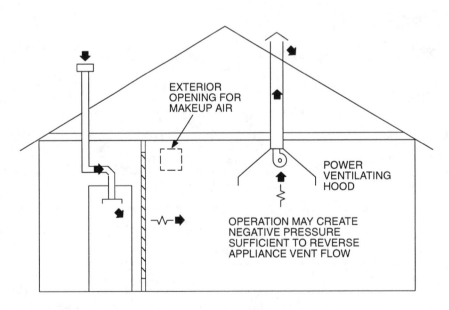

EXTERIOR
OPENING FOR
MAKEUP AIR

POWER
VENTILATING
HOOD

OPERATION MAY CREATE
NEGATIVE PRESSURE
SUFFICIENT TO REVERSE
APPLIANCE VENT FLOW

Solution:
Provide opening for makeup air large enough to prevent negative
pressure at appliance location

**FIGURE 7-11**

*(Continued from page 68)*

put of the appliances. Stated differently, infiltration may be assumed to provide combustion air in buildings of ordinary tightness when freely communicating interior spaces provide at least 50 cubic feet per 1,000 Btu/h (4.831 L/W) of appliance input rating.

## SECTION 704 — COMBUSTION-AIR DUCTS

The provisions of this section give specific requirements for the installation of combustion air ducts. A review of the commentary on previous sections of this chapter will answer most of the questions regarding this section. Understanding that the flow of combustion air is into the space containing the appliance, through the lower combustion air opening and out of the same space through the upper opening and that the flow into the lower opening supplies the air for the flow out of the upper opening will usually provide the logic required to answer questions on this section.

In regard to Section 704.2, Dampers, see UMC Section 702.2 and the commentary provided therein.

## SECTION 706 — CONDITIONS CREATED BY MECHANICAL EXHAUSTING

This section gives the building official great latitude in evaluating conditions that could cause unsatisfactory operation of an appliance. Obviously, providing an exterior opening of adequate size as illustrated in Figure 7-11 will solve the problem illustrated, but additional requirements for makeup air for other conditions such as bathrooms and kitchen vents in buildings of unusually tight construction and fireplaces require more detailed analysis. Therefore, the building official must recognize that there are conditions that are not specifically covered in the code, but are regulated by the general requirements of Section 701.1 where it states that "fuel-burning equipment shall be assured a sufficient supply of combustion air." Since this is a very general statement, there is a great deal of explanation that is not covered by the code and cannot be the subject of an interpretation or application because the code does not have requirements to be interpreted. This leaves the approval of a proposed installation in the hands of the building official using Section 105, which covers alternate methods.

It must be emphasized that the effect of the operation of air-moving devices, such as clothes dryers, exhaust hoods, ventilating fans and fireplaces, can produce a reduced pressure zone in the building that affects combustion and venting of gas-fired appliances. The static head for 7 feet (2134 mm) of vent height with 450°F (232°C) flue gases is only about $^{47}/_{1,000}$-inch (0.047) water column (11.7 Pa). In a vent 4 inches (102 mm) in diameter, the total lifting force would be approximately $^{1}/_{3}$ ounce. It does not require very much pressure reduction to overcome such a small head and to reverse the flow of flue gases. (See also the commentary on Section 703.3.)

## SECTION 707 — AREA OF COMBUSTION-AIR OPENINGS

**707.1 General.** This section determines the size and free area of the openings or combustion air ducts. The 1991 edition was simplified by the addition of Table 7-A, which in previous editions had been covered by some rather complex language. Even though Section 702.3 is specifically referenced in this section, all previous sections of this chapter are relevant and special care should be exercised when using Table 7-A not to overlook the footnotes. Any effort herein to summarize these sizing requirements would be a repetition of what is tabulated in a well-organized manner in Table 7-A.

To determine the required combustion air openings or duct sizes, proceed as follows:

1. Categorize the building as being of ordinary tightness or of unusually tight construction as defined in Section 223. Buildings having the construction features described in the definition are of unusually tight construction. Other buildings should be categorized as ordinarily tight.

2. Enter the table at either "Column I" or "Column II" as determined above on the left, selecting the appropriate "condition," and in the case of buildings of ordinary tightness, the subcategory selected (1, 2 or 3).

3. Note the minimum size of combustion air openings or ducts indicated in the block to the right of the condition selected. There are five methods for sizing the openings or ducts for appliances in confined spaces in buildings of unusually tight construction.

Figure 7-12 illustrates an outside air duct connected to the return-air duct as permitted and noted in Table 7-A for appliances in unconfined spaces in buildings of unusually tight construction. Outside air may also be brought into the building in this manner as permitted in Table 7-A for appliances in unconfined spaces in buildings of ordinary tightness (Condition Option 2).

It should be noted that the current wording of Table 7-A in regard to this method of supplying outside air is not mandatory (i.e., "may be connected to the cold-air return"). If these options are selected and the outdoor air duct is not connected to the cold-air return, it should be ducted to a point within the lower 12 inches (305 mm) of the appliance enclosure or the unconfined space containing the appliance.

The reasons for the various size openings required in Table 7-A are as follows:

1. An appliance in an enclosure having less than 50-cubic-foot per 1,000 Btu/h (4.831 L/W) input rating (i.e., one installed in a confined space of a building of unusually tight construction) must have openings large enough to ventilate the appliance enclosure [1-square-inch per 4,000 Btu/h (0.55 mm²/W) input rating]. When the appliance is in-

stalled in an unconfined space, the need for air to prevent overheating of the appliance enclosure is less demanding and less combustion air is needed [hence the 1-square-inch per 5,000 Btu/h (0.44 mm²/W) input rating].

2. The difference between 1 square inch per 4,000 Btu/h (0.55 mm²/W) and 1 square inch per 2,000 Btu/h (1.1 mm²/W) for appliances installed in confined spaces of buildings of unusually tight construction is based on the way ducts installed vertically will tend to establish thermosyphonic circulation through the appliance enclosure because of the different density between warm and cool air. Horizontal ducts do not encourage syphonic flow through them despite the fact that the warmest (least dense) air will tend to rise toward the ceiling of the appliance enclosure.

3. For appliances installed in confined spaces of buildings of ordinary tightness, the 1-square-inch per 1,000 Btu/h (2.2 mm²/W) opening to other interior spaces is established by the method of testing central furnaces under ANSI Z21.47, when listed for closet installation. The test standard requires an upper and lower opening, each having the code-specified 1-square-inch per 1,000 Btu/h (2.2 mm²/W) input, but not less than 100 square inches (0.0645 m²) each.

The heavy margin marking adjoining Table 7-A in the code indicates the addition of an exception, which allows use of a single combustion-air opening or duct to the outside located in the upper 12 inches (305 mm) of the furnace compartment. The research was conducted by Battelle-Columbus and reported in a Gas Research Institute Topical Report entitled *Analysis of Combustion Air Openings to the Outdoors: Preliminary Report.*

**707.2 Designed Installations.** Chapter 7 requirements are based on supplying combustion air by means of gravity-induced flow (i.e., the density of the air in the appliance compartment will be somewhat less than that of the air outside of the compartment and less than that of outdoor air). These subtle differences in density act as a small driving force causing air to enter the lower combustion air opening and to flow outward through the upper combustion air opening. The same buoyancy principle is used in gravity venting of the flue gases in an appliance venting system except, of course, that larger temperature differences ($\Delta t$'s) are encountered in a vent. Because the $\Delta t$ through an appliance enclosure is small, the driving forces for gravity induction of combustion air to an appliance compartment are very small indeed. Section 707 and Table 7-A provide openings that are adequately sized to permit air to flow into and out of an appliance enclosure by gravity alone.

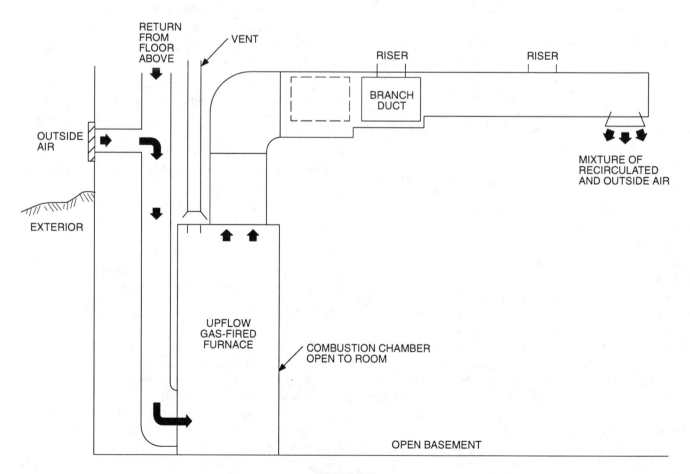

**FIGURE 7-12**

Designed systems for the provision of combustion air to an appliance compartment rely on a much larger pressure difference created by a fan, pump, compressor or an injector. In a designed system, the ducts and openings generally may be smaller because the driving force is not gravity, but a mechanical device that imparts energy to the air stream by pressurizing it. Therefore, the size and location of openings for combustion air and the duct sizing should not be changed unless a concurrent change from a gravity to a designed mechanically driven combustion-air system is proposed.

# Chapter 8
# CHIMNEYS AND VENTS

## SECTION 801 — VENTING SYSTEMS—GENERAL

This chapter regulates the installation of venting systems that convey products of combustion from appliances to the exterior of the building. The *Uniform Mechanical Code* distinguishes between *chimneys* and *vents*. The second paragraph of this section makes the following distinction: "Venting systems shall consist of approved chimneys, Type B vents, Type BW vents," etc. Although a chimney and a vent accomplish the same purpose, they have separate and distinct definitions in Chapter 2, and it is recommended that the reader review the definitions of the various classifications and types of vents and chimneys for a clear understanding of the differences. Table 8-1 is provided for this purpose and lists terms that have a specific meaning in the UMC relative to venting systems, including the definition or a paraphrase of the definition of the term.

Another distinction made in the second paragraph of Section 801 is that of venting systems fabricated from "plastic pipe recommended by the manufacturer of listed condensing appliances." There are no specific definitions related to plastic pipe venting systems in the UMC, but

they represent a distinct category of venting systems and are permitted to be used when complying with the requirements of the second and fifth paragraphs of Section 801 and Section 802.5, Plastic Venting Systems for Use with Listed Condensing Appliances.

Confusion often arises in applying the requirements of Chapter 8 because definitions are disregarded. The following basic requirements must be remembered:

- A *venting system* includes systems using vents, chimneys and plastic venting systems.

- A *vent* is not a chimney and the word means a listed vent pipe for use only with gas- or oil-burning appliances in accordance with its listing.

- A *chimney* is not a vent as defined in the UMC. With the proper designation, a chimney can convey flue gases from any kind of an appliance, unless the appliance listing requires a specific kind of venting system.

- *Plastic venting systems* are a distinct category of venting systems and must be installed in accordance with the terms of the appliance listing and the manufacturer's installation instructions.

## TABLE 8-1—SUMMARY OF UMC VENTING SYSTEM TERMS/DEFINITIONS

| TERM | UMC | DEFINITION[1] |
|---|---|---|
| **Chimney** | Section 205 | a vertical shaft enclosing one or more flues for conveying flue gases to the outside atmosphere |
| Factory-built chimney | | a listed chimney |
| Masonry chimney | | a chimney of solid masonry units, bricks, stones, listed masonry units or reinforced concrete, lined with suitable flue liners |
| Metal chimney (smoke stack) | | a job-built chimney constructed of metal with a minimum thickness not less than 0.127-inch (3.23 mm) (No. 10 manufacturer's standard gage) steel sheet |
| **Chimney Classifications** | Section 205 | |
| Chimney, residential appliance-type | | a factory-built or masonry chimney suitable for conveying products of combustion at temperatures not exceeding 1,000°F (538°C) |
| Chimney, low-heat appliance-type | | a factory-built, masonry or metal chimney suitable for conveying products of combustion whose temperature does not exceed 1,000°F (538°C), intermittent to 1,400°F (760°C) |
| Chimney, medium-heat appliance-type | | a factory-built, masonry or metal chimney suitable for conveying products of combustion whose temperature does not exceed 2,000°F (1093°C) |
| Chimney, high-heat appliance-type | | a factory-built, masonry or metal chimney suitable for conveying products of combustion whose temperatures exceed 2,000°F (1093°C) |
| **Chimney Connector** | Section 205 | the pipe that connects a fuel-burning appliance to a chimney |
| **Draft Hood** | Section 206 | a device built into an appliance or made a part of the vent connector from an appliance, which is designed to ensure proper venting of the appliance |
| **Vent** | Section 224 | a listed factory-made vent pipe and vent fittings for conveying flue gases to the outside atmosphere |
| Type B Gas Vent | | a listed gas vent for use only with gas-burning appliances |
| Type BW Gas Vent | | a listed gas vent for use only with gas-burning wall furnaces |
| Type L Vent | | a listed vent for use with oil-burning and gas-burning appliances |
| **Vent Connector, Gas** | Section 224 | that portion of a gas-venting system that connects a listed gas appliance to a gas vent |
| **Venting Collar** | Section 224 | the outlet opening of an appliance provided for connection to the venting system |
| **Venting System** | Section 224 | the vent or chimney and its connectors assembled to form a continuous open passageway from an appliance to the outside atmosphere for the purpose of removing products of combustion. This definition also shall include a venting assembly which is an integral part of an appliance |
| **Venting System—Gravity-Type** | Section 224 | a system that depends entirely on the heat from the fuel being used to provide the energy required to vent an appliance |
| **Venting System—Power-Type** | Section 224 | a system that depends on a mechanical device to provide a positive draft within the venting system |

[1]Some of these definitions have been paraphrased. Complete definitions can be found in Chapter 2 of the UMC.

Figure 8-1 illustrates the operation of a basic gravity-type venting system.

Figure 8-2 illustrates an induced draft or power-type venting system.

## SECTION 802 — TYPES OF VENTING SYSTEMS REQUIRED

**802.1 General.** This section provides requirements for selecting a venting system that will comply with the code.

**802.2 Limitations.** The reasons for these limitations can easily be understood by reviewing the definition of a Type B gas vent.

**802.3 Vent Connector.** This section provides the requirements for vent connectors used with gas-burning appliances. Listed conversion-burner-equipped appliances are heating boilers and furnaces that have been modified by the installation of a listed gas-burning burner and control system.

Because the *Uniform Mechanical Code* does not specify a vent connector suitable for use with oil-burning appliances, it may be concluded that a vent connector from an oil-fired appliance to a Type L venting system must also be fabricated from listed Type L materials. Such a conclusion is not necessarily correct. UMC Section 815 permits the use of single-wall metal pipe connectors subject to some limitations, principally those contained in Sections 815.2.1, 815.2.2 and 815.3, which establish the thickness requirements for single-wall connectors.

**802.4 Solid Fuel.** This section prohibits the interconnection of a solid-fuel-burning appliance with a venting system serving a gas- or oil-burning appliance.

**802.5 Plastic Venting Systems for Use with Listed Condensing Appliances.** See commentaries on the definition of "condensing appliance" in Section 205 and the second paragraph of Section 801.

See definition of vented gas appliance categories in Section 205.

Listed Categories III and IV appliances do operate with a positive pressure in the vent and, therefore, cannot use Type B vents that are not designed to operate under positive pressure; listed Categories I and II vented appliances operate with nonpositive vent pressure, and hence, may be used with Type B vents. Figure 8-3 illustrates a typical listed condensing central furnace. This design often operates with a positive pressure in the venting system and hence requires disposal of liquid condensate. These units may operate with flue gas temperatures less than 140°F (60°C) above the dew point (specifically Categories II and IV appliances), and hence will produce condensate which must be disposed of.

## SECTION 803 — INSTALLATION AND CONSTRUCTION REQUIREMENTS

**803.1 General.** This section states specifically how each kind of venting system is to be installed except plas-tic venting systems (see commentary on Section 802.5.) The 1991 edition of the UMC added Section 803.2 to incorporate a cross-reference to sections regulating the installation of unlisted metal chimneys (smokestacks) and masonry chimneys. Section 803.2 clarifies the distinction between listed venting systems that may be fabricated from metal (factory-built chimneys) and unlisted metal chimneys (smokestacks) that are job-built by welding or riveting steel plates almost $^1/_8$-inch (3.2 mm) thick.

Type B vents are to be used only with gas-fired appliances that are equipped with a draft hood and designed to operate at pressures at or below atmospheric in the connector. The absence of a draft hood should alert an inspector to ask for the manufacturer's installation instructions. When the pressure at the appliance vent collar exceeds atmospheric, the appliances should not be manifolded with appliances having a gravity-venting system. Positive-pressure flue gases must be conveyed to a masonry chimney constructed as required by UBC Chapter 31, to a smokestack constructed as specified in UMC Section 813 or 814, or to a venting system approved for operation at pressures above atmospheric. The chimney connector must also be gastight to prevent the products of combustion under pressure from leaking into the building.

Type B listed vents are marked as B-0, B-1, B-1$^1/_2$, B-2 or B-3 on each pipe section to indicate 0-inch, 1-inch (25 mm), 1$^1/_2$-inch (38 mm), 2-inch (51 mm) or 3-inch (76 mm) minimum clearances to combustible construction, respectively.

Commonly, two kinds of Type B vents have been installed: (1) double-walled metallic vents and (2) single-walled nonmetallic vents, which are not being produced currently, although thousands of such venting systems are in use. Figures 8-4, 8-5, 8-6 and 8-7 show typical installation details for the double-walled metallic type. Figures 8-8 and 8-9 show typical installation details for the single-walled nonmetallic type and are provided because of the many existing installations which will be encountered in the field. Installation details are shown in wood-framed walls using either 2 by 4 (50 by 102) or 2 by 6 (50 by 150) studs. The listing reads "Type B-2 × 4" (50 × 102) or "Type B-2 × 6" (50 × 150) pipe. The proper clearances are established by integral spacers embossed on each vent section and fire-stop spacers that must be installed at the level of each floor or ceiling penetrated by a vent.

The spacers shown in Figures 8-5 and 8-7 are usually intended only as fire stops and vent spacers. When employed as plate straps as described in Section 2320.11.7 of the *Uniform Building Code*, the spacers must meet all Building Code requirements.

Type L vents are also of double-walled metallic construction, and the typical installation drawings shown in Figures 8-4 and 8-5 are representative.

The other types of venting systems referenced in this section are discussed and illustrated in the following sections:

*(Continued on page 84)*

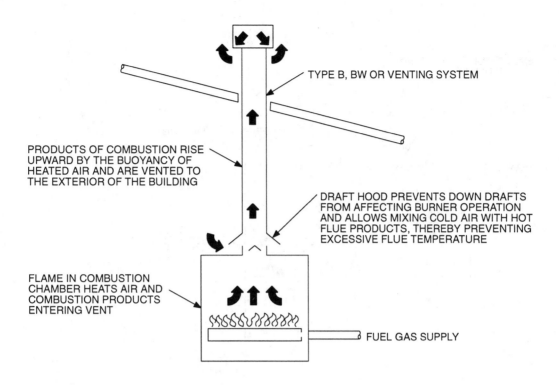

TYPE B, BW OR VENTING SYSTEM

PRODUCTS OF COMBUSTION RISE UPWARD BY THE BUOYANCY OF HEATED AIR AND ARE VENTED TO THE EXTERIOR OF THE BUILDING

DRAFT HOOD PREVENTS DOWN DRAFTS FROM AFFECTING BURNER OPERATION AND ALLOWS MIXING COLD AIR WITH HOT FLUE PRODUCTS, THEREBY PREVENTING EXCESSIVE FLUE TEMPERATURE

FLAME IN COMBUSTION CHAMBER HEATS AIR AND COMBUSTION PRODUCTS ENTERING VENT

FUEL GAS SUPPLY

**TYPICAL VENTING SYSTEM—GRAVITY TYPE**

**FIGURE 8-1**

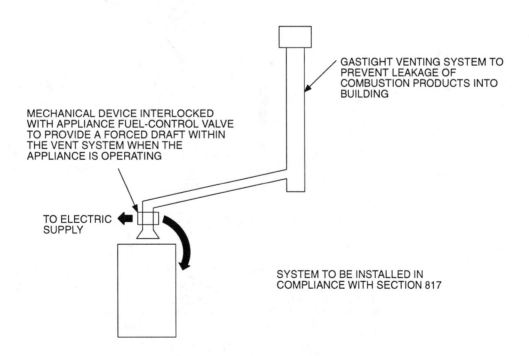

GASTIGHT VENTING SYSTEM TO PREVENT LEAKAGE OF COMBUSTION PRODUCTS INTO BUILDING

MECHANICAL DEVICE INTERLOCKED WITH APPLIANCE FUEL-CONTROL VALVE TO PROVIDE A FORCED DRAFT WITHIN THE VENT SYSTEM WHEN THE APPLIANCE IS OPERATING

TO ELECTRIC SUPPLY

SYSTEM TO BE INSTALLED IN COMPLIANCE WITH SECTION 817

**TYPICAL VENTING SYSTEM—POWER TYPE**

**FIGURE 8-2**

FLUE GAS TEMPERATURES LESS THAN
140°F (60°C) ABOVE DEWPOINT

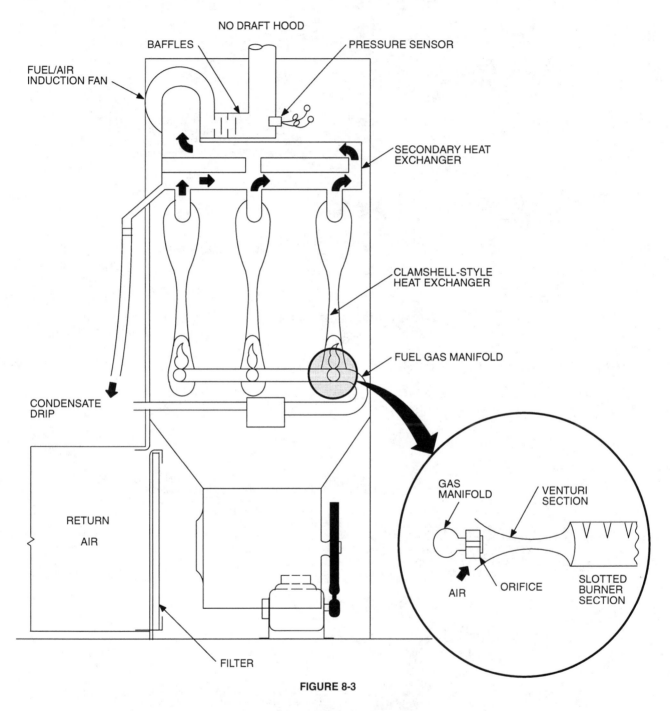

FIGURE 8-3

**LISTED CONDENSING CENTRAL FURNACE**
(Schematic diagram only—does not reflect a specific manufacturer's product)

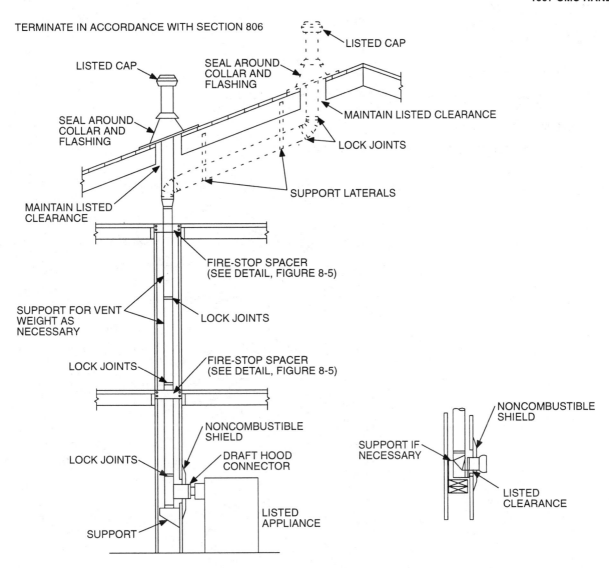

TERMINATE IN ACCORDANCE WITH SECTION 806

LISTED CAP

LISTED CAP

SEAL AROUND COLLAR AND FLASHING

MAINTAIN LISTED CLEARANCE

SEAL AROUND COLLAR AND FLASHING

LOCK JOINTS

MAINTAIN LISTED CLEARANCE

SUPPORT LATERALS

FIRE-STOP SPACER (SEE DETAIL, FIGURE 8-5)

SUPPORT FOR VENT WEIGHT AS NECESSARY

LOCK JOINTS

LOCK JOINTS

FIRE-STOP SPACER (SEE DETAIL, FIGURE 8-5)

NONCOMBUSTIBLE SHIELD

NONCOMBUSTIBLE SHIELD

LOCK JOINTS

DRAFT HOOD CONNECTOR

SUPPORT IF NECESSARY

LISTED CLEARANCE

LISTED APPLIANCE

SUPPORT

**TYPICAL TYPE B ROUND VENTING SYSTEM**

**FIGURE 8-4**

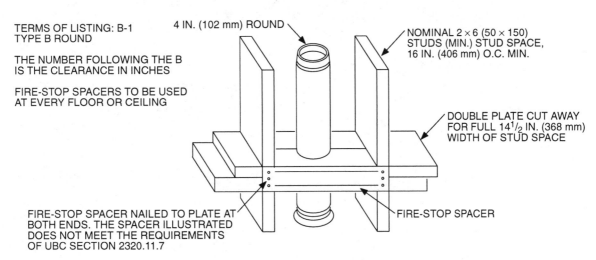

TERMS OF LISTING: B-1 TYPE B ROUND

THE NUMBER FOLLOWING THE B IS THE CLEARANCE IN INCHES

FIRE-STOP SPACERS TO BE USED AT EVERY FLOOR OR CEILING

4 IN. (102 mm) ROUND

NOMINAL 2 × 6 (50 × 150) STUDS (MIN.) STUD SPACE, 16 IN. (406 mm) O.C. MIN.

DOUBLE PLATE CUT AWAY FOR FULL 14$^1$/$_2$ IN. (368 mm) WIDTH OF STUD SPACE

FIRE-STOP SPACER NAILED TO PLATE AT BOTH ENDS. THE SPACER ILLUSTRATED DOES NOT MEET THE REQUIREMENTS OF UBC SECTION 2320.11.7

FIRE-STOP SPACER

**TYPICAL TYPE B ROUND VENTING SYSTEM FIRE-STOP SPACER**

**FIGURE 8-5**

TYPE B INSTALLATION REQUIREMENTS. DOUBLE-WALL METAL VENT 4 IN.
OVAL IN FRAME WALL, FOR SINGLE OR MULTISTORY USE.

TERMS OF LISTING: TYPE B—2 × 4

TYPE B VENTS LISTED FOR INSTALLATION IN 2 × 4 FRAME WALLS.

SEE MANUFACTURER'S INSTRUCTIONS

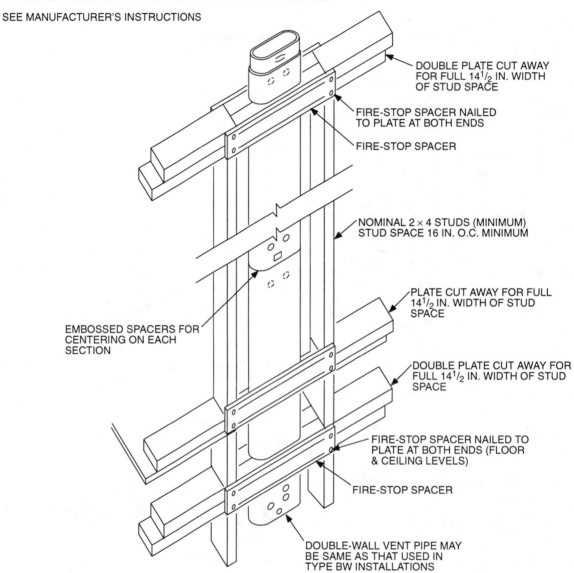

DOUBLE PLATE CUT AWAY
FOR FULL 14$\frac{1}{2}$ IN. WIDTH
OF STUD SPACE

FIRE-STOP SPACER NAILED
TO PLATE AT BOTH ENDS

FIRE-STOP SPACER

NOMINAL 2 × 4 STUDS (MINIMUM)
STUD SPACE 16 IN. O.C. MINIMUM

PLATE CUT AWAY FOR FULL
14$\frac{1}{2}$ IN. WIDTH OF STUD
SPACE

DOUBLE PLATE CUT AWAY FOR
FULL 14$\frac{1}{2}$ IN. WIDTH OF STUD
SPACE

EMBOSSED SPACERS FOR
CENTERING ON EACH
SECTION

FIRE-STOP SPACER NAILED TO
PLATE AT BOTH ENDS (FLOOR
& CEILING LEVELS)

FIRE-STOP SPACER

DOUBLE-WALL VENT PIPE MAY
BE SAME AS THAT USED IN
TYPE BW INSTALLATIONS

For **SI:** 1 inch = 25.4 mm.

**FIGURE 8-6**

**TYPICAL TYPE B OVAL VENTING SYSTEM**

TYPE B INSTALLATION REQUIREMENT.
DOUBLE-WALL METAL VENT 2 × 6 (50 × 150) WALL CONSTRUCTION

MUST BE LISTED FOR 0 IN. (0 mm) OR 1 IN. (25 mm) CLEARANCE

FIRE-STOP SPACERS TO BE USED AT EVERY FLOOR OR CEILING

TERMS OF LISTING: TYPE B—2 × 6 (50 × 150)

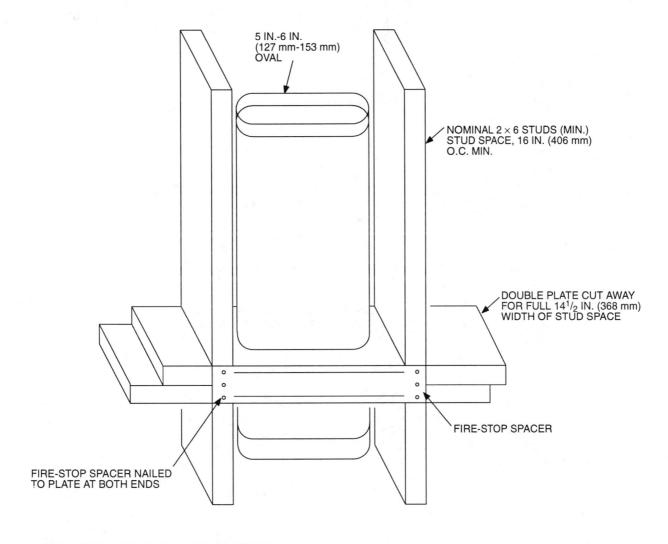

5 IN.-6 IN.
(127 mm-153 mm)
OVAL

NOMINAL 2 × 6 STUDS (MIN.)
STUD SPACE, 16 IN. (406 mm)
O.C. MIN.

DOUBLE PLATE CUT AWAY
FOR FULL 14$^1$/$_2$ IN. (368 mm)
WIDTH OF STUD SPACE

FIRE-STOP SPACER

FIRE-STOP SPACER NAILED
TO PLATE AT BOTH ENDS

THE SPACER ILLUSTRATED DOES NOT MEET THE
REQUIREMENTS OF UBC SECTION 2320.11.7

**FIGURE 8-7**

**TYPICAL TYPE B OVAL VENTING SYSTEM FIRE-STOP SPACER**

LISTED SINGLE-WALL TYPE B VENTS

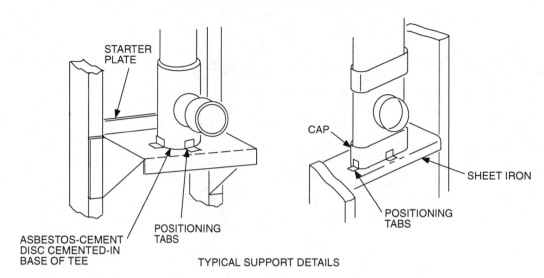

STARTER PLATE

CAP

SHEET IRON

POSITIONING TABS

POSITIONING TABS

ASBESTOS-CEMENT DISC CEMENTED-IN BASE OF TEE

TYPICAL SUPPORT DETAILS

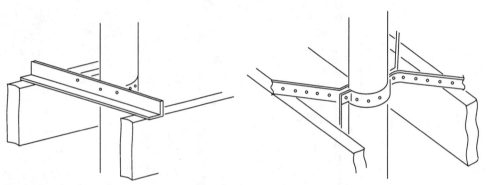

ANGLE IRON AND LIGHT STRAPPING OR RISER CLAMPS OF HANGER IRON CAN BE USED IN VARIOUS WAYS FOR SUPPORTING THE VENT

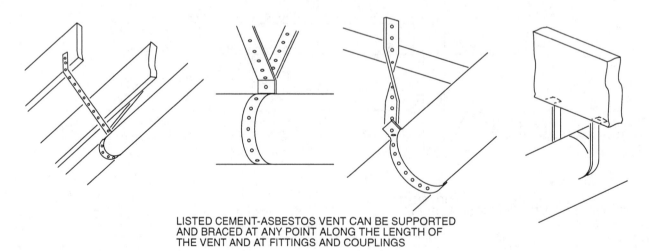

LISTED CEMENT-ASBESTOS VENT CAN BE SUPPORTED AND BRACED AT ANY POINT ALONG THE LENGTH OF THE VENT AND AT FITTINGS AND COUPLINGS

WHEN BASE OF VENT EXTENDS TO GROUND, IT SHALL BE SUPPORTED ON 2 IN. (51 mm) OF SOLID MASONRY OR CONCRETE

WHEN SUPPORTING VENT, MINIMUM CLEARANCES MUST BE OBSERVED

**NOTE:** Pipe and fittings are listed for either $1^1/_2$-in. or 3-in. (38 mm or 76 mm) clearance to combustible construction.

**TYPICAL DETAILS FOR SUPPORT OF SINGLE-WALL NONMETALLIC TYPE B VENTS**

**FIGURE 8-8**

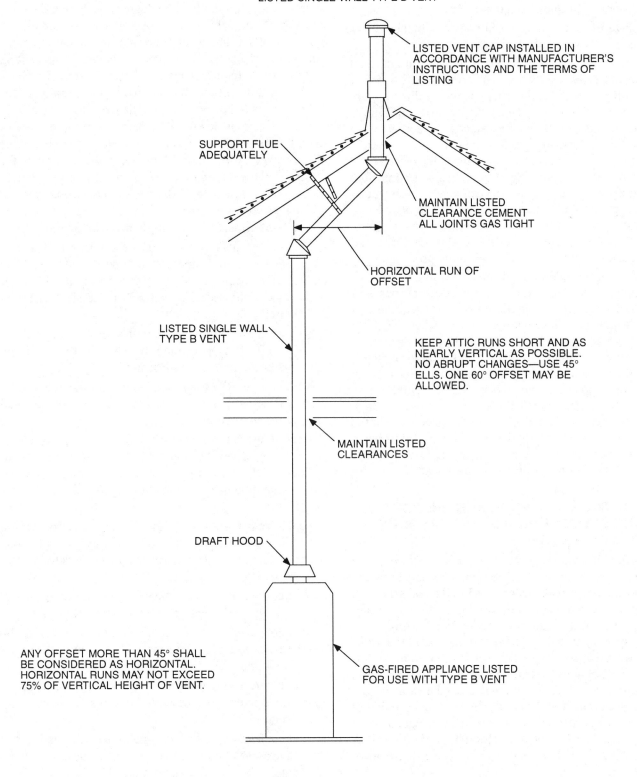

LISTED SINGLE-WALL TYPE B VENT

LISTED VENT CAP INSTALLED IN ACCORDANCE WITH MANUFACTURER'S INSTRUCTIONS AND THE TERMS OF LISTING

SUPPORT FLUE ADEQUATELY

MAINTAIN LISTED CLEARANCE CEMENT ALL JOINTS GAS TIGHT

HORIZONTAL RUN OF OFFSET

LISTED SINGLE WALL TYPE B VENT

KEEP ATTIC RUNS SHORT AND AS NEARLY VERTICAL AS POSSIBLE. NO ABRUPT CHANGES—USE 45° ELLS. ONE 60° OFFSET MAY BE ALLOWED.

MAINTAIN LISTED CLEARANCES

DRAFT HOOD

ANY OFFSET MORE THAN 45° SHALL BE CONSIDERED AS HORIZONTAL. HORIZONTAL RUNS MAY NOT EXCEED 75% OF VERTICAL HEIGHT OF VENT.

GAS-FIRED APPLIANCE LISTED FOR USE WITH TYPE B VENT

**NOTE:** Pipe and fittings are listed for either $1^1/_2$-in. or 3-in. (38 mm or 76 mm) clearance to combustible construction.

**TYPICAL DETAILS FOR INSTALLATION OF SINGLE-WALL NONMETALLIC TYPE B VENTS**

**FIGURE 8-9**

- The Type BW Gas Vent, Section 807
- Masonry Chimneys, Section 813
- Job-fabricated Metal Chimneys (smokestacks), Section 814

Type B vents are also produced in an oval configuration to fit conveniently in 2 by 4 or 2 by 6 (50 by 102 or 50 by 150) wood stud walls and partitions and are illustrated in Figures 8-6 and 8-7. The 4-inch (102 mm) oval Type B vent has similar capacity and resistance characteristics to 4-inch (102 mm) round pipe; 5-inch (127 mm) and 6-inch (153 mm) oval B vents can be sized using the 6-inch (153 mm) round tables. Centering in frame walls is controlled by integral spacers embossed on each vent section and by fire-stop spacers that must be installed at each plate level. The oval Type B vents are listed for 0-inch or 1-inch (25 mm) clearance. However, Type B-0 is not now listed in directories (i.e., they are not now being produced).

**803.3 Dampers.** Vent dampers used with gas- and oil-fired appliance venting systems are used for purposes of energy conservation and are designed to prevent the loss of heat from the appliance heat exchanger when the appliance is not being fired by closing the venting system except when the appliance is firing. This section regulates the installation of these dampers to ensure that the damper is in the open position when the appliance is fired. These requirements are not intended to prevent the use of listed, thermally activated dampers that are designed to be in the open position while the appliance is being fired or barometric dampers designed to regulate the negative pressure in the venting system for oil-fired equipment.

## SECTION 804 — LOCATION AND SUPPORT OF VENTING SYSTEMS, INCLUDING MASONRY VENTING SYSTEMS

A portion of a venting system may not pass through an air duct or plenum except a combustion-air duct. There are two separate objectives incorporated in the one sentence: (1) to prevent contamination of clean air in the duct or plenum by outward leakage from the joints or seams of the venting system, and (2) to prevent reduction in the minimum required area of a duct or plenum caused by the inclusion of the venting system. The intent is that if a portion of a venting system passed through a combustion air duct then the overall area of the combustion air duct should not be reduced by construction that would reduce the plenum or duct area below that area required in Section 707. Figures 8-10, 8-11, 8-12 and 8-13 illustrate the requirements of this section.

## SECTION 805 — GRAVITY VENTING SYSTEMS—LENGTH, PITCH AND CLEARANCES

**805.1 Offsets in a Gravity Vent.** Types B and L venting systems may be installed three ways: (1) with as many offsets as required that are less than 45 degrees from vertical, (2) with one offset not more than 60 degrees from vertical, and (3) with a total offset that is greater than 45 degrees and not more than 60 degrees, including the horizontal portion of the vent connector. The horizontal projection of offsets in the connector plus that in the vent must not exceed 75 percent of the vertical height of the venting system. These requirements are illustrated in Figure 8-14. If the building official has approved the installation of Type B vents to be made in compliance with Appendix C, Chapter 8, as provided for in Section 801, the allowance of overall horizontal run of the vent connector is more liberal. However, Appendix C does not make provisions for offsets in the vent, and the predominant interpretation is that offsets of less than 45 degrees are considered vertical and that offsets exceeding 45 degrees require that the venting system be installed in compliance with Section 805.1.

Vent offsets in Type BW vents are not permitted. Where Type BW vents are connected to Type B vents after they emerge from within a wall, the Type B vent may be offset in the attic as allowed in Section 805.1. (See UMC Section 807, Item 9.)

Factory-built chimneys and plastic venting systems may be offset as permitted by their listing and the manufacturer's installation instructions.

Metal chimneys (smokestacks) are not intended to be built with offsets, and their connectors are to be installed as required in Section 815.

According to UBC Section 3102.4.4, masonry chimneys may be offset at a slope of not more than 4 inches in 24 inches (102 mm in 610 mm), but not more than one third of the dimension of the chimney, in the direction of the offset.

**805.2 Vent Connector Rise.** Vent connectors serving Types B and L venting systems shall have a continuous rise of not less than $^1/_4$ unit vertical in 12 units horizontal (2% slope).

Vent connectors may not be used to connect a wall furnace to a Type BW vent. (See Section 807, Item 1.)

Vent connectors serving factory-built chimneys shall be installed according to the terms of their listing. (See Sections 812.1 and 815.1.)

Vent connectors serving plastic venting systems are to be installed in compliance with the terms of their listing. (See Section 802.3.)

Vent connectors serving metal chimneys (smokestacks) shall have a rise of not less than $^1/_4$ unit vertical in 12 units horizontal (2% slope). (See Section 815.8.)

Vent connectors serving masonry chimneys shall be pitched upwards from the appliance at least $^1/_4$ unit vertical in 12 units horizontal (2% slope). (See Sections 815.2 and 816.5.)

**805.3 Clearance.** Single-wall unlisted metal vent connectors connected to Types B and L venting systems shall be provided with clearances from combustible material of not less than that set forth in Table 3-C.

(*Continued on page 87*)

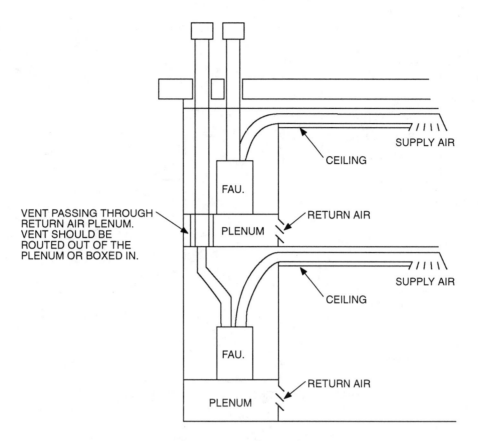

SUPPLY AIR

CEILING

VENT PASSING THROUGH
RETURN AIR PLENUM.
VENT SHOULD BE
ROUTED OUT OF THE
PLENUM OR BOXED IN.

FAU.

RETURN AIR

PLENUM

SUPPLY AIR

CEILING

FAU.

RETURN AIR

PLENUM

**VENT PASSING THROUGH AIR PLENUM**

**FIGURE 8-10**

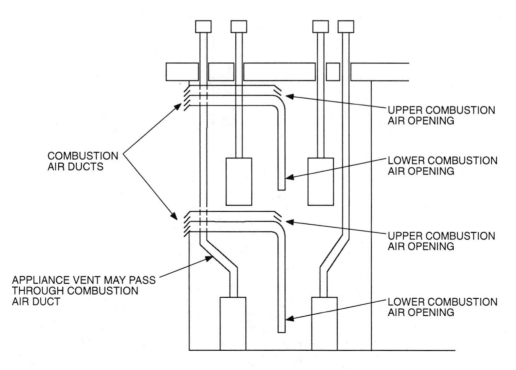

COMBUSTION
AIR DUCTS

UPPER COMBUSTION
AIR OPENING

LOWER COMBUSTION
AIR OPENING

UPPER COMBUSTION
AIR OPENING

APPLIANCE VENT MAY PASS
THROUGH COMBUSTION
AIR DUCT

LOWER COMBUSTION
AIR OPENING

**VENT PASSING THROUGH COMBUSTION AIR DUCT**

**FIGURE 8-11**

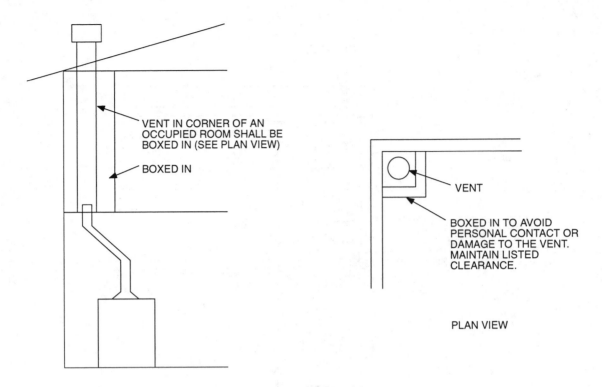

VENT IN CORNER OF AN
OCCUPIED ROOM SHALL BE
BOXED IN (SEE PLAN VIEW)

BOXED IN

VENT

BOXED IN TO AVOID
PERSONAL CONTACT OR
DAMAGE TO THE VENT.
MAINTAIN LISTED
CLEARANCE.

PLAN VIEW

**ENCLOSING VENTING SYSTEM, SECTION 804.2**

**FIGURE 8-12**

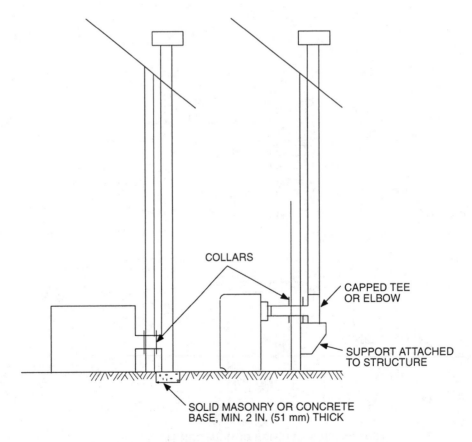

COLLARS

CAPPED TEE
OR ELBOW

SUPPORT ATTACHED
TO STRUCTURE

SOLID MASONRY OR CONCRETE
BASE, MIN. 2 IN. (51 mm) THICK

**SUPPORT OF VENTING SYSTEM BASE, SECTION 804.2**

**FIGURE 8-13**

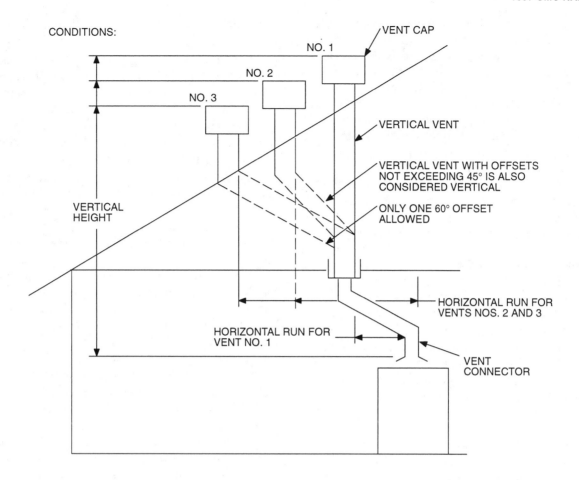

CONDITIONS:

**FIGURE 8-14**

*(Continued from page 84)*

Single-wall unlisted metal vent connectors are not permitted to be used with Type BW vents. (See Section 807, Item 1.)

Single-wall unlisted metal vent connectors are not permitted to be used with factory-built chimneys unless they are specifically allowed by the manufacturer's installation instructions. (See Sections 812.1 and 815.1.)

Single-wall unlisted metal vent connectors are not permitted to be used with plastic venting systems unless they are specifically allowed by the manufacturer's installation instructions. (See Section 802.5.)

Single-wall unlisted metal vent connectors connected to metal chimneys and masonry chimneys "shall be connected to a chimney or vent in such a manner as to maintain the clearance to combustibles as required in Table 3-C." (See Section 815.1.)

## SECTION 806 — VENT TERMINATION

**806.1 General.** Types B, BW and L vents shall extend through the roof and terminate in listed vent caps.

**806.2 Gravity-type Venting Systems.** All venting systems except

• Type BW venting systems,

• Venting systems that are an integral part of a listed appliance and

• Mechanical draft systems regulated by Section 817

shall terminate not less than 5 feet (1524 mm) above the highest vent collar which it serves. This requirement includes all of the various kinds of venting systems regulated by this code except Type BW venting systems (Type B, Type L, factory-built chimneys, metal chimneys/smokestacks and masonry chimneys). See Section 806.3 for termination of Type BW vents.

Figure 8-15 illustrates the required minimum vent height.

**806.3 Wall Furnace.** Section 807 of the UMC, which is referenced in this section, does not contain requirements that affect the 12 feet (3658 mm) above the bottom of the furnace requirement contained in this section.

**806.4 Type B or BW Gas Vents.** The provisions of this section were revised to conform with testing requirements contained in UL 441, "Gas Vents," and are more restrictive with respect to minimum dimensions except those provided in Table 8-C.

The principal reasons for not locating a vent cap adjoining a vertical wall surface or in the lee of a parapet wall are the varying effect of wind on venting action and the problem of snow accumulations in cold climate areas. Also, a vent protruding from a flat wall surface is subject to increased static pressure as wind strikes the building wall. Conversely, in the lee of a parapet wall, an area of stagnation and reduced atmospheric pressure may be created which increases draft and may produce undesired effects on gas appliances that are not equipped with a draft hood.

The slope of roof surfaces has been expressed traditionally as the ratio of the rise of the rafter to the entire width of the building (that is, a building having a one-half pitch roof has roof surfaces 45 degrees from horizontal). More recent usage has changed the word *pitch* to *slope* and it now refers to the ratio of the span of a rafter to its rise. The variations in terminology for roof framing are so general that in order to avoid confusion, the UMC ceased using the term *pitch* and has adopted the term *slope*.

The requirements of Section 806.4 and Table 8-A are illustrated in Figures 8-16 and 8-17. Figure 8-16 raises the question of how far a portion of the building may extend past the vertical Line A toward the vent as long as the 8-foot or 10-foot (2438 mm or 3048 mm) distance is maintained. The wording of this section does not specifically answer this question. The conservative response would be that no portion of the building should extend beyond Line A.

The least conservative response would be to allow projections toward the vent as long as they do not cross the arc indicating the minimum 8-foot or 10-foot (2438 mm or 3048 mm) distance and extend to a point directly over the vent. Probably the best decision would be something between the foregoing alternatives, such as allowing projections to extend half the distance from Line A to directly above the vent as long as they are not closer than the

minimum 8 feet or 10 feet (2438 mm or 3048 mm) requirement.

**806.5 Type L Venting Systems.** This section provides the requirements for termination of Type L vents serving oil-fired appliances. This section was updated in the 1991 edition to conform with NFPA 31 and ANSI/UL Standard No. 641, *Type L Low Temperature Venting Systems*. The requirements of this section are illustrated in Figure 8-18.

**806.6 Vent Terminals.** This section has not been amended to correlate with changes made to Sections 806.4 and 806.5. The purpose of this section is to prevent products of combustion from re-entering the building by requiring adequate separation from vent terminals to openings into the building. The requirements of Sections 806.4 and 806.5 are not more restrictive than this section for required separation of vent openings from all portions of the building, which would include doors, windows, etc., except for an outside- or makeup-air inlet and property lines. Also, the only kind of vent termination that is not regulated by the code in other sections is vent terminals for direct vent appliances. Therefore, a suggested editorial change to this section would be as follows:

*Vent terminals of direct-vent appliances are properly called vent-air intake terminals because they perform both functions. In addition to conveying the products of combustion to the exterior, the vent-air intake terminal admits air for combustion. Location of an exterior wall should be such as to avoid recirculation of flue gases through other building openings. The ground clearance ensures that grass and weeds will not obstruct either intake or exhaust. Shrubbery closely planted could also interfere with operation of the vent-air intake terminal.* Figure 8-19 illustrates the requirements of this section.

*(Continued on page 91)*

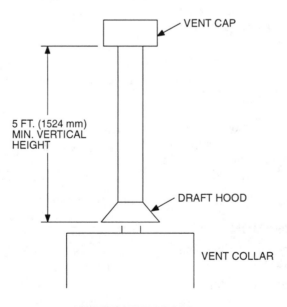

**MINIMUM VENT HEIGHT**

**FIGURE 8-15**

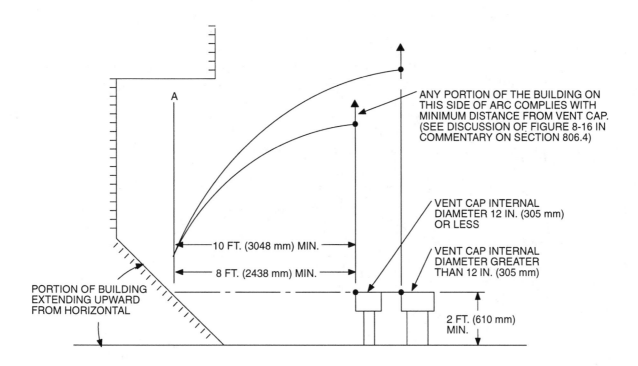

ANY PORTION OF THE BUILDING ON THIS SIDE OF ARC COMPLIES WITH MINIMUM DISTANCE FROM VENT CAP. (SEE DISCUSSION OF FIGURE 8-16 IN COMMENTARY ON SECTION 806.4)

VENT CAP INTERNAL DIAMETER 12 IN. (305 mm) OR LESS

VENT CAP INTERNAL DIAMETER GREATER THAN 12 IN. (305 mm)

10 FT. (3048 mm) MIN.

8 FT. (2438 mm) MIN.

PORTION OF BUILDING EXTENDING UPWARD FROM HORIZONTAL

2 FT. (610 mm) MIN.

**TERMINATION OF TYPE B OR BW VENTS THROUGH SLOPING OR FLAT ROOFS**

**FIGURE 8-16**

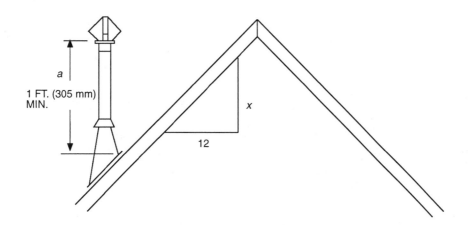

1 FT. (305 mm) MIN.

NOTE THAT THE ENTRIES IN TABLE 8-A ARE BASED ON MEASUREMENT "$a$" IN FEET (meters) AND INCHES (millimeters).

ROOF SLOPE = $x$ UNITS VERTICAL IN 12 UNITS HORIZONTAL

EXAMPLE: IF ROOF SLOPE = $^{18}/_{12}$ FROM TABLE 8-A, THEN MEASUREMENT "$a$" SHOULD BE A MINIMUM OF 7 FT. (2134 mm)

Listed gas vent caps up to 12 in. (305 mm) internal diameter have been found to be satisfactory for installation on listed gas vents with which they are compatible, terminating a sufficient distance from the roof so that no discharge opening is less than 1 ft. (305 mm) above the roof surface, and the lowest discharge opening will be no closer than the minimum height specified in Table 8-C. These minimum heights may be used, provided that the vent is not less than 8 ft. (2438 mm) from any portion of building which extends vertically upward. Vent caps over 12 in. (305 mm) in internal diameter are to be installed at least 10 ft. (3048 mm) from any portion of a building extending vertically upward. If closer than 10 ft. (3048 mm), the termination must be extended at 2 ft. (610 mm) higher than any portion within 10 ft. (3048 mm).

**TERMINATION OF TYPE B OR BW VENTS THROUGH SLOPING ROOFS**

**FIGURE 8-17**

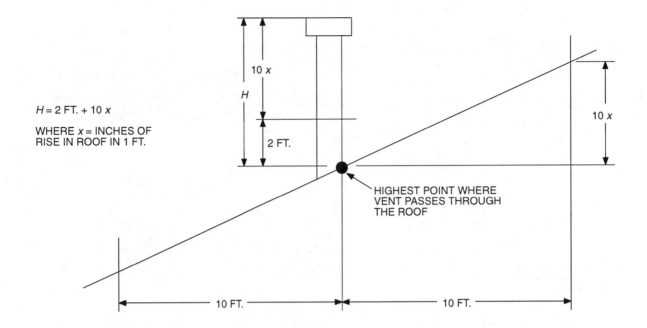

$H = 2$ FT. $+ 10 \, x$

WHERE $x$ = INCHES OF RISE IN ROOF IN 1 FT.

10 $x$

$H$

2 FT.

10 $x$

HIGHEST POINT WHERE VENT PASSES THROUGH THE ROOF

10 FT.

10 FT.

**NOTE:** The required height of the vent cap will be 2 ft. plus 10 times the inches of rise in 1 ft.

For **SI:** 1 inch = 25.4 mm, 1 foot = 305 mm.

**VENT TERMINATION OF TYPE L VENT SERVING OIL-BURNING APPLIANCE**

**FIGURE 8-18**

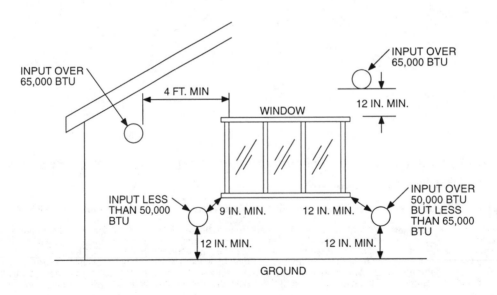

INPUT OVER 65,000 BTU

INPUT OVER 65,000 BTU

4 FT. MIN

12 IN. MIN.

WINDOW

INPUT LESS THAN 50,000 BTU

9 IN. MIN.

12 IN. MIN.

INPUT OVER 50,000 BTU BUT LESS THAN 65,000 BTU

12 IN. MIN.

12 IN. MIN.

GROUND

For **SI:** 1 inch = 25.4 mm, 1 foot = 305 mm.

**VENT TERMINATION—DIRECT-VENT APPLIANCES**

**FIGURE 8-19**

*(Continued from page 88)*

**806.7 Outdoor Appliances with Integral Vents.** The purpose of this section is to prevent products of combustion from entering the building. Figure 8-20 illustrates the requirements of this section.

# SECTION 807 — VENTED WALL FURNACE (TYPE BW) SYSTEMS

This section provides specific requirements for installing venting systems for listed wall furnaces. In addition to these requirements, the furnace and venting system must also be installed according to the terms of the listing and the manufacturer's installation instructions for both the furnace and the venting system, which will duplicate many of the requirements of this section.

The designation BW conveys information that the venting system is a Type B system located in the wall cavity. The venting systems are intended for use with listed recessed wall heaters. The venting system is listed for either single-story or multistory installation. The single-story kit can also be installed in the topmost story of a multistory building.

The requirements of Section 807 will require special consideration for systems installed when construction is required to be fire rated. The requirements of this section will affect the integrity of fire-rated construction, especially Items 5 and 6 with respect to fire-rated floor/ceiling assemblies.

Figures 8-21 and 8-22 illustrate the requirements of this section and Section 806.3. A cross-reference to UBC Section 2320.11.7 should be marked in the margin beside Item 2 regarding metal ties required to maintain the continuity of soles and plates in conventional wood framing. Ceiling plate spacers and firestops furnished with a BW venting system are not adequate to perform the function of framing straps (metal ties) spanning cut plates.

# SECTION 809 — COMMON VENTING SYSTEM

The requirements of this section determine when and how a multiple-appliance venting system may be installed and are summarized as follows:

1. Two or more gas-fired appliances may be connected to the same venting system.

2. Two or more oil-fired appliances may be connected to the same venting system.

3. Automatically controlled gas appliances may be connected into the same chimney serving liquid-fuel-fired appliances. The converse of this is not true unless the venting system materials were approved for use with oil-fired appliances. In addition, a strict interpretation of chimney would include only those chimneys defined in Section 205. However, the intent is to also include Type L vents for this application.

4. In addition, for systems described in Items 1, 2 and 3 above, it is also required that:

- Gas appliances be equipped with safety shut-off devices.

- Each oil-fired appliance be equipped with primary safety control.

- The venting system be designed in accordance with accepted engineering methods as provided for in Section 801 (fourth and sixth paragraphs), or the venting system is to be installed to comply with paragraphs 1 through 4 of Section 809.

It needs to be recognized that Appendix C, Chapter 8, is applicable only to venting systems serving gas-burning appliances and should not be used to design a mixed-fuel system. In addition, the venting system material used for a mixed gas or oil-fuel-burning system must be satisfactory for use with oil-burning appliances that include either Type L venting system materials or chimney materials approved for venting of oil-burning appliances.

Combined vents of gas-burning appliances in which two or more appliances are joined in a common vertical vent can be sized in accordance with Appendix C, Chapter 8, Table C8-D, C8-E or C8-F when approved by the building official. Correct sizing of connectors is critical to efficient and properly operating combined systems. The most undesirable operating condition occurs when the smallest (input) appliance is operating by itself because it must heat a larger column of air in the vertical common vent portion to produce venting action. For this reason, installations should always be arranged to maximize the rise of each connector, and the appliance having the smaller input rating should be located, whenever possible, directly below the vertical common vent.

Figures 8-23 and 8-24 illustrate some of the provisions of this section.

# SECTION 811 — DRAFT HOODS

Figure 8-25 illustrates the requirements of this section.

# SECTION 812 — TYPES OF CHIMNEYS

**812.1 Factory-built Chimneys.** There are several different factory-built chimneys available for different applications. Section 205 defines the types of chimneys that are currently in common use. Care must be exercised with the terms of listing of all chimneys, especially those that are not in common use such as chimneys marked as *Building Heating Appliance Only,* which are listed for nonresidential-type building heating appliances, steam boilers operating at less than 50 pounds per square inch (344 kPa) gage, and pressing machine boilers. Figure 8-26 illustrates typical installation details for a listed factory-built chimney.

The specific requirement in this section that factory-built chimneys shall terminate as required for unlisted single-wall metal chimneys in Table 8-D has resulted in questions concerning listed terminations that appear not to conform with the requirements of Table 8-D. Those cases

*(Continued on page 94)*

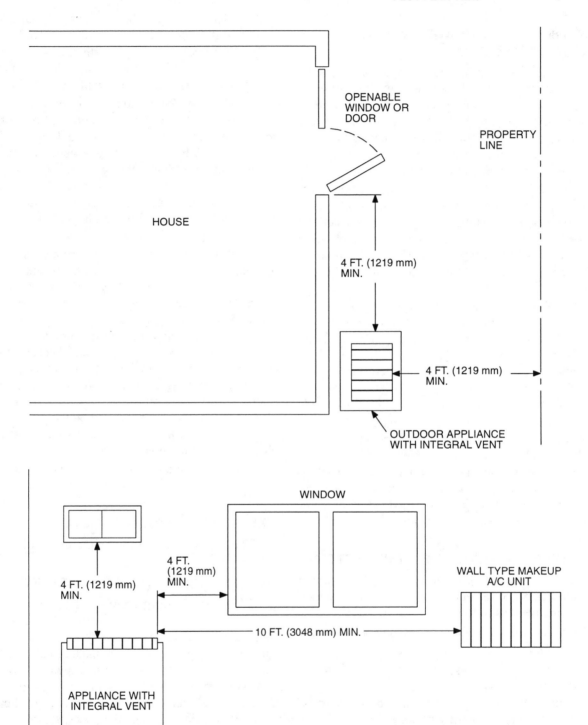

PLOT PLAN VIEW

OPENABLE
WINDOW OR
DOOR

PROPERTY
LINE

HOUSE

4 FT. (1219 mm)
MIN.

4 FT. (1219 mm)
MIN.

OUTDOOR APPLIANCE
WITH INTEGRAL VENT

WINDOW

4 FT.
(1219 mm)
MIN.

4 FT. (1219 mm)
MIN.

WALL TYPE MAKEUP
A/C UNIT

10 FT. (3048 mm) MIN.

APPLIANCE WITH
INTEGRAL VENT

**OUTDOOR VENT TERMINATION—APPLIANCES WITH INTEGRAL VENT**

**FIGURE 8-20**

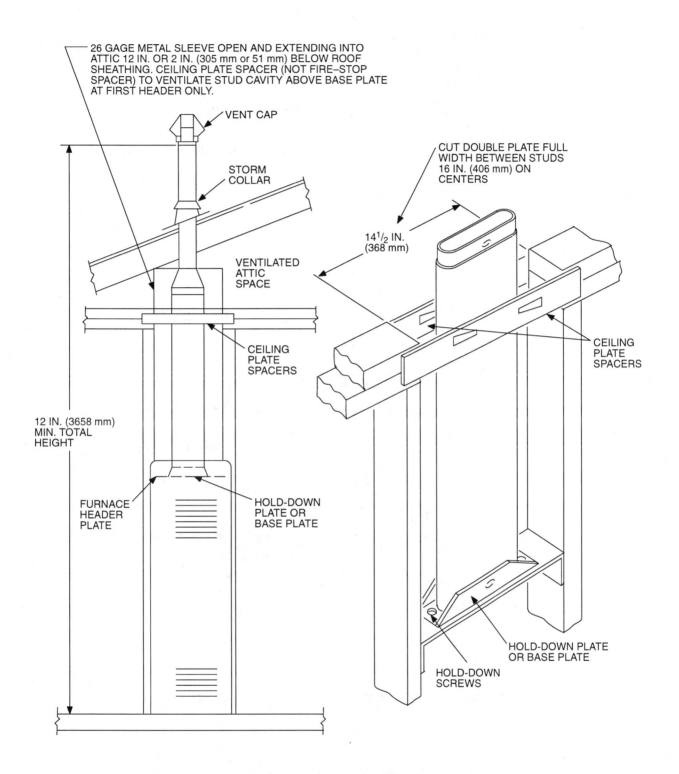

26 GAGE METAL SLEEVE OPEN AND EXTENDING INTO ATTIC 12 IN. OR 2 IN. (305 mm or 51 mm) BELOW ROOF SHEATHING. CEILING PLATE SPACER (NOT FIRE–STOP SPACER) TO VENTILATE STUD CAVITY ABOVE BASE PLATE AT FIRST HEADER ONLY.

VENT CAP

STORM COLLAR

CUT DOUBLE PLATE FULL WIDTH BETWEEN STUDS 16 IN. (406 mm) ON CENTERS

14 1/2 IN. (368 mm)

VENTILATED ATTIC SPACE

CEILING PLATE SPACERS

CEILING PLATE SPACERS

12 IN. (3658 mm) MIN. TOTAL HEIGHT

FURNACE HEADER PLATE

HOLD-DOWN PLATE OR BASE PLATE

HOLD-DOWN PLATE OR BASE PLATE

HOLD-DOWN SCREWS

**TYPICAL TYPE BW INSTALLATION REQUIREMENTS FOR ONE STORY OR TOP STORY OF MULTISTORY BUILDINGS**

**FIGURE 8-21**

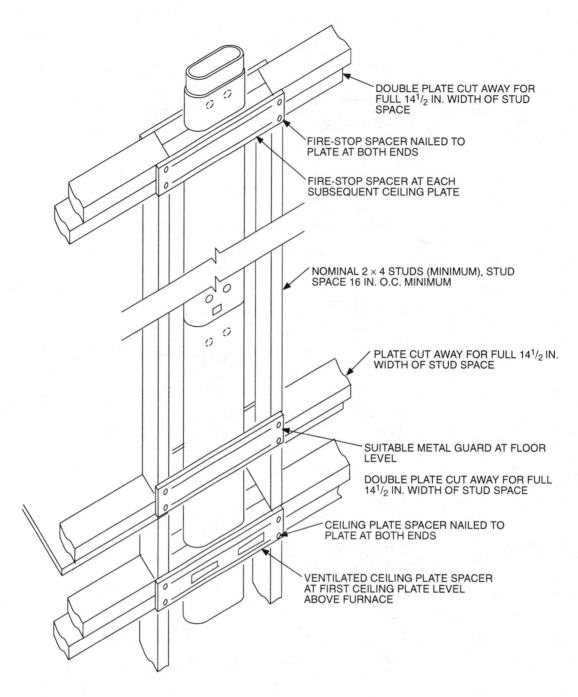

DOUBLE PLATE CUT AWAY FOR FULL 14¹/₂ IN. WIDTH OF STUD SPACE

FIRE-STOP SPACER NAILED TO PLATE AT BOTH ENDS

FIRE-STOP SPACER AT EACH SUBSEQUENT CEILING PLATE

NOMINAL 2 × 4 STUDS (MINIMUM), STUD SPACE 16 IN. O.C. MINIMUM

PLATE CUT AWAY FOR FULL 14¹/₂ IN. WIDTH OF STUD SPACE

SUITABLE METAL GUARD AT FLOOR LEVEL

DOUBLE PLATE CUT AWAY FOR FULL 14¹/₂ IN. WIDTH OF STUD SPACE

CEILING PLATE SPACER NAILED TO PLATE AT BOTH ENDS

VENTILATED CEILING PLATE SPACER AT FIRST CEILING PLATE LEVEL ABOVE FURNACE

For **SI:** 1 inch = 25.4 mm.

**TYPICAL TYPE BW INSTALLATION REQUIREMENTS FOR BW VENTS IN BUILDINGS MORE THAN ONE STORY IN HEIGHT**

**FIGURE 8-22**

*(Continued from page 91)*

reviewed indicate that the listed profile terminations (see Figure 8-27) are of noncombustible construction and would conform with the requirements of Table 8-D. When a listed termination fails to satisfy the requirements of Table 8-D, it would be up to the building official as provided in Section 302 to approve or disapprove the installation. Factory-built chimneys that serve appliances in which solid or liquid fuel is burned must have spark arrest-

ers. Masonry chimneys so utilized also require spark arresters in accordance with UBC Section 3102.3.8.

It is important that the reader understand that a factory-built chimney and fireplace are listed assemblies that must be installed in accordance with the terms of their listing and the manufacturer's installation instructions. There are no generic instructions that apply to such equipment;

*(Continued on page 97)*

WHERE TWO OR MORE APPLIANCES ARE CONNECTED TO ONE VENTING SYSTEM, THE VENTING SYSTEM AREA SHALL NOT BE LESS THAN THE AREA OF THE LARGEST VENT CONNECTOR PLUS 50 PERCENT OF THE AREAS OF THE ADDITIONAL VENT CONNECTORS. (AN OVAL MAY BE USED PROVIDED ITS AREA IS NOT LESS THAN THE AREA OF THE ROUND PIPE FOR WHICH IT IS BEING SUBSTITUTED.)

**EXCEPTION:** SYSTEMS DESIGNED BY METHODS APPROVED BY THE BUILDING OFFICIALS AS PROVIDED FOR IN SECTION 801.

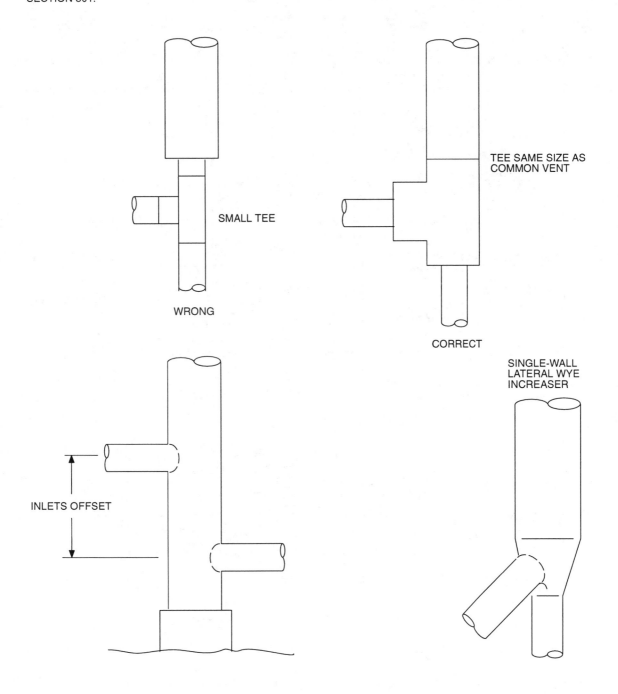

**TYPICAL MANIFOLDS FOR MULTIPLE-APPLIANCE VENTING SYSTEMS**

**FIGURE 8-23**

TERMINATE IN ACCORDANCE WITH SECTION 806

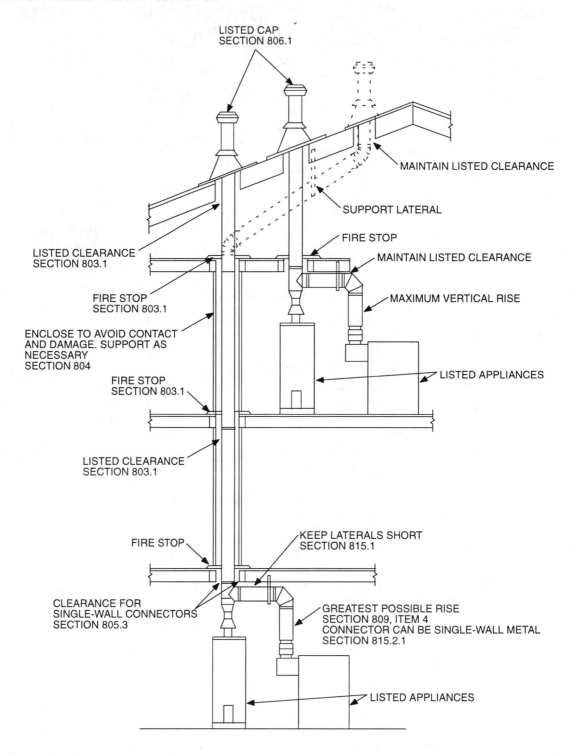

**NOTE:** Building occupancy could require fire-resistive shaft construction. See UBC Section 711.

**TYPICAL TYPE B OR TYPE L VENT SERVING MULTIPLE APPLIANCES**

**FIGURE 8-24**

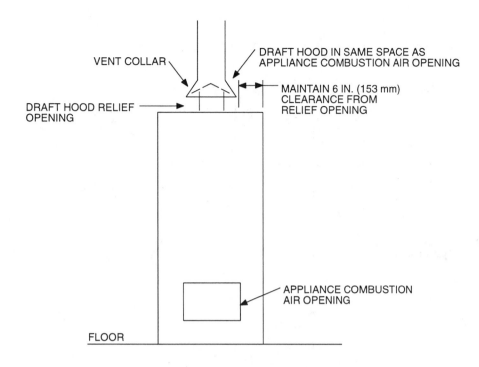

**TYPICAL DRAFT HOOD INSTALLATION**

**FIGURE 8-25**

*(Continued from page 94)*

each manufacturer's product is unique in its installation requirements.

It is also important from a terminology viewpoint to understand that factory-built chimneys, although fabricated from metal and other materials, are not called "metal chimneys." This title is reserved for use when discussing unlisted job-fabricated smokestacks.

**812.2 Masonry Chimneys.** See UMC Sections 205 and 813.

**812.3 Unlisted Smokestacks.** See UMC Sections 205 and 814.

## SECTION 813 — EXISTING MASONRY CHIMNEYS FOR GAS VENTING

**813.1 Design.** The design and construction of masonry chimneys are regulated by Section 3102 of the UBC. The reference chapters in Section 813 are incomplete (UBC Chapter 21, Masonry, regulates masonry construction); however, UBC Section 3102.3.1 references all of the relevant chapters required for design and construction of masonry chimneys. *Uniform Building Code* Section 3102 would probably be a sufficient reference for this section.

**813.2 Gas Venting into Existing Masonry Chimneys.** This section provides requirements for existing chimneys to be used for venting of gas-fired appliances. New masonry chimneys would probably not be constructed for this purpose for economic reasons, but if such a chimney were constructed, the requirements of this section would apply.

There are two frequently asked questions about the requirements of this section:

- What is an approved liner?

Comment: Most building officials will accept liners listed for this purpose. The manufacturer's installation instructions usually require that the void between the liner and surrounding masonry be filled with mineral insulation, supporting and centering the liner in the chimney.

Other alternatives that could be approved as liners would be vitrified clay tile as prescribed in UBC Chapter 31, Table 31-B, and those lined with galvanized steel pipe equivalent to that required for chimney connectors in UMC Section 815.2.1.

- When is a chimney not safe for the intended application?

Comment: An unlined masonry chimney or one parged (coated) with mortar on the interior should be thoroughly inspected for deterioration of the mortar joints and parging, particularly if the previous fuel was wood or coal. Parging that has fallen from the interior of flue passages is ordinarily a sign of serious deterioration. The chimney passages should be cleaned before inspection and a light source lowered course by course to detect disintegrating mortar, damp spots or failure of the mortar bond. This method of lining chimneys is no longer an approved method, and in most cases, chimneys lined in this manner will require relining.

A masonry chimney lined with vitrified clay tile should be cleaned and inspected for cracking of the clay tile liner.

*(Continued on page 100)*

DEFINITION: A FACTORY-BUILT CHIMNEY IS A LISTED CHIMNEY—SECTION 205

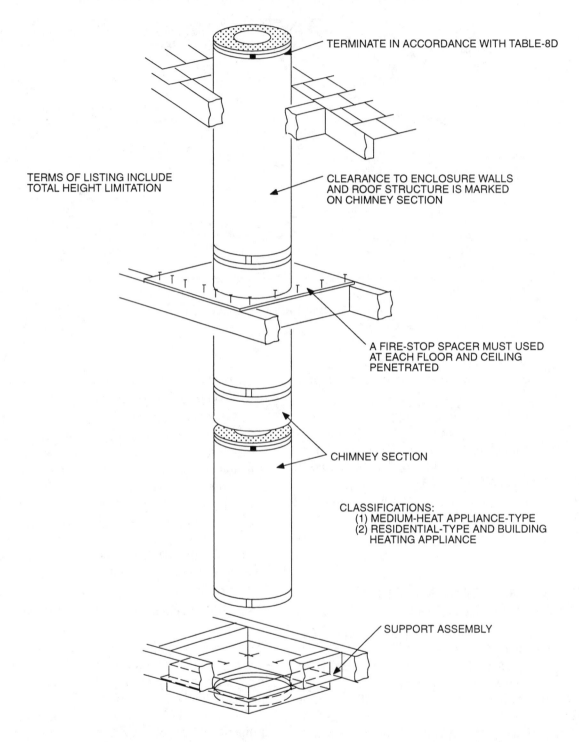

TERMINATE IN ACCORDANCE WITH TABLE-8D

TERMS OF LISTING INCLUDE
TOTAL HEIGHT LIMITATION

CLEARANCE TO ENCLOSURE WALLS
AND ROOF STRUCTURE IS MARKED
ON CHIMNEY SECTION

A FIRE-STOP SPACER MUST USED
AT EACH FLOOR AND CEILING
PENETRATED

CHIMNEY SECTION

CLASSIFICATIONS:
  (1) MEDIUM-HEAT APPLIANCE-TYPE
  (2) RESIDENTIAL-TYPE AND BUILDING
      HEATING APPLIANCE

SUPPORT ASSEMBLY

**NOTE:** Chimneys marked as building heating appliance only are not suitable for installation
in one- or two-family dwellings. Such chimneys must be enclosed in a noncombustible
(masonry) shaft and treated as metal chimneys (smokestacks). Section 814.1.9.

**TYPICAL INSTALLATION DETAILS—FACTORY-BUILT CHIMNEY**

**FIGURE 8-26**

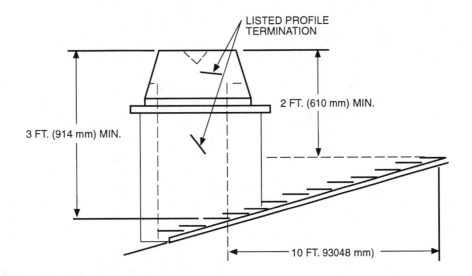

LISTED PROFILE
TERMINATION

2 FT. (610 mm) MIN.

3 FT. (914 mm) MIN.

10 FT. 93048 mm)

**NOTE:** Since the entire termination is listed, the 3-foot (914 mm) measurement is from the roof surface to the top of the termination.

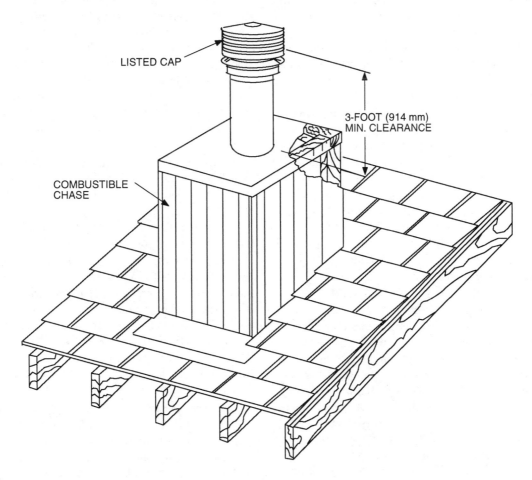

LISTED CAP

3-FOOT (914 mm)
MIN. CLEARANCE

COMBUSTIBLE
CHASE

**NOTE:** The combustible chase requires that the 3-foot (914 mm) clearance be measured in the manner indicated. This clearance may be reduced if a listed termination is used and approved by the building official.

**TERMINATION OF FACTORY-BUILT CHIMNEYS**

**FIGURE 8-27**

*(Continued from page 97)*

Cracks in a liner usually indicate that a chimney fire has occurred. The inspection should also include checking wood members near the chimney for charring or indications of exposure to high heat. Any discolorations of masonry or adjacent construction indicate that the masonry is not tight. Section 302 of the *Uniform Code for the Abatement of Dangerous Buildings* also addresses defects. The final decision is a judgment call by the building official; however, if inspections are made as discussed above, very likely it will be judged that reasonable and prudent enforcement has been performed.

In addition to the requirements of this section, the exception in UMC Section 902.2.1 requires that existing chimneys used to vent small domestic type incinerators shall have "at least 4-inch (102 mm) nominal brick walls." Considerations of air quality have virtually eliminated domestic incinerators in many localities.

## SECTION 814 — UNLISTED SMOKESTACKS

**814.1 Prohibited Use.** This section contains design requirements for metal chimneys that are unlisted chimneys usually fabricated on site by welding or riveting for a specific industrial or commercial application requiring individual review and approval by the building official. These chimneys should not be confused with factory-built chimneys and vents that are also fabricated from metal.

*Uniform Building Code* Section 3102.6 refers to the *Uniform Mechanical Code* as the main document for construction and installation requirements related to metal chimneys. Section 814.1.3 references UBC Chapters 16 and 22 as design criteria for metal chimneys.

The first paragraph of Section 814.1 prohibits the installation of a metal chimney within a Group R Occupancy; however, this requirement would not exclude a metal chimney from serving a Group R Occupancy if installed on the exterior of the building (i.e., for venting an incinerator or central heating plant, etc.).

Sections 814.1.5, 814.1.6 and 814.1.7 refer to Table 8-D with respect to lining, termination and clearances required for metal chimneys. The height and clearance of smokestacks are based on possible fire hazards from radiant heat and hot gases and also provide minimum clearances that will locate the termination of the chimney a reasonable distance from the influence of adjoining buildings and structures, thereby aiding in dispersal of flue products. Use of these minimums will not necessarily ensure that the stack action will be unaffected by tall structures on an adjoining tract or by surrounding terrain features. Professional judgment is required to evaluate the myriad variables that might affect smokestack operation.

Figures 8-28, 8-32, 8-34 and 8-35 illustrate termination requirements.

When used with incinerators, steel smokestacks also have specific requirements based on the severity of service. Residential-type incinerators are considered to impose less severe service conditions than commercial and industrial service. Inspectors should incorporate a marginal note cross-referencing Sections 814.5, 814.7 and 814.8 to Chapter 9, Part II, in the *Uniform Mechanical Code*.

Section 814.1 requires a fire-resistance rating of not less than three hours for supporting members of metal chimneys (other than masonry or reinforced concrete). Acceptable methods for providing this protection are provided in UBC Chapter 7, Table 7-A.

Depending on the appliance it serves, metal chimneys may be classified as (1) building heating appliance type, which is the same classification of service as a low-heat industrial appliance type; (2) medium-heat appliance type; and (3) high-heat appliance type. The specific requirements for these classifications of smokestacks are provided in Sections 814.2, 814.3 and 814.4, respectively.

Figures 8-29, 8-30 and 8-31 illustrate some of the general requirements for metal chimneys.

**814.2 Metal Chimneys for Building Heating and Industrial-type Low-heat Appliances.** This section provides an additional method for roof penetrations of metal chimneys serving low-heat appliances. The clearance requirements provided in the first paragraph of this section are the same as those provided in Table 8-D. The second paragraph provides for an alternative method of penetrating through a roof and adds the requirement that the ventilating thimble at the roof be of galvanized steel or approved corrosion-resistant metal. An illustration of a ventilating thimble is provided in Figure 8-31, and Figure 8-32 illustrates the termination requirements provided in UMC Table 8-D.

**814.3 Unlisted Smokestacks for Medium-heat Appliances.** This section essentially restates the requirements provided in UMC Table 8-D except for the requirement that the ventilating thimble (illustrated in Figure 8-31) at the roof be fabricated "of galvanized iron or approved corrosion-resistant metal."

The lining requirements for metal chimneys are illustrated in Figure 8-33. Even though this section does not state specific requirements as it does for chimneys serving high-heat appliances in Section 814.1 and although the degree of hazard is less than for chimneys serving high-heat appliances, the intent of the code is that metal chimneys serving medium-heat appliances may terminate 25 feet (7620 mm) or less above a chimney connector entrance and shall be lined to the top.

The last paragraph of this section implies that the 36-inch (914 mm) clearance requirement from combustibles would only apply to the chimney in the same story in which the appliance is installed. Section 814.1.7 refers to Table 8-D, which clearly requires the 36-inch (914 mm) clearance from combustibles at all interior locations. Figure 8-34 illustrates the termination requirements provided in UMC Table 8-D.

**814.4 Unlisted Smokestacks for High-heat Appliances.** Metal chimneys for high-heat appliances should be lined as illustrated in Figure 8-33. There is a conflict in the code in regard to the required height of the chimney lining. This section would allow the lining to be termi-

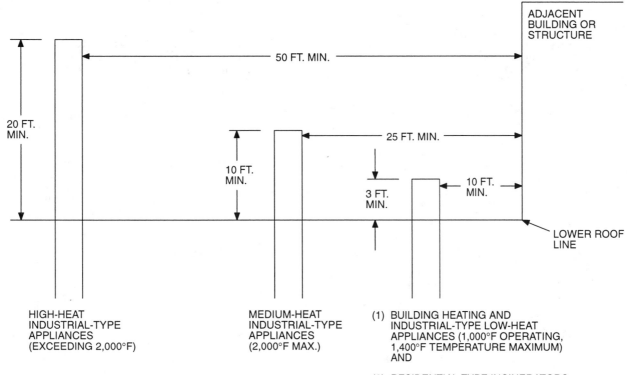

NOTE: See Figures 8-32, 8-34 and 8-35 for other termination configurations.

For **SI:** 1 inch = 25.4 mm.

**TYPICAL METAL CHiMNEY (SMOKESTACK) TERMINATIONS**

**FIGURE 8-28**

nated "25 feet (7620 mm) above the highest chimney connector entrance," while Table 8-D requires in Footnote 2 that metal chimneys serving high-heat appliances be lined "from bottom to top of chimney." The code would, therefore, be interpreted in accordance to Section 103, which requires that where this code specifies different materials, methods of construction or other requirements, the most restrictive shall govern, and chimneys serving high-heat appliances would be required to be lined to the top, regardless of height.

Termination and clearance requirements are provided in UMC Table 8-D and are illustrated in Figure 8-35.

**814.5 Unlisted Smokestacks for Residential-type Incinerators.** The requirements for installing metal chimneys for residential-type incinerators are the same requirements previously discussed for chimneys serving building heating and industrial-type low-heat appliances in Section 814.2.

**814.6 Commercial and Industrial-type Incinerators.** The requirements for installing metal chimneys for commercial and industrial-type incinerators are the same requirements previously discussed for chimneys serving medium-heat appliances in Section 814.3, except that:

- Chimneys shall be lined with medium-duty firebrick not less than $4^1/_2$ inches (114 mm) thick, regardless of the diameter of the chimney.

- The lining should always start at the base of the chimney and extend continuously to the top.

## SECTION 815 — CONNECTORS

**815.1 General.** This section of the code provides the general installation requirements for connecting appliances to venting systems. Subjects covered include:

- Explanation of terminology. See also definitions in Section 205 for chimney connector and in Section 224 for vent connector.

- Acceptable and prohibited locations.

- Required clearances (refers to UMC Table 3-C).

- Connection to venting system served by a power exhauster (see Figures 8-39 through 8-41).

- Quality of work requirements such as routing, support and fastening.

- Concealed connectors in attics and crawl spaces and connectors passing through walls (references UMC Sections 815.10 and 815.12).

This section and the following Sections 815.2 and 816 are confusing, as the outline format implies that the original intent was that Section 815.1 would contain requirements that would apply to both chimney and vent connectors, while Sections 815.2 and 816 would contain

*(Continued on page 105)*

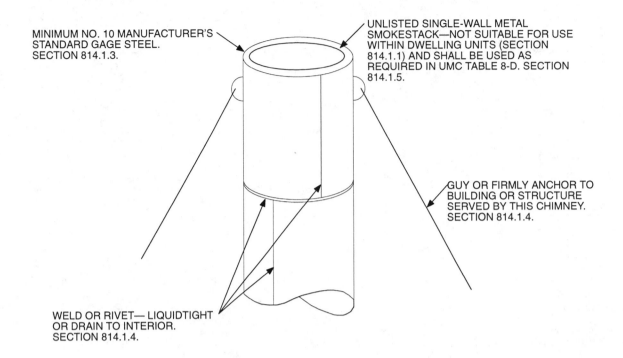

MINIMUM NO. 10 MANUFACTURER'S
STANDARD GAGE STEEL.
SECTION 814.1.3.

UNLISTED SINGLE-WALL METAL
SMOKESTACK—NOT SUITABLE FOR USE
WITHIN DWELLING UNITS (SECTION
814.1.1) AND SHALL BE USED AS
REQUIRED IN UMC TABLE 8-D. SECTION
814.1.5.

GUY OR FIRMLY ANCHOR TO
BUILDING OR STRUCTURE
SERVED BY THIS CHIMNEY.
SECTION 814.1.4.

WELD OR RIVET— LIQUIDTIGHT
OR DRAIN TO INTERIOR.
SECTION 814.1.4.

**UNLISTED SMOKESTACKS—GENERAL LIMITATIONS, DESIGN, CONSTRUCTION, LINING**

**FIGURE 8-29**

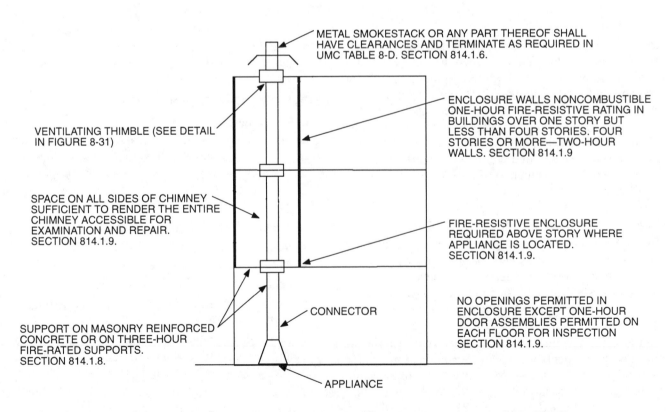

METAL SMOKESTACK OR ANY PART THEREOF SHALL
HAVE CLEARANCES AND TERMINATE AS REQUIRED IN
UMC TABLE 8-D. SECTION 814.1.6.

VENTILATING THIMBLE (SEE DETAIL
IN FIGURE 8-31)

ENCLOSURE WALLS NONCOMBUSTIBLE
ONE-HOUR FIRE-RESISTIVE RATING IN
BUILDINGS OVER ONE STORY BUT
LESS THAN FOUR STORIES. FOUR
STORIES OR MORE—TWO-HOUR
WALLS. SECTION 814.1.9

SPACE ON ALL SIDES OF CHIMNEY
SUFFICIENT TO RENDER THE ENTIRE
CHIMNEY ACCESSIBLE FOR
EXAMINATION AND REPAIR.
SECTION 814.1.9.

FIRE-RESISTIVE ENCLOSURE
REQUIRED ABOVE STORY WHERE
APPLIANCE IS LOCATED.
SECTION 814.1.9.

CONNECTOR

NO OPENINGS PERMITTED IN
ENCLOSURE EXCEPT ONE-HOUR
DOOR ASSEMBLIES PERMITTED ON
EACH FLOOR FOR INSPECTION
SECTION 814.1.9.

SUPPORT ON MASONRY REINFORCED
CONCRETE OR ON THREE-HOUR
FIRE-RATED SUPPORTS.
SECTION 814.1.8.

APPLIANCE

**UNLISTED SMOKESTACKS—GENERAL TERMINATION CLEARANCE, SUPPORT, ENCLOSURE**

**FIGURE 8-30**

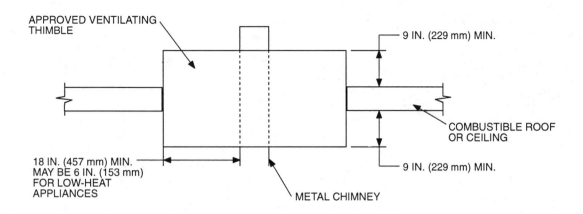

APPROVED VENTILATING
THIMBLE

9 IN. (229 mm) MIN.

COMBUSTIBLE ROOF
OR CEILING

18 IN. (457 mm) MIN.
MAY BE 6 IN. (153 mm)
FOR LOW-HEAT
APPLIANCES

9 IN. (229 mm) MIN.

METAL CHIMNEY

**VENTILATING THIMBLE**

**FIGURE 8-31**

1,000°F (538°C)—OPERATING TEMPERATURE

1,400°F (760°C)—MAXIMUM PEAK TEMPERATURE

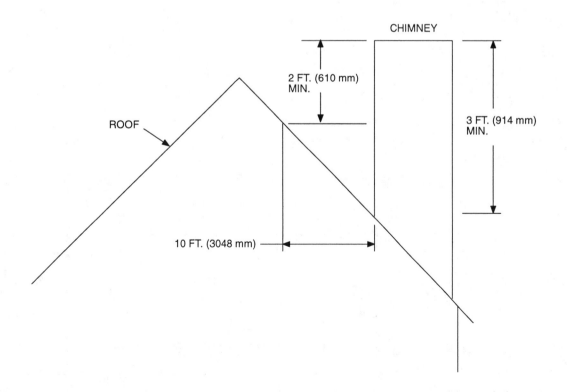

CHIMNEY

2 FT. (610 mm)
MIN.

ROOF

3 FT. (914 mm)
MIN.

10 FT. (3048 mm)

**TERMINATION—UNLISTED SMOKESTACKS SERVING BUILDING HEATING AND
INDUSTRIAL-TYPE LOW-HEAT APPLIANCES**

**FIGURE 8-32**

**NOTE:** Chimneys to be lined with medium-duty firebrick complying with the standard for fire clay refractories, ASTM C27-60.

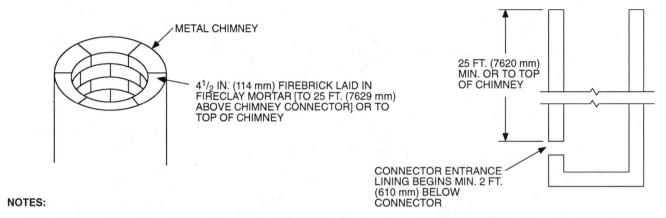

METAL CHIMNEY

$4^1/_2$ IN. (114 mm) FIREBRICK LAID IN FIRECLAY MORTAR [TO 25 FT. (7629 mm) ABOVE CHIMNEY CONNECTOR] OR TO TOP OF CHIMNEY

25 FT. (7620 mm) MIN. OR TO TOP OF CHIMNEY

CONNECTOR ENTRANCE LINING BEGINS MIN. 2 FT. (610 mm) BELOW CONNECTOR

**NOTES:**

1.  Metal chimneys for minimum-heat appliances up to 18 in. (457 mm) in diameter may be lined with $2^1/_2$ in. (64 mm) firebrick.

2.  Metal chimneys for high-heat appliances are to be lined to the top of chimney, regardless of height (Footnote 2, UMC Table 8-D).

**METAL CHIMNEY LINING REQUIREMENTS**

**FIGURE 8-33**

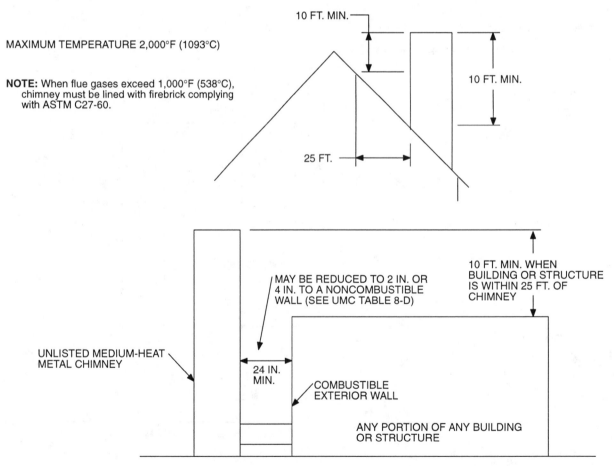

MAXIMUM TEMPERATURE 2,000°F (1093°C)

**NOTE:** When flue gases exceed 1,000°F (538°C), chimney must be lined with firebrick complying with ASTM C27-60.

10 FT. MIN.

10 FT. MIN.

25 FT.

MAY BE REDUCED TO 2 IN. OR 4 IN. TO A NONCOMBUSTIBLE WALL (SEE UMC TABLE 8-D)

10 FT. MIN. WHEN BUILDING OR STRUCTURE IS WITHIN 25 FT. OF CHIMNEY

UNLISTED MEDIUM-HEAT METAL CHIMNEY

24 IN. MIN.

COMBUSTIBLE EXTERIOR WALL

ANY PORTION OF ANY BUILDING OR STRUCTURE

For **SI:** 1 inch = 25.4 mm, 1 foot = 305 mm.

**TERMINATION—METAL CHIMNEYS SERVING MEDIUM-HEAT APPLIANCES**

**FIGURE 8-34**

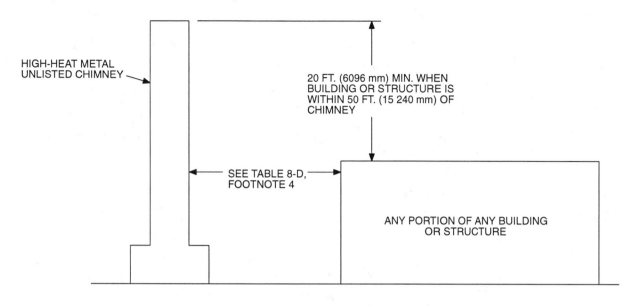

**TERMINATION—METAL CHIMNEYS SERVING HIGH-HEAT APPLIANCES**

**FIGURE 8-35**

*(Continued from page 101)*

requirements specific to chimney and vent connectors, respectively. This format has not been followed in some cases. This commentary is not intended to provide specific code change recommendations; however, the following examples may be worthwhile to those who may consider reorganizing these sections to follow what appears to be the original intended format:

- The last sentence of the first paragraph of Section 815.1 specifically addresses chimney connectors and would be more appropriate in Section 815.2.

- The last sentence of the first paragraph of Section 815.2 references Section 816 as an acceptable way to connect listed gas appliances to chimneys as well as vents. These requirements could be included in Section 815.1 since they apply to both chimneys and vents.

- The referenced Sections 815.10 and 815.12 in Section 815.1 are contained in the section intended to be specific for chimneys. If they apply to both vents and chimneys as indicated by this reference, the proper location would be in Section 815.1.

- Sections 815.2 and 816 contain a "pitch" requirement of $1/4$ inch per foot ($1/4$ unit vertical in 12 units horizontal) (2% slope). This general requirement would be more appropriate in Section 815.1.

The minimum pitch for all gravity chimney connectors is $1/4$ inch per foot ($1/4$ unit vertical in 12 units horizontal) (2% slope) to assure that the natural buoyancy of heated gases will fill the connector, and it further assures that any condensate which forms will be drained back toward the appliance and will probably be reevaporated. Reversed slope (i.e., slope from an appliance downward toward the

chimney or vent) forms a trap. If an appliance having a draft hood were connected in this way, the products of combustion would spill from the draft hood and, in the case of appliances not having a draft hood, could prevent proper operation. (See Figure 8-36.)

**815.2 Chimney Connector Materials.** This section provides specific requirements for the installation of connectors between appliances and chimneys as defined in the UMC.

**815.9 Entering Masonry Chimneys.** The requirements of Section 815.9 are illustrated in Figure 8-37. The requirement for a cleanout at the base of a masonry chimney, which is also required in UBC Section 3102.3, exists because masonry chimneys can be used in applications where products of combustion contain suspended solid matter such as ash, soot, etc.

**815.10 Passage through Walls or Partitions.** Section 815.10 permits connectors for listed gas appliances with draft hoods to pass through combustible construction if made of Type B or L material and installed with their listed clearances to combustible materials to reach a masonry chimney provided certain methods of protection are used. By cross-reference in Section 816.7, vent connectors entering gas vents may also pass through combustible construction if made of Type B or L materials. Table 8-E provides detailed methods for penetrating through walls of combustible construction. These methods are illustrated in Figures 8-38, 8-39, 8-40 and 8-41.

The requirements of Section 815.11 are illustrated in Figure 8-42. These maximum length requirements also apply to connectors connecting to vent systems and are referenced in Section 816.4.

*(Continued on page 109)*

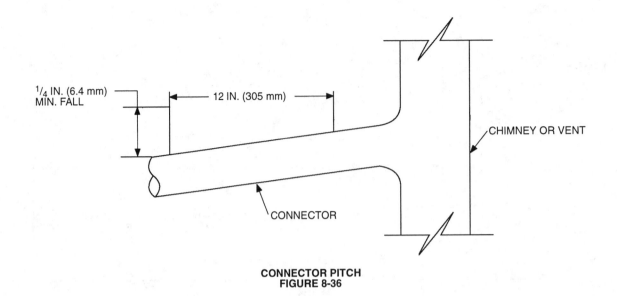

**CONNECTOR PITCH**
**FIGURE 8-36**

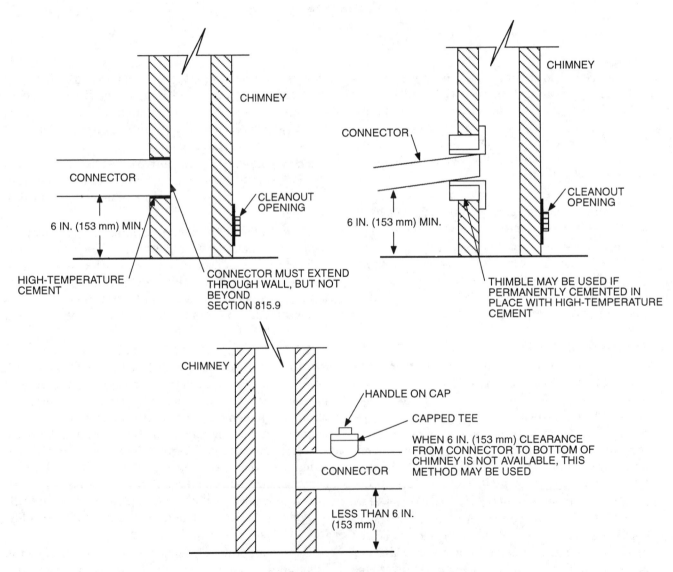

**ENTERING A MASONRY CHIMNEY**

**FIGURE 8-37**

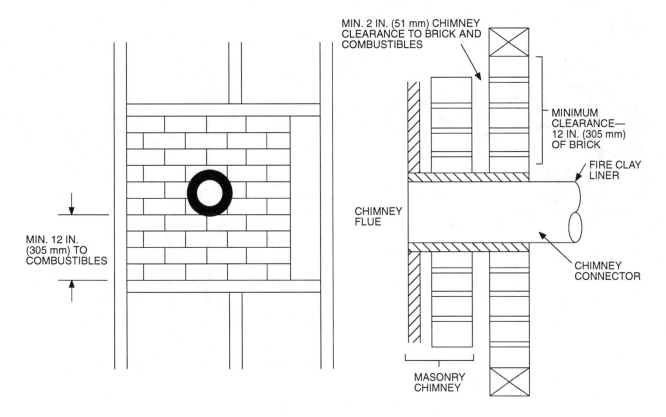

**SYSTEM A, UMC TABLE 8-E**

**FIGURE 8-38**

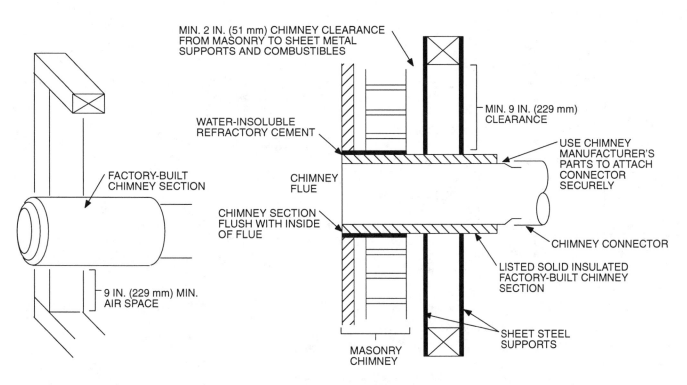

**SYSTEM B, UMC TABLE 8-E**

**FIGURE 8-39**

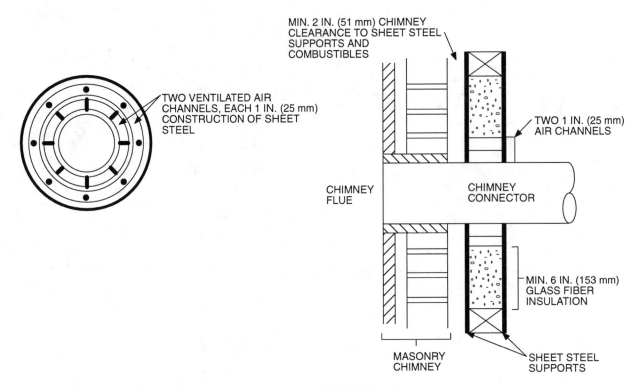

TWO VENTILATED AIR CHANNELS, EACH 1 IN. (25 mm) CONSTRUCTION OF SHEET STEEL

MIN. 2 IN. (51 mm) CHIMNEY CLEARANCE TO SHEET STEEL SUPPORTS AND COMBUSTIBLES

TWO 1 IN. (25 mm) AIR CHANNELS

CHIMNEY FLUE

CHIMNEY CONNECTOR

MIN. 6 IN. (153 mm) GLASS FIBER INSULATION

MASONRY CHIMNEY

SHEET STEEL SUPPORTS

**SYSTEM C, UMC TABLE 8-E**

**FIGURE 8-40**

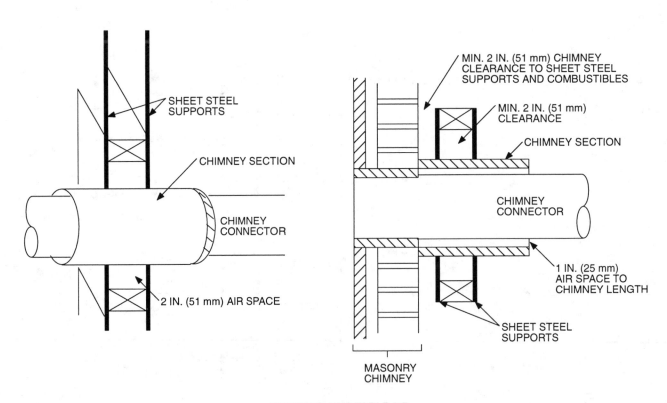

SHEET STEEL SUPPORTS

CHIMNEY SECTION

CHIMNEY CONNECTOR

2 IN. (51 mm) AIR SPACE

MIN. 2 IN. (51 mm) CHIMNEY CLEARANCE TO SHEET STEEL SUPPORTS AND COMBUSTIBLES

MIN. 2 IN. (51 mm) CLEARANCE

CHIMNEY SECTION

CHIMNEY CONNECTOR

1 IN. (25 mm) AIR SPACE TO CHIMNEY LENGTH

SHEET STEEL SUPPORTS

MASONRY CHIMNEY

**SYSTEM D, UMC TABLE 8-E**

**FIGURE 8-41**

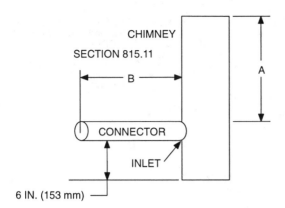

CHIMNEY

SECTION 815.11

B

A

CONNECTOR

INLET

6 IN. (153 mm)

UNINSULATED CONNECTOR:
"B" DIMENSION MAY NOT EXCEED 75% OF
"A" DIMENSION (UNLESS PART OF AN
APPROVED ENGINEERED VENTING
SYSTEM)

INSULATED CONNECTOR:
"B" DIMENSION MAY NOT EXCEED 100% OF
"A" DIMENSION (UNLESS PART OF AN
APPROVED ENGINEERED VENTING
SYSTEM)

**MAXIMUM LENGTH CONNECTORS TO CHIMNEYS AND VENTS**

**FIGURE 8-42**

*(Continued from page 105)*

## SECTION 816 — VENT CONNECTORS

The *Uniform Mechanical Code* does not specify connectors for Type L vents as it does for chimney connectors in Section 205 and gas vent connectors in Section 224, but it is generally agreed that single-wall connectors as provided in Section 815.2.1 may be used; however, UMC Table 3-C provides required clearances for connectors from combustible materials and requires single-wall metal pipe connectors from oil-fired appliances when connected to chimneys to have 18-inch (457 mm) clearance. This requirement is not found in the body of the code. The application of Table 3-C follows:

- Residential low-heat appliance single-wall connectors serving oil-burning or solid-fuel appliances should maintain a minimum 18 inches (457 mm) from combustible materials.

- If a connector serving an oil-burning appliance is provided with a listed Type L vent connector that enters a masonry chimney, the clearance to combustible materials may be reduced to 9 inches (229 mm) [from 18 inches (457 mm)].

## SECTION 817 — MECHANICAL DRAFT SYSTEMS

A power exhauster or an induced draft fan raises the pressure on its discharge side above atmospheric pressure. If the inlet of a gravity-vented appliance were connected on the pressurized side of the fan, it would force the products of combustion back to the gravity-vented appliance instead of allowing them to flow in a normal direction.

A new generation of central forced-air furnaces with a built-in air fuel inducer fan causes the flow of the air/gas mixture into the atmospheric firebox and draws the burning gases through the heat exchanger. It has baffles in its venting passage just beyond the fan outlet which are designed to reduce the static and velocity pressure to atmospheric at the appliance vent collar so that the appliances are suitable for use with a Type B venting system. An "induced-draft" furnace is not the same as an induced-draft fan in a venting system. An induced-draft furnace is illustrated in Figure 8-3. Such a design reduces the pressure to atmospheric at the appliance vent collar.

Figure 8-43 illustrates some of the requirements of this section.

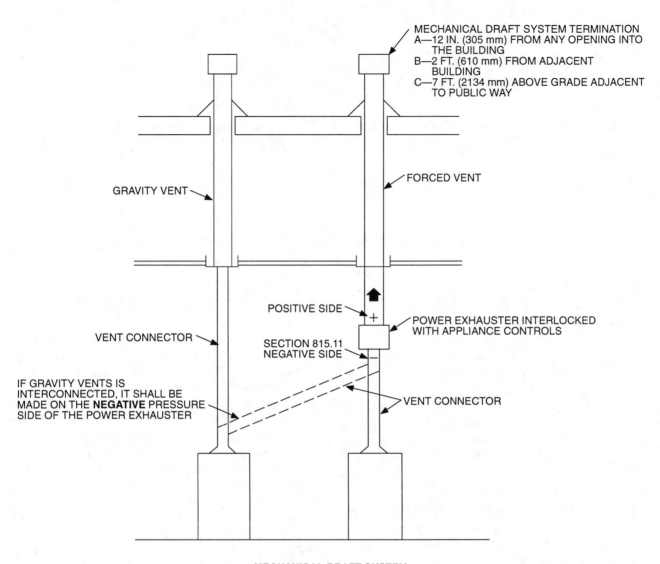

MECHANICAL DRAFT SYSTEM TERMINATION
A—12 IN. (305 mm) FROM ANY OPENING INTO THE BUILDING
B—2 FT. (610 mm) FROM ADJACENT BUILDING
C—7 FT. (2134 mm) ABOVE GRADE ADJACENT TO PUBLIC WAY

FORCED VENT

GRAVITY VENT

POSITIVE SIDE

POWER EXHAUSTER INTERLOCKED WITH APPLIANCE CONTROLS

VENT CONNECTOR

SECTION 815.11
NEGATIVE SIDE

VENT CONNECTOR

IF GRAVITY VENTS IS INTERCONNECTED, IT SHALL BE MADE ON THE **NEGATIVE** PRESSURE SIDE OF THE POWER EXHAUSTER

**MECHANICAL DRAFT SYSTEM**

**FIGURE 8-43**

# Chapter 9
# SPECIAL FUEL-BURNING EQUIPMENT

### Part I—Factory-built and Masonry Fireplaces

## SECTION 901 — VENTED DECORATIVE APPLIANCES, DECORATIVE GAS APPLIANCES FOR INSTALLATION IN SOLID-FUEL-BURNING FIREPLACES AND GAS-FIRED LOG LIGHTERS

Vented decorative appliances, although usually designed to resemble solid-fuel-burning fireplaces, are actually gas burning and are subject to applicable requirements for the installation of gas-fired appliances. See Section 701.3. Vented decorative appliances are listed for compliance with ANSI Z21.50.

Installation of approved (not necessarily listed) gas logs is permitted in solid-fuel-burning fireplaces. Listed zero-clearance fireplaces and fireplace stoves, designed with provisions for gas piping to the firebox, may be included in this category, provided the installation, along with the installation in the solid-fuel-burning fireplace, complies with the requirements of this section. It is not the intent of the code that this section regulate the installation of gas log lighters.

Can vented decorative appliances be installed in bedrooms? Yes, see Section 701.3, in a building of ordinary tightness where infiltration can be counted on as a source of combustion air and provided that the room or space meets the criteria of Section 703.4.1 [that is, the volume is equal to or greater than 50 cubic feet per 1,000 Btu/h (4.831 L/w) input]. If the building is of unusually tight construction, provisions must be made to admit combustion air from outdoors by means of ducts or openings as required by Section 702.1 (that is, the combustion air should be admitted through two openings, one high and one low). This kind of an arrangement is not normally used because of energy conservation requirements. Note that the newly added exception to Section 702.1 regarding a single combustion air opening does not apply to gas-fired appliances installed in fireplaces.

### Part II—Incinerators

## SECTION 902 — INCINERATORS, GENERAL

**902.1 Scope.** Incinerators which burn refuse, garbage or other waste are regulated by the provisions of this chapter, except for materials and structural design, which must meet the requirements of the Building Code.

Air pollution control agencies have actively and successfully sought to limit expansion of such devices and have phased out most existing incinerators. Domestic-type incinerators are now prohibited in many areas and are almost completely phased out in the western United States.

This chapter provides a reasonable basis for regulating incinerators whose installation may still be allowed in rural areas or small communities not subject to air quality controls.

**902.2 Small Domestic-type Incinerators.** Small, uninsulated incinerators installed indoors in residences are to be constructed, mounted, installed and vented according to the applicable requirements for room-heating stoves burning solid fuel and room heaters burning liquid fuel as specified in UMC Chapter 3, Part I; Chapter 3, Part III; Chapters 7 and 8, except that mounting must be on a noncombustible and fire-resistive floor with minimum clearances to combustible materials of 36 inches (914 mm) above, 48 inches (1219 mm) in front, and 36 inches (914 mm) at the back and sides. This requirement also applies to incinerators installed as part of other appliances.

Small domestic incinerators, or those that are part of other appliances, which have been tested and listed for installation on a combustible floor or with lesser clearances must be installed in accordance with their listing and the manufacturer's installation instructions, and connected to a chimney complying with the requirements of UMC Chapter 8 and UBC Section 3102.

> **EXCEPTION:** Existing unlined chimneys having at least 4-inch-thick (102 mm) brick walls may be used for venting gas-fired freestanding incinerators when other requirements of this chapter have been met and when they have been inspected and approved by the building official.

Small outdoor domestic incinerators and their location must be approved by the agency having jurisdiction, which may be a local health department or an air quality management district.

## SECTION 903 — INCINERATORS USING THE FLUE AS A REFUSE CHUTE

**903.1 Construction.** Incinerators which combine the function of refuse chute and smoke flue, and which use no fuel other than normal refuse and a gas flame or similar means to accomplish ignition (excluding oil, liquid fuels or solid fuels such as coal or wood), must be built to meet the following requirement:

The enclosing walls of the primary combustion chamber must be constructed of clay or shale brickwork not less than:

(a) 4 inches (102 mm) thick where there is a horizontal grate area not more than 9 square feet (0.8 m²) and

(b) 8 inches (203 mm) thick where there is a horizontal grate area exceeding 9 square feet (0.84 m$^2$).

In both cases, lining of firebrick not less than 4 inches (102 mm) thick must be installed. Case (b) also requires an air space between the outer clay or shale brick, and the inner firebrick sufficient to compensate for the different rates of expansion and contraction of the two types of brick.

Experience has shown that in the larger combustion chamber sizes requiring an outer clay or shale brick wall 8 inches (203 mm) thick or greater, an air space is required to keep the two types of brick from separating due to their different rates of expansion and contraction.

*Uniform Building Code* Section 3102 on incinerator chimneys regulates the construction of the combined chute and flue portion of the incinerators. Such chutes and flues must be constructed straight and plumb and must be finished with a smooth interior.

All flues must terminate in a substantially constructed spark arrestor with a mesh which will not stop a sphere having a diameter less than $3/8$ inch (10 mm), but will stop a sphere having a diameter of $1/2$ inch (13 mm). See UMC Section 814.7.

Service openings into the chute-flue must be approved self-closing hoppers constructed so that the openings are closed off completely while the hopper is being charged (loaded) and so that no part projects into the chute-flue. The area of the service opening cannot exceed one third of the area of the chute or flue to prevent clogging by the refuse.

## SECTION 904 — COMMERCIAL AND INDUSTRIAL INCINERATORS

Commercial and industrial incinerators are grouped into two types:

1. Those which burn not more than 250 pounds (113 kg) of refuse per hour and have a horizontal grate area not exceeding 9 square feet (0.8 m$^2$) and
2. Those which burn more than 250 pounds (113 kg) of refuse per hour and have a horizontal grate area exceeding 9 feet (2743 mm).

The following requirements apply to both categories:

1. The enclosing walls of the combustion chamber must be constructed of clay or shale brick not less than 8 inches (203 mm) thick.
2. The outer 4 inches (102 mm) of clay or shale brickwork may be replaced by steel plate casing not less than $3/16$ inch (5 mm) in thickness.

The two categories differ in their firebrick lining thickness requirements.

The first, smaller category requires a firebrick lining not less than 4 inches thick (102 mm); the second, larger category requires a minimum 8-inch-thick (203 mm) firebrick lining.

Incinerators and their waste material bins or containers must be located in a room or space used for no other purpose or in a room exclusively devoted to boilers and the heating plant. This room must be separated from the rest of the building by at least a one-hour fire-resistive occupancy separation because incinerators are obviously a higher-than-average source of fire hazard in an occupied building and should be isolated to some degree.

The following requirements apply to flue connections or breechings from the combustion chamber:

1. When they do not exceed 12 inches (305 mm) in diameter or greatest dimension, they must be constructed of material no lighter than 0.055-inch (1.40 mm) (No. 16 carbon sheet steel) gage.
2. When they exceed 12 inches (305 mm) in diameter or greatest dimension, they must be constructed of material no lighter than 0.097-inch (2.46 mm) (No. 12 carbon sheet steel) gage.
3. They must be lined with firebrick laid in fireclay mortar not less than $2^1/2$ inches (64 mm) thick when they are between 12 and 18 inches (305 and 457 mm) in diameter or greatest dimension and not less than $4^1/2$ inches (114 mm) thick when they are larger.

If they lead into and combine with flue connections or breechings from other appliances, such other connection or breeching must also be lined as required above for direct-flue connections, unless the cross-sectional area for the connection into which they lead is at least four times the area of the incinerator connection.

Clearances to combustibles such as woodwork or other combustible construction on all sides of flue connections or breechings must be at least 36 inches (914 mm). Clearances may be reduced as set forth in Table 3-B.

Refuse chutes cannot feed directly into the incinerator combustion chamber, but must discharge into a room or bin which is enclosed and separated from the incinerator room by floors, ceilings and walls of not less than two-hour fire-resistive construction. The opening between this storage room and the incinerator room must be equipped with a fire assembly having a three-hour fire-resistive rating.

Refuse chutes for large commercial and industrial incinerators must rest on substantial noncombustible foundations. The enclosing walls for refuse chutes must be of clay or shale brickwork not less than 8 inches (203 mm) thick. These chutes must extend at least 4 feet (1219 mm) above the roof and must be covered by a metal skylight glazed with a single thick pane of glass, presumably to allow ample light for repair work.

The Building Code governs the location, construction and protection of service openings for chutes. Automatic sprinkler systems are required for refuse chutes.

## SECTION 905 — OTHER TYPES OF INCINERATORS

**905.1 Design.** Incinerators not regulated by any of the above categories must be constructed and installed in accordance with the requirements of the Building Code, except that special large-capacity incinerators and refuse burners used in connection with sawmills, woodworking plants and other applications require special approval of the building official.

## Part III—Miscellaneous Heat-producing Appliances

Chapter 9, Part III, considers various types of heat-producing appliances. The most common are the domestic freestanding or built-in gas ranges or counter cooking tops and domestic clothes dryers. The chapter also covers built-in broilers or barbecue units, direct gas-fired makeup heaters, industrial air heaters, and small ceramic kilns.

The appliances regulated by this chapter have unique installation requirements which limit their use and require special provisions to assure their safe installation and operation within the permitted occupancies.

## SECTION 906 — DOMESTIC RANGE AND COOK TOP UNIT INSTALLATION

**906.1 Vertical Clearance above Cooking Top.** The installation of a domestic gas or electric range or a cooking top requires a vertical clearance above the cooking surface of at least 30 inches (762 mm) to unprotected combustible materials. This vertical clearance may be reduced to 24 inches (610 mm) when combustible material is protected with $^1/_4$-inch-thick (6.4 mm) insulating millboard, covered with 28 gage metal, or with a metallic ventilating hood. Section 504.1 covers requirements pertaining to the exhaust duct. It should be noted that even if domestic kitchen cabinets were constructed of noncombustible material (e.g., steel), care should be exercised so as not to allow a reduced clearance greater than what is required here since the contents of the cabinets may overheat to such an extent that the contents or packaging material ignites.

**906.2 Horizontal Clearance of Built-in Top Cooking Units.** The minimum horizontal distance from the center of the burners of a top or surface cooking unit to adjacent vertical combustible surfaces cannot be less than the distance specified by the permanent marking on the unit. Figure 9-1 illustrates two types of hoods often installed in domestic kitchens. Note specifically that neither the UBC nor the UMC requires a domestic range hood. Figures 9-2, 9-3 and 9-4 illustrate other domestic kitchen ventilation systems.

*(Continued on page 117)*

**DUCTED HOOD**

THIS HOOD COLLECTS HEAT, STEAM, GREASE, SMOKE AND ODORS AT THEIR SOURCE BEFORE THEY CAN FILL THE COOKING AREA AND SPREAD TO ADJACENT ROOMS. DUCTED HOODS DISCHARGE THE HEAT, VAPOR AND CONTAMINANTS THROUGH DUCTS TO THE BUILDING'S EXTERIOR.

**DUCTLESS HOOD AND EXHAUST SYSTEMS**

A DUCTLESS HOOD OR EXHAUST SYSTEM CONDUCTS THE GREASE, SMOKE AND ODORS THROUGH AN ACTIVATED CHARCOAL FILTER OR AN ELECTRONIC AIR FILTER THAT REMOVES THE CONTAMINANTS FROM THE AIR STREAM. IT THEN RETURNS THE CLEANED AIR TO THE KITCHEN AREA.

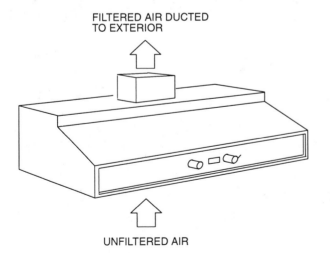

FILTERED AIR DUCTED TO EXTERIOR

UNFILTERED AIR

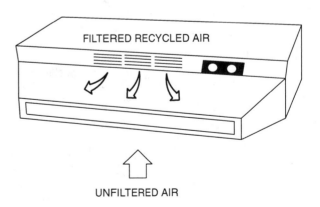

FILTERED RECYCLED AIR

UNFILTERED AIR

**DOMESTIC RANGE HOODS**

**FIGURE 9-1**

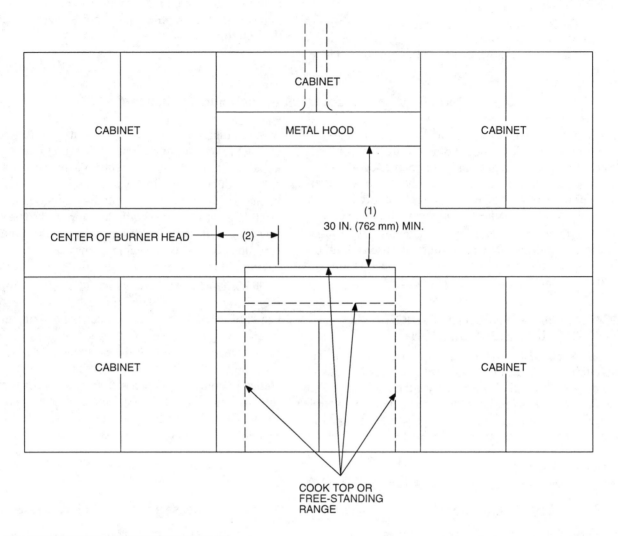

*TO UNPROTECTED COMBUSTIBLE MATERIAL

(1)  MAY BE REDUCED TO 24 IN. (610 mm) BY PLACING $1/4$ IN. (6.4 mm) THICK INSULATING MILLBOARD COVERED WITH NO. 28 U.S. GAGE SHEET STEEL OR WITH A STEEL HOOD.

(2)  HORIZONTAL CLEARANCE TO VERTICAL SURFACES IMMEDIATELY ADJACENT TO COOK TOP SHALL BE NOT LESS THAN THAT DISTANCE SPECIFIED BY THE PERMANENT MARKING ON COOKING UNIT.

**FIGURE 9-2**

### DOWNFLOW OR COUNTERRLOW EXHAUST SYSTEM

THE DOWNFLOW EXHAUST SYSTEM IS A COMPONENT PART OF THE RANGE OR COUNTER TOP. THIS SYSTEM COLLECTS THE CONTAMINANTS AT THE COOKING SURFACE AND DISCHARGES THEM IN A DOWNWARD DIRECTION. THE CONTAMINANTS ARE CONDUCTED BY DUCTS TO THE BUILDING'S EXTERIOR.

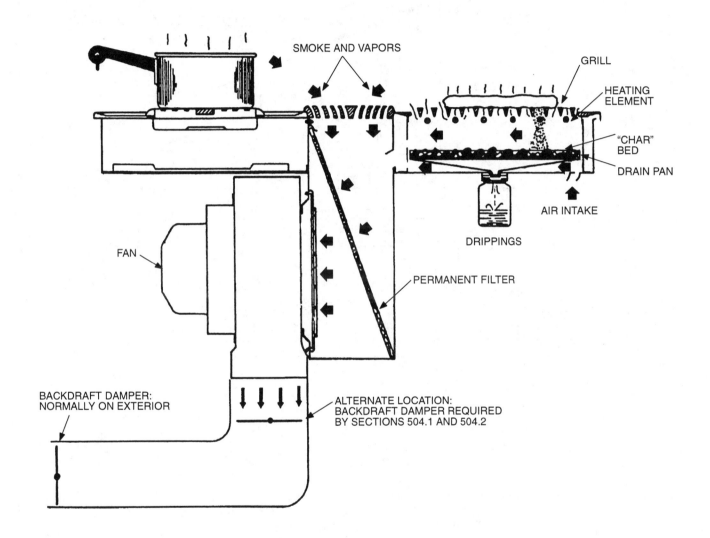

**DOWNFLOW EXHAUST SYSTEM**

**FIGURE 9-3**

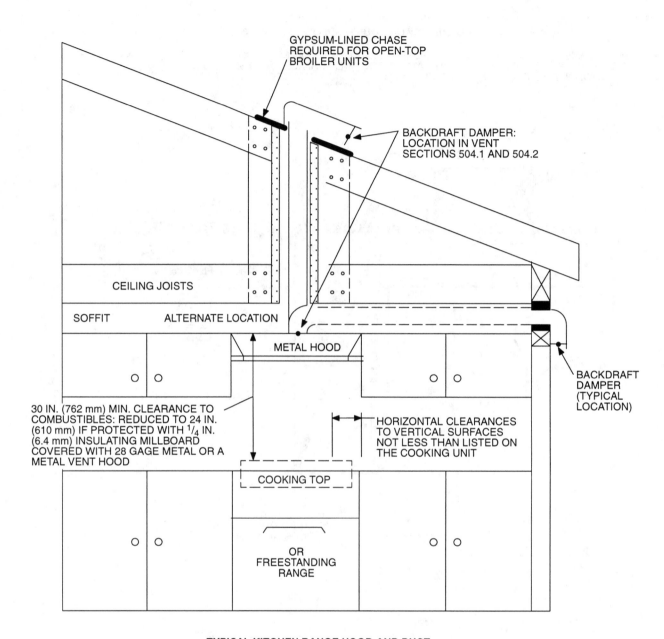

GYPSUM-LINED CHASE
REQUIRED FOR OPEN-TOP
BROILER UNITS

BACKDRAFT DAMPER:
LOCATION IN VENT
SECTIONS 504.1 AND 504.2

CEILING JOISTS

SOFFIT       ALTERNATE LOCATION

METAL HOOD

BACKDRAFT
DAMPER
(TYPICAL
LOCATION)

30 IN. (762 mm) MIN. CLEARANCE TO
COMBUSTIBLES: REDUCED TO 24 IN.
(610 mm) IF PROTECTED WITH $1/4$ IN.
(6.4 mm) INSULATING MILLBOARD
COVERED WITH 28 GAGE METAL OR A
METAL VENT HOOD

HORIZONTAL CLEARANCES
TO VERTICAL SURFACES
NOT LESS THAN LISTED ON
THE COOKING UNIT

COOKING TOP

OR
FREESTANDING
RANGE

**TYPICAL KITCHEN RANGE HOOD AND DUCT**

**FIGURE 9-4**

*(Continued from page 113)*

**906.3 Installation of a Listed Cooking Appliance or Microwave Oven above a Listed Cooking Appliance.** The installation of a microwave oven over a cooking top is based on the conditions of listing and the manufacturer's installation instructions for the upper appliance. Permanent markings on the appliances specify clearances from combustibles.

## SECTION 907 — DOMESTIC OPEN-TOP BROILER UNITS AND HOODS

Domestic open-top broiler units and hoods must be installed in accordance with their listing and the manufacturer's installation instructions. Figure 9-5 shows a typical indoor broiler ventilation system.

An exhaust duct and a fan having a minimum capacity of 100 cfm per square foot [508 L/(s•m$^2$)] of hood intake area are required for a broiler or barbecue unit. If the duct penetrates a ceiling or floor, it must be enclosed in a fire-resistive shaft and protected on the inside as required for a one-hour fire-resistive construction, without other combustible material used within the shaft. The shaft must be separated from the duct by at least 1 inch (25 mm) of air space vented to the outside, and the duct must terminate at least 18 inches (457 mm) above the roof surface. A minimum 24-inch (610 mm) clearance must be maintained between the cooking surface and combustible materials. The hood must be at least as wide as the broiler unit and centered above it.

The operation of an open-top broiler unit produces a significant amount of grease and smoke which must be removed from the kitchen or cooking area. The stringent requirement for installation exists because the grease accumulates on the exhaust duct walls as it cools, thereby providing fuel for a potential grease fire.

## SECTION 908 — CLOTHES DRYERS

**908.1 Domestic Clothes Dryers.** When a compartment or space for a domestic clothes dryer is provided, a minimum 4-inch-diameter (102 mm) exhaust duct of approved material must be installed in accordance with this section and the requirements of Section 504.

**908.2 Makeup Air.** Clothes dryers installed in a compartment require makeup air because the air used to entrain moisture vapor is taken directly from the appliance enclosure.

**908.3 Commercial Clothes Dryers.** Installations of commercial clothes dryers must comply with the manufacturer's installation instructions.

When clothes dryers are installed in a room with other fuel-burning appliances, combustion air openings must be sized to prevent the creation of negative pressure within the compartment. See Section 706.

## SECTION 909 — DIRECT GAS-FIRED MAKEUP AIR HEATERS AND INDUSTRIAL AIR HEATERS

**909.1 General.** A direct gas-fired makeup air heater is a commercial or industrial appliance in which all the combustion products generated by the gas-burning device are released into the air stream being heated. See Figure 9-6.

These heaters may be installed in commercial and industrial occupancies which use heated makeup air from outside of the building to replace air exhausted from the interior space.

A direct gas-fired industrial air heater is an appliance, a device or a piece of equipment used in an industrial, a manufacturing or a commercial occupancy for applying heat to materials being processed; this does not include water heaters, boilers or portable equipment used by artisans in pursuit of a trade. They may be installed in commercial and industrial occupancies to offset building heat loss, to provide fresh air ventilation or to do both. Neither an industrial nor a direct-fired air heater should be used to supply an occupancy containing sleeping quarters.

**909.2 Relief Openings.** The design of the installation must include adequate provisions to permit the equipment to operate at rated capacity by considering the structure's designed infiltration rate; providing properly designed relief openings or an interlocked power exhaust system; or a combination of these methods. If adequate relief is not provided, the pressure within the building will increase, thus decreasing the airflow rate of the heater, creating a potentially unsafe condition.

Relief openings may be louvers or counterbalanced gravity dampers. If the dampers are motorized, they must be electrically interlocked so as not to permit equipment blower and main burner operation until they are proven to be in the open position.

**909.3 Clearance.** Direct-fired and industrial makeup air heaters must be located so that the temperatures of surrounding combustible material will not be raised higher than 90°F (32°C) above ambient.

## SECTION 910 — SMALL CERAMIC KILNS

**910.1 General.** This section applies to the installation of ceramic kilns that have a maximum interior volume of 20 cubic feet (0.566 m$^3$) and are used for hobby or noncommercial purposes. See Figures 9-7, 9-8 and 9-9.

**910.2 Installation.** Kilns must be installed in accordance with applicable code requirements and the manufacturer's installation instructions.

Kilns which exceed 20 cubic feet (0.566 m$^3$) capacity will probably be unlisted and used for commercial or industrial applications. The building official may require that the design and installation be prepared by a licensed professional. The guidance contained in Table 10-C may be applied in designing the controls and limit devices required for automatic (unattended) operation.

*(Continued on page 123)*

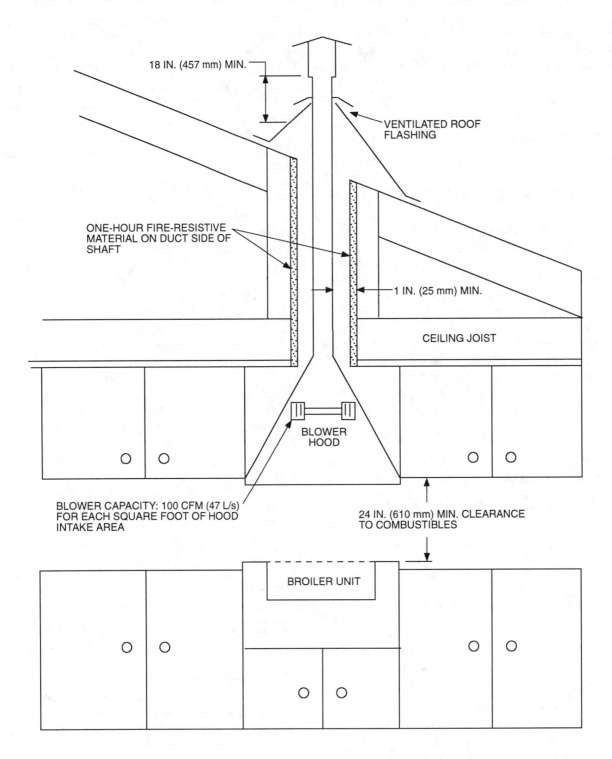

18 IN. (457 mm) MIN.

VENTILATED ROOF FLASHING

ONE-HOUR FIRE-RESISTIVE MATERIAL ON DUCT SIDE OF SHAFT

1 IN. (25 mm) MIN.

CEILING JOIST

BLOWER HOOD

BLOWER CAPACITY: 100 CFM (47 L/s) FOR EACH SQUARE FOOT OF HOOD INTAKE AREA

24 IN. (610 mm) MIN. CLEARANCE TO COMBUSTIBLES

BROILER UNIT

**OPEN-TOP BROILER UNIT**

**FIGURE 9-5**

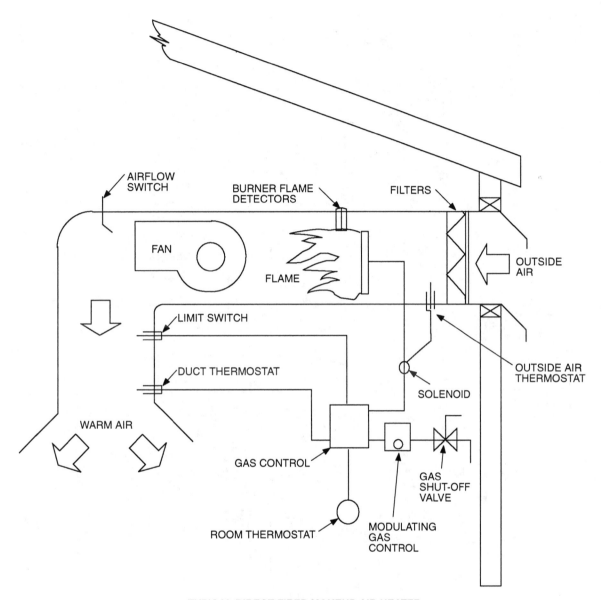

AIRFLOW SWITCH

BURNER FLAME DETECTORS

FILTERS

FAN

FLAME

OUTSIDE AIR

LIMIT SWITCH

DUCT THERMOSTAT

OUTSIDE AIR THERMOSTAT

SOLENOID

WARM AIR

GAS CONTROL

GAS SHUT-OFF VALVE

ROOM THERMOSTAT

MODULATING GAS CONTROL

**TYPICAL DIRECT-FIRED MAKEUP AIR HEATER**

**FIGURE 9-6**

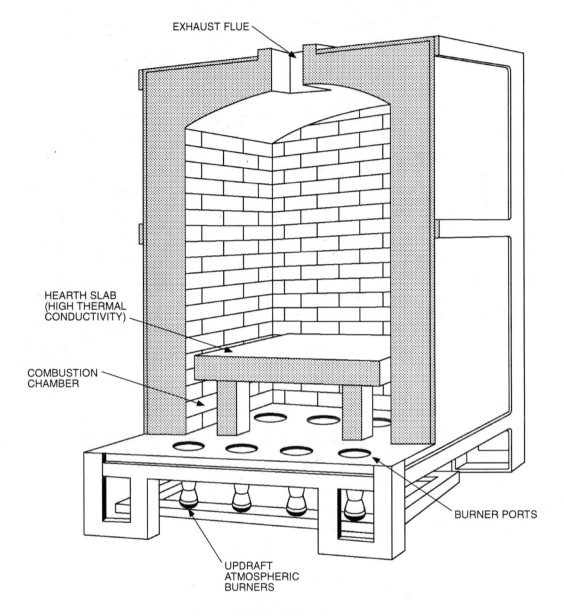

EXHAUST FLUE

HEARTH SLAB
(HIGH THERMAL
CONDUCTIVITY)

COMBUSTION
CHAMBER

BURNER PORTS

UPDRAFT
ATMOSPHERIC
BURNERS

**TYPICAL SMALL KILN**

**FIGURE 9-7**

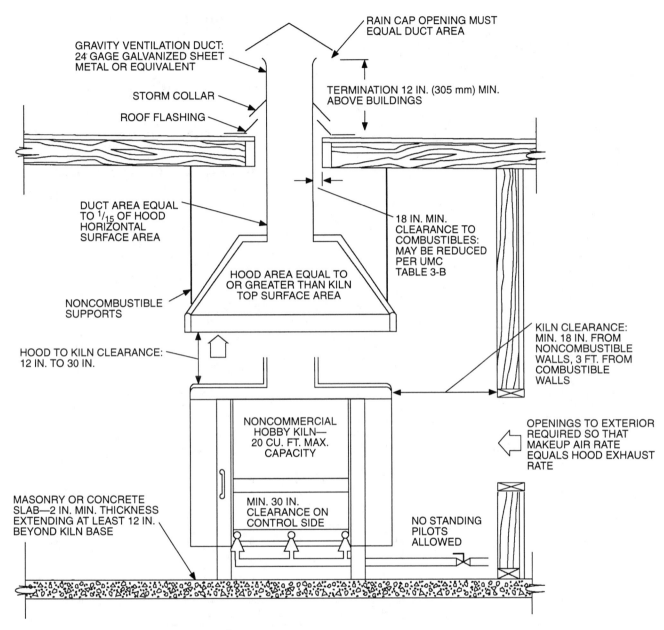

RAIN CAP OPENING MUST EQUAL DUCT AREA

GRAVITY VENTILATION DUCT: 24 GAGE GALVANIZED SHEET METAL OR EQUIVALENT

STORM COLLAR

ROOF FLASHING

TERMINATION 12 IN. (305 mm) MIN. ABOVE BUILDINGS

DUCT AREA EQUAL TO $1/15$ OF HOOD HORIZONTAL SURFACE AREA

18 IN. MIN. CLEARANCE TO COMBUSTIBLES: MAY BE REDUCED PER UMC TABLE 3-B

HOOD AREA EQUAL TO OR GREATER THAN KILN TOP SURFACE AREA

NONCOMBUSTIBLE SUPPORTS

KILN CLEARANCE: MIN. 18 IN. FROM NONCOMBUSTIBLE WALLS, 3 FT. FROM COMBUSTIBLE WALLS

HOOD TO KILN CLEARANCE: 12 IN. TO 30 IN.

NONCOMMERCIAL HOBBY KILN— 20 CU. FT. MAX. CAPACITY

OPENINGS TO EXTERIOR REQUIRED SO THAT MAKEUP AIR RATE EQUALS HOOD EXHAUST RATE

MASONRY OR CONCRETE SLAB—2 IN. MIN. THICKNESS EXTENDING AT LEAST 12 IN. BEYOND KILN BASE

MIN. 30 IN. CLEARANCE ON CONTROL SIDE

NO STANDING PILOTS ALLOWED

For **SI:** 1 inch = 25.4 mm, 1 cubic foot = 0.028 m$^3$.

**TYPICAL INDOOR HOBBY KILN INSTALLATION—NOT FOR COMMERCIAL APPLICATIONS**

**FIGURE 9-8**

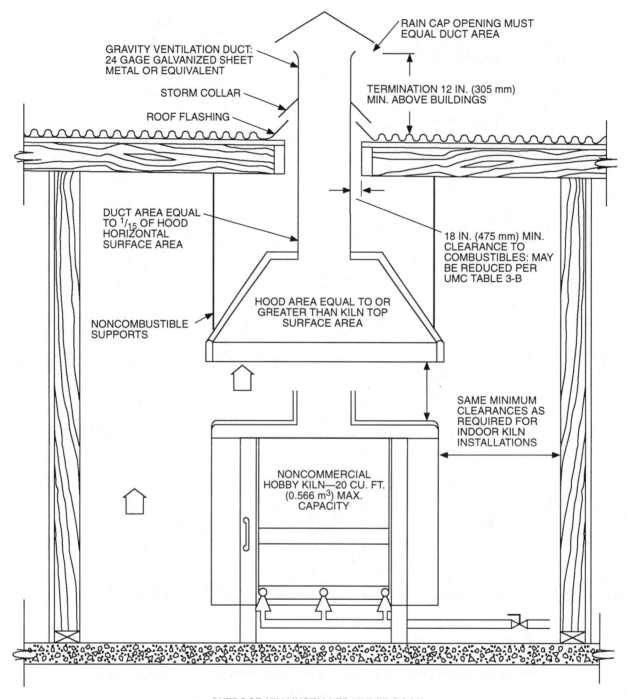

**OUTDOOR KILN INSTALLED UNDER ROOF**
(Partially Enclosed by More than Two Vertical Wall Surfaces)

**FIGURE 9-9**

*(Continued from page 117)*

**910.3 Installations inside Buildings.** Small hobby kilns installed inside a building must also meet the following requirements:

1. **Kiln clearances.** The kiln sides and top must have an 18-inch (457 mm) minimum clearance from noncombustible wall surfaces and a 3-foot (914 mm) minimum clearance from combustible wall surfaces. The flooring must be noncombustible material of at least 2 inches (51 mm) of solid masonry or concrete extending at least 12 inches (305 mm) beyond the base or supporting members of the kiln. Clearances may be reduced when the kiln is installed according to the conditions of its listing or when installed according to test results acceptable to the building official.

In no case can the clearance on the gas or electrical control side be reduced to less than 30 inches (762 mm).

2. **Hoods.** A canopy hood sized to at least equal the top horizontal surface area of the kiln must be installed directly above the kiln. The hood is to be constructed from at least 0.024-inch (0.61 mm) (No. 24 United States gage) galvanized steel or an equivalent material and supported with noncombustible supports at a height not less than 12 inches (305 mm) or more than 30 inches (762 mm) above the kiln.

> **EXCEPTION:** Electric kilns installed with listed exhaust blowers may be used when marked as being suitable for the kiln and installed in accordance with the manufacturer's instructions.

3. **Gravity ventilation ducts.** A gravity ventilation duct must be connected to the hood and extendd vertically to outside of the building. The duct must be of the same material as the hood and sized to equal at least one fifteenth of the face opening area of the hood. The duct is to terminate at least 12 inches (305 mm) above any part of the building within 4 feet (1219 mm) and at least 4 feet (1219 mm) from any openable window or opening into the building or adjacent property line. The opening to the outside must be shielded to prevent the entry of rain without reducing the opening area of the duct. Each section of the duct must be supported with noncombustible supports.

4. **Makeup air.** Openings or supply fans must be provided so that makeup air can enter the room at a rate equal to the rate of air removed from the room through the kiln hood.

5. **Hood and duct clearances.** A hood or duct serving a fuel-burning kiln must have a clearance from combustibles of at least 18 inches (457 mm); this clearance may be reduced in accordance with Table 3-B.

**910.3.4 Exterior installations.** Kilns installed in exterior locations must have the same minimum clearances from combustible constructions as kilns installed indoors.

When a kiln is located under a roofed area and such area is enclosed by more than two vertical wall surfaces, a hood and gravity exhaust duct which comply with all requirements for indoor installation are required. The same minimum clearances apply for indoor kiln installations. (See Figure 9-9.)

# Chapter 10
# BOILER/WATER HEATERS

Chapter 10 was previously located in UMC Appendix B. By relocating the appendix chapter to the main body of the code, the requirements became an enforceable part of the code instead of merely guidance for the building official.

The scope of Part I is water heaters; Part II deals with steam and hot-water boilers that burn or utilize any fuel. Note the similarity between 1997 UMC Sections 1003 and 1018 and 1994 UMC Section 315, Item 5. The similarity arises from the fact that the equipment being regulated are fuel-burning devices, which normally obtain their combustion air from the room in which they are located. These devices have an atmospheric fire box located in the room or space in which the devices are located. Therefore, this discussion does not apply to direct-vented appliances but only to fuel-burning devices having an atmospheric combustion chamber. Combustion air requirements are now set forth in Chapter 7.

## SECTION 1010 — EXPANSION TANKS

Expansion tanks are a safety measure used with water heating boilers to accommodate the expansion of the liquid when it is heated. Frequently the liquid in boilers is water, but in industrial boilers it may heat any fluid including mercury, a metal. Such a system is most frequently seen in electric power generating applications. Expansion tanks serve to modulate the wide pressure swings that would occur if the pressure-relief valve were to open. Hot-water boilers and piping systems operate with the system full of the heat transfer fluid, usually water. There are two common types of expansion tanks; one is an elevated reservoir in which the static head of liquid expands into the reservoir as the pressure inside the boiler increases. The other type of expansion tank is a two-chamber closed reservoir separated by a flexible diaphragm. In this type, the heated boiler fluid compresses a reservoir of air, and if the pressure exceeds the design pressure, some air is released. This type of closed tank may become waterlogged when the diaphragm no longer has an air cushion. To correct the waterlogged condition, compressed air must be added to the expansion tank air space. This raises the pressure of the boiler's fluid charge to the extent that some boiler water may have to be bled off so that the boiler's fluid is not forced back into a potable water supply system.

## SECTION 1013 — GAS-PRESSURE REGULATORS

If fuel gas is supplied to a boiler at a pressure higher than that at which the boiler's main burner is designed to operate, a separate approved gas-pressure regulator for the main burner should be installed. A boiler-burner unit assembled by a manufacturer does not require a separate pilot gas pressure regulator.

Exception 8 in Table 10-C relating to boilers used in Group R Occupancies of less that six units is an indirect reference to ANSI Z21.13(a), *Gas-fired Low-pressure Steam and Hot-water Boilers,* which is listed in Chapter 16, and ANSI/ASME CSD-1 entitled *Controls and Safety Devices for Automatically Fired Boilers.* The scope and content of ANSI/ASME CSD-1 constitute the basis for UMC Chapter 10 because it deals with the scope of controls and safety devices installed on automatically operated boilers fired with gas, oil, gas-oil or electricity whereas ANSI Z21.13(a) is applicable only to gas-fired low-pressure steam and hot-water boilers. Thus, ANSI/ASME CSD-1 has a much broader scope than ANSI Z21.13(a).

Appendix Table A-1 in ANSI/ASME CSD-1 contains a comparison between ANSI Z21.13(a) and ANSI/ASME CSD-1 requirements. ANSI/ASME CSD-1 and UMC Chapter 10 indicate when ANSI Z21.1 requirements satisfy the requirements of ANSI/ASME CSD-1.

# Chapter 11
# REFRIGERATION

### Part I—Mechanical Refrigeration Systems

## SECTION 1101 — GENERAL

The changes in Section 1101 arise from revisions to comply with the common code format. In addition to the general requirements of Chapter 3, Part I, Chapter 11 regulates mechanical refrigeration systems and equipment. It explains the safety classifications of refrigerants and discusses special requirements for each category and the requirements for installation, alteration and replacement of components of such systems or equipment. The listing and label of an approved agency attached to refrigeration equipment may be accepted as evidence that the equipment meets the applicable standards.

Refrigerants are the vital working fluids in refrigeration, air-conditioning and heat-pumping systems. They absorb heat from one area, such as an air-conditioned space, and reject it into another, such as outdoors, usually through evaporation and condensation processes, respectively.

The environmental consequences of a refrigerant that leaks from a system must be considered. Because of their great stability, fully halogenated compounds (called CFCs or chlorofluorocarbons) persist in the atmosphere for many years and eventually diffuse into the stratosphere. The molecules of CFCs, such as R-11 and R-12, contain only carbon and the halogens chlorine, fluorine and bromine or a combination. Once in the upper atmosphere, the refrigerant molecule breaks down and releases chlorine, which destroys ozone. In the lower atmosphere, these molecules absorb infrared radiation, which may contribute to the warming of the earth (the greenhouse effect).

The refrigeration industry is currently in transition because of the Montreal Protocol, which is an international agreement to phase out the environmentally damaging chlorofluorocarbon refrigerants and replace them with refrigerants that are more environmentally benign. President George Bush's Executive Order has further accelerated the phaseout in the United States, which has given rise to accelerated development of national consensus standards for refrigeration safety and a newly developed nomenclature for the flammability and toxicity hazards of refrigerants. Under the heading "N" in UMC Section 1603 is the title *Number Designation and Safety Classification of Refrigerants*, ANSI/ASHRAE 34-1992, which provides the basis for refrigerant safety classifications employed in Section 1102.

Figure 11-1 illustrates the principal parts of a direct refrigeration (also designated high-probability system in Section 1103) or air-conditioning system. These include the compressor, condenser, receiver and the evaporator. By definition, a high-probability refrigerating system is one in which the refrigerant evaporator is in direct contact with the material or space to be refrigerated or is located in air-circulating passages communicating with such space. A condensing unit is defined as a specific refrigerating machine combination for a given refrigerant, consisting of one or more power-driven compressors, condensers, liquid receivers, when required, and the pertinent accessories. Refrigerant flow is shown by the arrows and is routed from the compressor to the condenser, receiver, evaporator coil and then back to the compressor.

An indirect refrigerating system (also designated as a low-probability system in Section 1103) is defined as one in which a fluid cooled by a refrigerating system is circulated to the material or space to be refrigerated or is used to cool air that is used to cool a space. The difference is that the evaporator coil, rather than being located in the refrigerated space, duct or plenum, is located in a heat exchanger, which cools a circulating brine, which in turn cools the refrigerated space, duct or plenum. The heat exchanger is located in the refrigeration machinery room.

How do you identify the individual parts of a refrigerating system? One of the easiest ways is to first identify the compressor. A compressor is nothing more than a pump. Compressors are found in two basic types—centrifugal and positive displacement. The centrifugal-type pump often looks like a large snail. A positive displacement pump simply looks like an internal combustion engine. To distinguish between the suction side and the discharge side of a compressor, simply look for an insulated line, which is the suction line; the other pipe is the discharge line. Centrifugal compressors are usually used in relatively large systems, while positive displacement compressors are commonly found in most others.

The next large piece of equipment is the condenser. Condensers are generally either water cooled or air cooled. Air-cooled condensers would normally be located outside of the building and often on the roof of the building. Air-cooled condensers generally resemble radiators and are either mounted in a vertical or horizontal position with a fan blowing across them. Water-cooled condensers are normally inside the building in the same room as the compressor. Most condensers simply look like a tank with an inlet and an outlet connection for refrigerant and an inlet and an outlet connection for cooling water. The inlet and outlet connections for cooling water are normally connected to a cooling tower. The condenser and cooling tower are sometimes combined through a pump system into one piece of equipment which is then called an evaporative condenser.

The next piece of equipment in the system is the receiver. The receiver is simply a storage tank for the liquid refrigerant which has been condensed in the condenser.

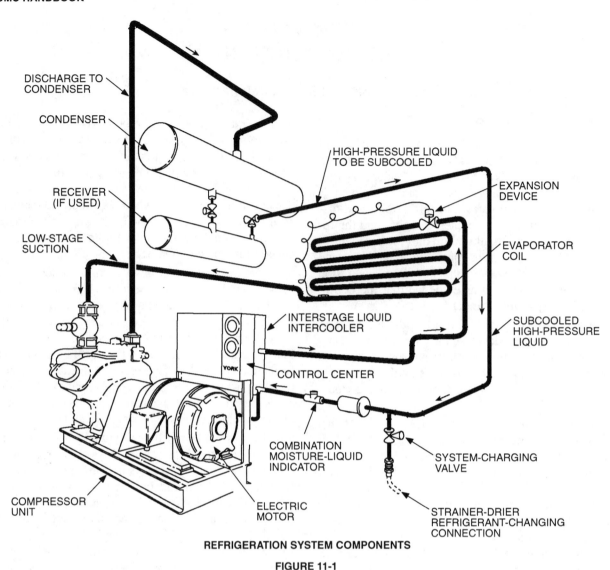

**REFRIGERATION SYSTEM COMPONENTS**

**FIGURE 11-1**

Next comes an evaporator coil or coils where the liquid refrigerant is expanded into vapor and the cooling effect takes place because of the phase change. From the evaporator coil, the expanded gas is returned to the suction side of the compressor, completing its cycle. The components of an indirect refrigerating system can be identified in the same manner as the components of the direct refrigerating system, except that the piece of equipment immediately downstream of the receiver is a heat exchanger which closely resembles a condenser. In this heat exchanger, water or brine is cooled by the evaporator coil, and this chilled water or brine is then pumped from the heat exchanger to the refrigerated space, duct or plenum, rather than cooling that space directly with refrigerant. When a compressor, condenser, receiver and heat exchanger containing the evaporative coil are combined by the manufacturer in a single unit, it is called a chiller.

## SECTION 1102 — REFRIGERANTS

The marginal line refers to text revisions to refer to ANSI/ASHRAE 34 as the source document for refrigerant safety classification and number designations as listed in Chapter 16. Section 1102.2 is a newly added requirement for new reclaimed and recovered refrigerants.

**1102.1 General.** Table 11-A contains the currently recognized refrigerant names, safety group designations, properties and allowable quantities. Notice that the revised safety groups are alphanumeric characters in which the capital letter designates the toxicity classification and the Arabic numeral denotes the flammability of the refrigerant.

**1102.3 Toxicity Classification.** The A designation represents refrigerants exhibiting lower toxicity while B represents higher toxicity refrigerants.

**1102.4 Flammability Classification.** Arabic number 1 is used to designate refrigerants having no flame propagation; Arabic number 2 designates refrigerants having lower flammability while Arabic number 3 designates those refrigerants exhibiting higher flammability. Note that Table 11-A does not recognize refrigerants exhibiting higher flammability characteristic (i.e., Safety Groups A3 and B3) as currently written. The following diagram illus-

| SAFETY GROUP | | |
|---|---|---|
| Higher Flammability | A3 | B3 |
| Lower Flammability | A2 | B2 |
| No Flame Propagation | A1 | B1 |
| | Lower Toxicity | Higher Toxicity |

INCREASING FLAMMABILITY →

INCREASING TOXICITY →

trates the safety classifications employed in ANSI/ ASHRAE 34-1992 and as used in the 1994 UMC, Chapter 11.

## SECTION 1103 — CLASSIFICATION OF REFRIGERATION SYSTEMS

**1103.1 General.** Refrigeration systems are classified according to the degree of probability that leakage of a refrigerant could enter a normally occupied area. Referring to the fifth paragraph of Section 1101, direct systems offer the highest probability of refrigerant leakage into occupied spaces because the refrigerant evaporator coil is located either in the space itself or in a duct communicating directly with the space. Section 1103.1.1 designates such a direct system as a high-probability system; Section 1103.1.2 designates an indirect system, as described in the sixth paragraph of Section 1101, as a low-probability system because the refrigerant does not enter the room or duct, but rather is confined in a heat exchanger through which is circulated a brine (note that the term *brine* does not necessarily refer to a saline solution) which cools the space to be refrigerated. A brine may also be circulated through another heat exchanger located in a duct or plenum, thereby cooling the air. See Figure 11-2 which illustrates various combinations of direct and indirect systems. Both the direct and double direct systems would be classified as high-probability systems. The various indirect systems would all be classified as low-probability systems.

## SECTION 1104 — REQUIREMENTS FOR REFRIGERANT AND REFRIGERATION SYSTEM USE

**1104.1 System Selection.** Table 11-B prescribes permissible systems, refrigerants and requirements for a refrigeration machinery room by occupancy group and division.

**1104.2 Volume of Occupied Space.** Table 11-A controls the maximum quantity of refrigerant in high-proba-

bility systems, i.e., in direct systems. The controlling entry is found in Column 10, entitled Pounds per 1,000 Cubic Feet (Kg/28.3 m$^3$) of Occupied Space. If the refrigerant charge weight exceeds the limits specified in Table 11-A, it would be theoretically possible to select a different refrigerant; however, the practical solution would usually be to select an indirect system. The consequences of that election will be that a refrigeration machinery room will be required to contain the entire quantity of refrigerant.

**1104.3 Refrigerated Process and Storage Areas.** This provision for unlimited refrigerant quantities for refrigerated processing and storage areas is, in effect, an exception to the limitations of Table 11-A for the specific occupancy. The rationale for the relaxation is, of course, the very low occupant load of the occupancy which reduces the life-safety exposure. Note that use of this provision also brings into play other life-safety measures, such as exiting provisions of UBC Chapter 10, refrigerant vapor detection and alarm systems, and vapor-tight isolation of the refrigerated space from other portions of the building.

## SECTION 1105 — GENERAL REQUIREMENTS

**1105.1 Human Comfort.** The cross-reference to UMC Sections 402, 403 and 404 establish requirements for return and outside air as specified for a central warm-air heating system. These requirements were repeated in Chapter 12 of the 1991 and preceding editions. Thus, the common code format and Chapter 11 rewrite were successful in reducing the size of the 1997 UMC.

Figures 11-3 through 11-17 show how domestic mechanical refrigeration systems for comfort cooling are to be installed.

Readers should note that the separate Chapter 12 in the 1991 edition covering cooling for human comfort has been eliminated by cross-references to Sections 402, 403 and 404 in the 1994 edition.

**1105.2 Supports and Anchorage.** Supports for compressors and condensing units must be designed to safely support the equipment. Supports from buildings or parts of buildings that are of noncombustible construction must be noncombustible. The reference to the occupancy categories in Chapter 16 of the UBC refers to Sections 1625 and 1629.2 in Volume 2 in which the occupancy importance categories are indicated in Table 16-K.

**1105.2.1 Support from ground.** A compressor or portion of a condensing unit supported from the ground must rest on a concrete or other approved base extending at least 3 inches (76 mm) above the adjoining grade level.

**1105.3 Access.** A minimum of 36 inches by 6 feet 8 inches (915 mm by 2032 mm) unobstructed access and passageway must be provided to any compressor, unless otherwise specified by the code.

**1105.4 Illumination and Service Receptacles.** Refrigeration equipment required to be accessible or readily accessible must have the electrical connections as required

*(Continued on page 134)*

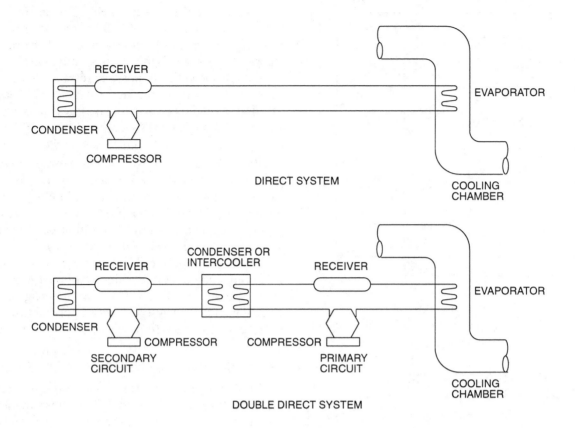

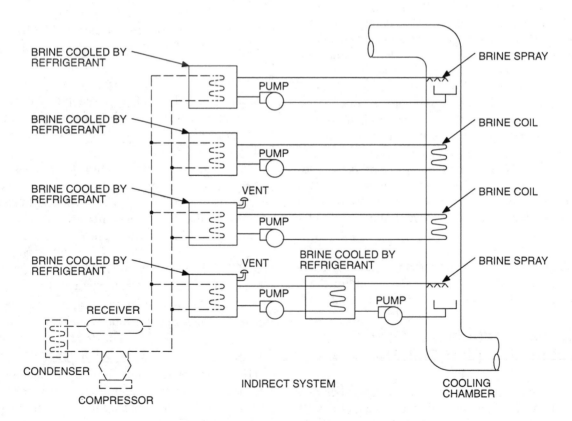

**TYPES OF REFRIGERATION SYSTEMS**

**FIGURE 11-2**

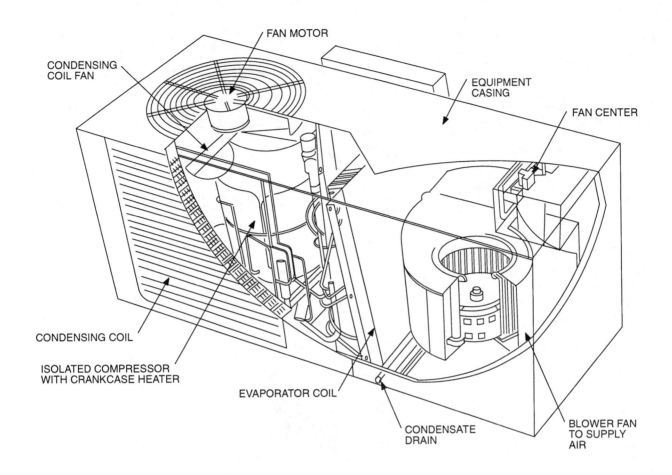

CONDENSING
COIL FAN

FAN MOTOR

EQUIPMENT
CASING

FAN CENTER

CONDENSING COIL

ISOLATED COMPRESSOR
WITH CRANKCASE HEATER

EVAPORATOR COIL

CONDENSATE
DRAIN

BLOWER FAN
TO SUPPLY
AIR

**REVERSIBLE AIR CONDITIONER/HEAT PUMP—TYPICAL "COOLING UNIT" FOR HUMAN COMFORT**

**FIGURE 11-3**

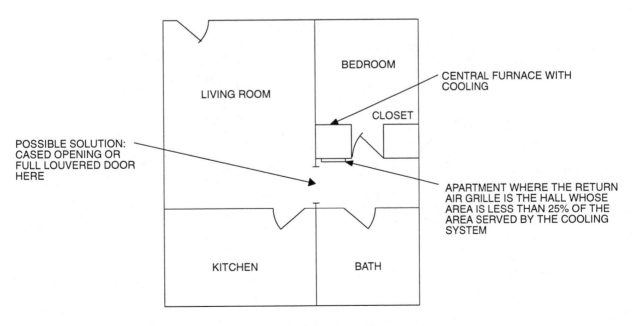

BEDROOM

CENTRAL FURNACE WITH
COOLING

LIVING ROOM

CLOSET

POSSIBLE SOLUTION:
CASED OPENING OR
FULL LOUVERED DOOR
HERE

APARTMENT WHERE THE RETURN
AIR GRILLE IS THE HALL WHOSE
AREA IS LESS THAN 25% OF THE
AREA SERVED BY THE COOLING
SYSTEM

KITCHEN

BATH

**NOTE:** Requirements for heating in Sections 403 and 404 also apply to cooling systems.

**FIGURE 11-4**

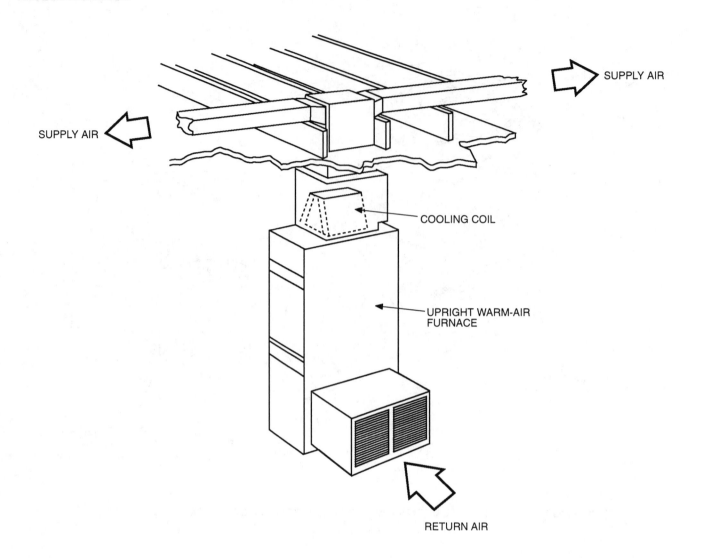

SUPPLY AIR

SUPPLY AIR

COOLING COIL

UPRIGHT WARM-AIR FURNACE

RETURN AIR

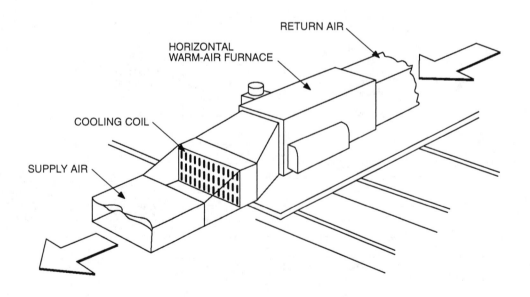

RETURN AIR

HORIZONTAL WARM-AIR FURNACE

COOLING COIL

SUPPLY AIR

**TYPICAL COOLING COILS WITH FURNACES**

**FIGURE 11-5**

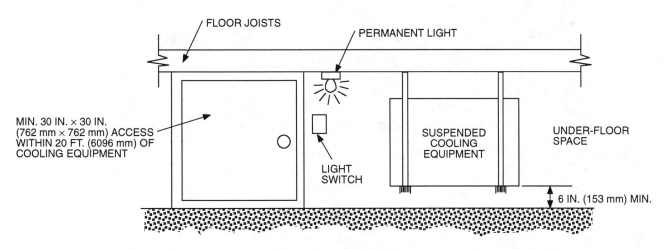

FLOOR JOISTS

PERMANENT LIGHT

MIN. 30 IN. × 30 IN.
(762 mm × 762 mm) ACCESS
WITHIN 20 FT. (6096 mm) OF
COOLING EQUIPMENT

LIGHT
SWITCH

SUSPENDED
COOLING
EQUIPMENT

UNDER-FLOOR
SPACE

6 IN. (153 mm) MIN.

**TYPICAL ACCESS UNDER FLOORS**
**(By cross reference to Section 307.4 and Section 1105.3) Exception 3**

**FIGURE 11-6**

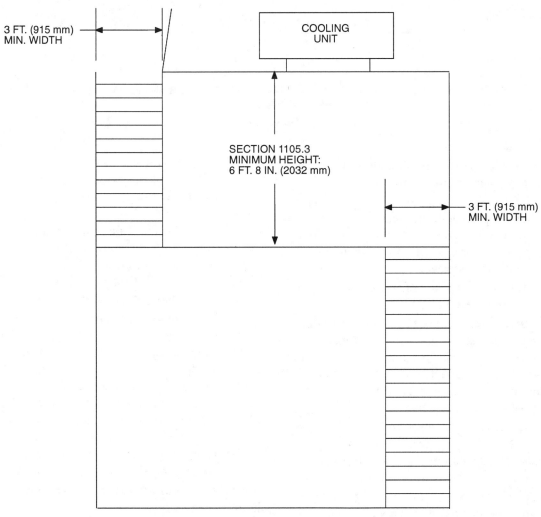

3 FT. (915 mm)
MIN. WIDTH

COOLING
UNIT

SECTION 1105.3
MINIMUM HEIGHT:
6 FT. 8 IN. (2032 mm)

3 FT. (915 mm)
MIN. WIDTH

SECTION VIEW

**TYPICAL ACCESS TO COOLING UNITS ON ROOFS**
**(By cross reference to Section 307.5)**

**FIGURE 11-7**

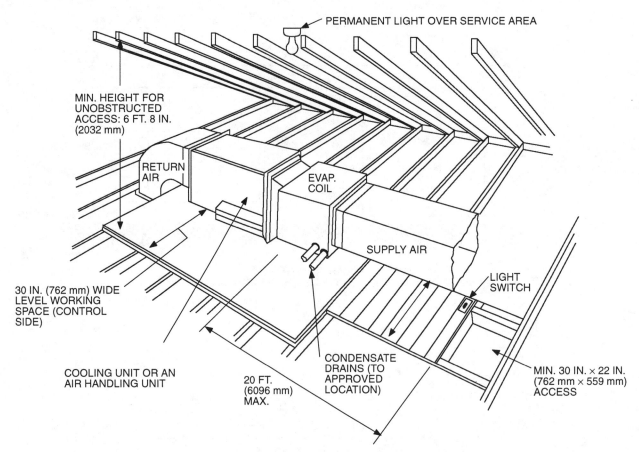

PERMANENT LIGHT OVER SERVICE AREA

MIN. HEIGHT FOR
UNOBSTRUCTED
ACCESS: 6 FT. 8 IN.
(2032 mm)

RETURN
AIR

EVAP.
COIL

SUPPLY AIR

LIGHT
SWITCH

30 IN. (762 mm) WIDE
LEVEL WORKING
SPACE (CONTROL
SIDE)

COOLING UNIT OR AN
AIR HANDLING UNIT

20 FT.
(6096 mm)
MAX.

CONDENSATE
DRAINS (TO
APPROVED
LOCATION)

MIN. 30 IN. × 22 IN.
(762 mm × 559 mm)
ACCESS

**TYPICAL ATTIC INSTALLATION OF HORIZONTAL COOLING UNIT OR AN AIR HANDLING UNIT**
**(By cross reference to Section 307.3)**

**FIGURE 11-8**

*(Continued from page 129)*

by Section 309.1, plus permanent lighting to safely perform the tasks for which access is requisite.

**1105.5 Protection from Mechanical Damage.** A refrigerating system or portion thereof cannot be located in an elevator shaft, a dumbwaiter shaft or any shaft having moving objects therein, or in any location where it might be subject to mechanical damage.

**1105.6 Electrical.** Electrically energized components shall comply with the Electrical Code.

**1105.7 Ventilation of Rooms Containing Condensing Units.** A room or space, other than a refrigeration machinery room complying with the requirements of this chapter, in which a refrigerant-containing portion of a condensing unit is located must be provided with ventilation by one of the following means:

1. Permanent gravity openings with not less than 2 square feet (0.19 m²) net free area opening directly to the outside of the building or extending to the outside of the building by continuous ducts.

2. A mechanical exhaust system providing a complete air change to the space at least every 20 minutes, discharging to the outside of the building.

**EXCEPTIONS:** 1. This requirement does not apply to a space exceeding 1,000 cubic feet per horsepower (8.05 m³/kW) of the unit.

2. To spaces with permanent gravity ventilation openings of at least 2 square feet (0.19 m²) connecting to other rooms or spaces exceeding 1,000 cubic feet per horsepower (8.05 m³/kW) of the unit.

**1105.8 Prohibited Locations.** Refrigerant compressors of more than 5 horsepower rating must be located at least 10 feet (3048 mm) from any exit in any Group A, B, Division 2, E, I, or R, Division 1 Occupancy, unless separated by a one-hour fire-resistive occupancy separation.

**1105.9 Condensation Control.** Refrigerant machinery piping and brine or coolant piping and fittings that could reach a surface temperature below the dew point of the surrounding air during normal operation, and are located in spaces or areas where condensate could cause a hazard to the building occupants, structure, electrical or other equipment must be protected to prevent such damage. The most common protection is thermal insulation overwrapped with a vapor-retardant barrier material.

**1105.10 Condensate.** In locations where the temperature can drop below freezing, heat tracing or insulation of drains may be required.

**1105.12 Overflows.** The 1997 text and Formula 11-1 specify the details for calculating condensate flows. When the cooling coil or air-conditioning unit is installed in an attic or a furred space where damage may result from con-

*(Continued on page 143)*

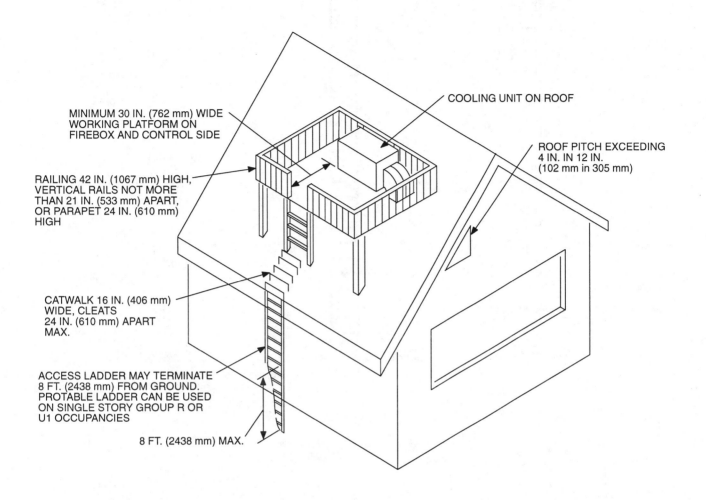

MINIMUM 30 IN. (762 mm) WIDE
WORKING PLATFORM ON
FIREBOX AND CONTROL SIDE

COOLING UNIT ON ROOF

ROOF PITCH EXCEEDING
4 IN. IN 12 IN.
(102 mm in 305 mm)

RAILING 42 IN. (1067 mm) HIGH,
VERTICAL RAILS NOT MORE
THAN 21 IN. (533 mm) APART,
OR PARAPET 24 IN. (610 mm)
HIGH

CATWALK 16 IN. (406 mm)
WIDE, CLEATS
24 IN. (610 mm) APART
MAX.

ACCESS LADDER MAY TERMINATE
8 FT. (2438 mm) FROM GROUND.
PROTABLE LADDER CAN BE USED
ON SINGLE STORY GROUP R OR
U1 OCCUPANCIES

8 FT. (2438 mm) MAX.

**TYPICAL COOLING EQUIPMENT ON ROOF OR EXTERIOR WALLS**

**FIGURE 11-9**

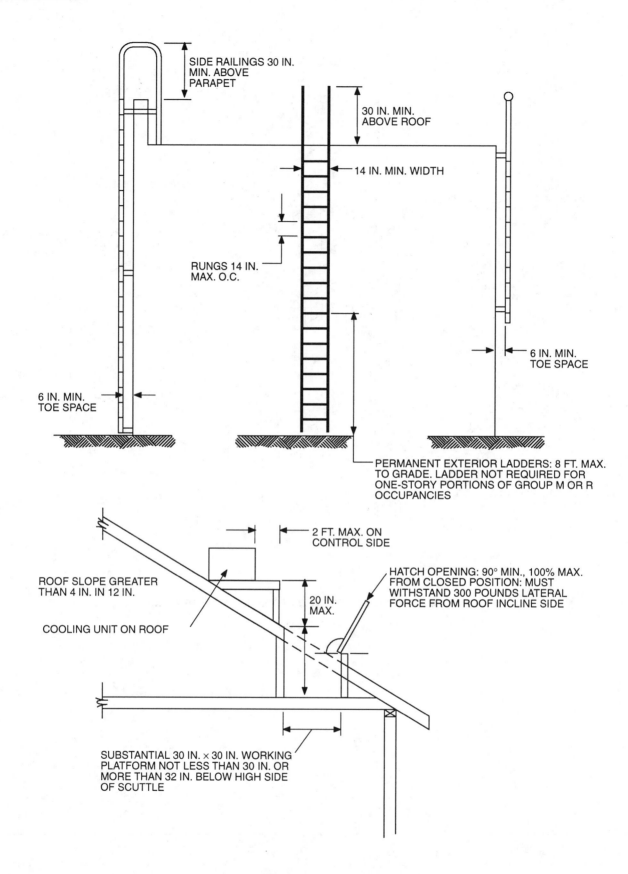

SIDE RAILINGS 30 IN. MIN. ABOVE PARAPET

30 IN. MIN. ABOVE ROOF

14 IN. MIN. WIDTH

RUNGS 14 IN. MAX. O.C.

6 IN. MIN. TOE SPACE

6 IN. MIN. TOE SPACE

PERMANENT EXTERIOR LADDERS: 8 FT. MAX. TO GRADE. LADDER NOT REQUIRED FOR ONE-STORY PORTIONS OF GROUP M OR R OCCUPANCIES

2 FT. MAX. ON CONTROL SIDE

ROOF SLOPE GREATER THAN 4 IN. IN 12 IN.

COOLING UNIT ON ROOF

20 IN. MAX.

HATCH OPENING: 90° MIN., 100% MAX. FROM CLOSED POSITION: MUST WITHSTAND 300 POUNDS LATERAL FORCE FROM ROOF INCLINE SIDE

SUBSTANTIAL 30 IN. × 30 IN. WORKING PLATFORM NOT LESS THAN 30 IN. OR MORE THAN 32 IN. BELOW HIGH SIDE OF SCUTTLE

**ACCESS TO ROOF-MOUNTED UNITS**

**FIGURE 11-10**

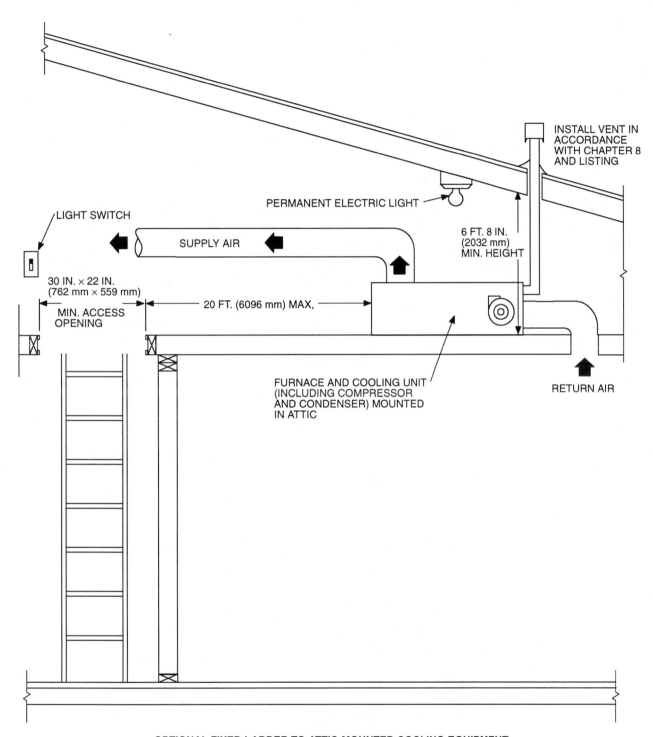

**OPTIONAL FIXED LADDER TO ATTIC-MOUNTED COOLING EQUIPMENT**

**FIGURE 11-11**

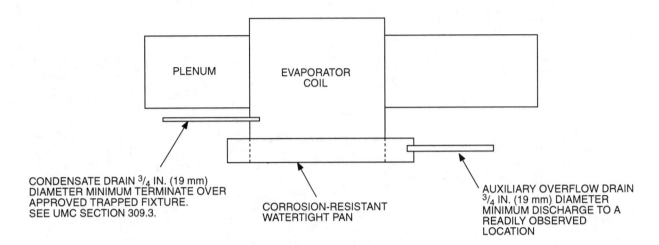

CONDENSATE DRAIN $^3/_4$ IN. (19 mm) DIAMETER MINIMUM TERMINATE OVER APPROVED TRAPPED FIXTURE. SEE UMC SECTION 309.3.

CORROSION-RESISTANT WATERTIGHT PAN

AUXILIARY OVERFLOW DRAIN $^3/_4$ IN. (19 mm) DIAMETER MINIMUM DISCHARGE TO A READILY OBSERVED LOCATION

**TYPICAL ATTIC INSTALLATION OF COOLING COILS LOCATED IN AN ATTIC OR FURRED SPACE**
**(Section 309.3 and Table 11-E)**

**FIGURE 11-12**

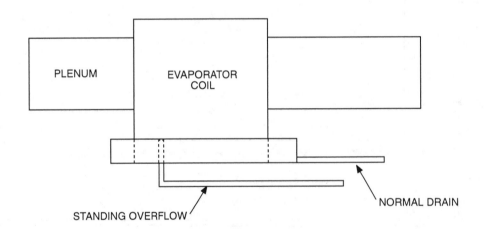

STANDING OVERFLOW

NORMAL DRAIN

**FIGURE 11-13**
**(Section 1105.12)**

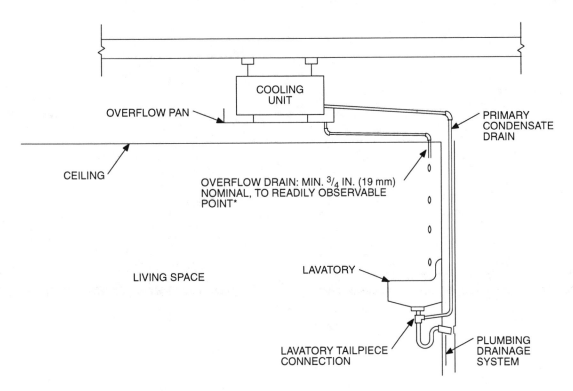

OVERFLOW PAN

COOLING
UNIT

PRIMARY
CONDENSATE
DRAIN

CEILING

OVERFLOW DRAIN: MIN. 3/4 IN. (19 mm)
NOMINAL, TO READILY OBSERVABLE
POINT*

LIVING SPACE

LAVATORY

LAVATORY TAILPIECE
CONNECTION

PLUMBING
DRAINAGE
SYSTEM

*NOTE: The overflow drain is most often taken to the exterior of the building, over a
doorway where any discharge will be noticed before damage is done to the attic or
ceiling below. Section 1105.12

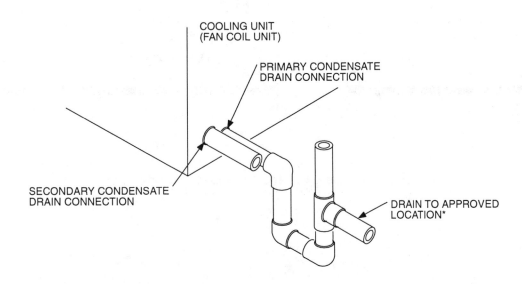

COOLING UNIT
(FAN COIL UNIT)

PRIMARY CONDENSATE
DRAIN CONNECTION

SECONDARY CONDENSATE
DRAIN CONNECTION

DRAIN TO APPROVED
LOCATION*

*NOTE: Trap shown here is to prevent cabinet pressure loss; install when required
by unit listing or instructions.

**PRIMARY AND SECONDARY CONDENSATE DRAINS**
**(By cross reference to Sections 1105.10 and 1105.12)**

**FIGURE 11-14**

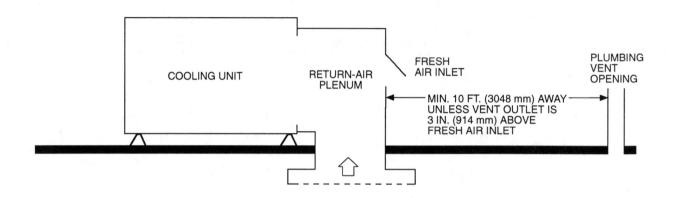

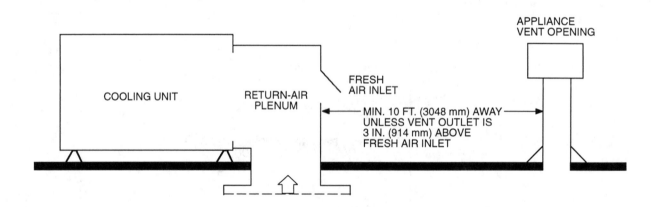

**TYPICAL OUTSIDE AIR INLET CLEARANCES—SECTION 1105.1
AND BY REFERENCE SECTION 403.2**

**FIGURE 11-15**

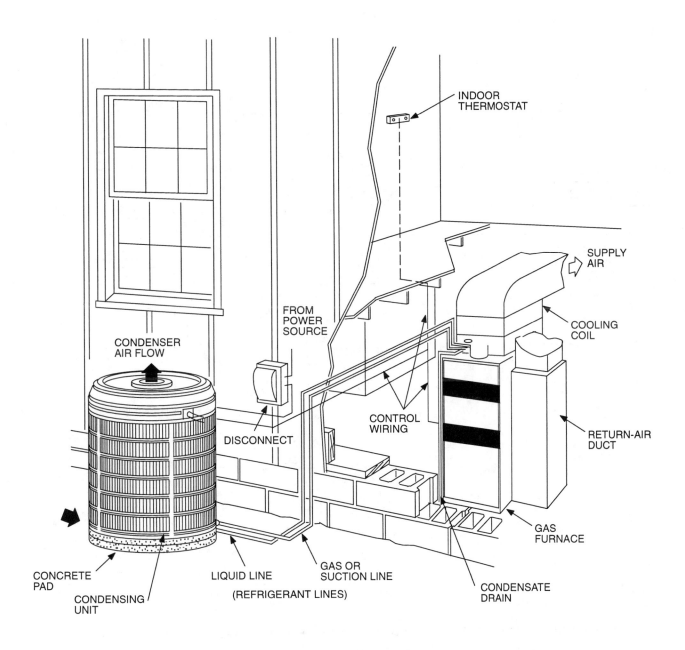

**TYPICAL "SPLIT SYSTEM" AIR-CONDITIONING SYSTEM: UPRIGHT GAS FURNACE WITH INTEGRAL COOLING COIL; CONDENSING UNIT ON EXTERIOR OF BUILDING**

**FIGURE 11-16**

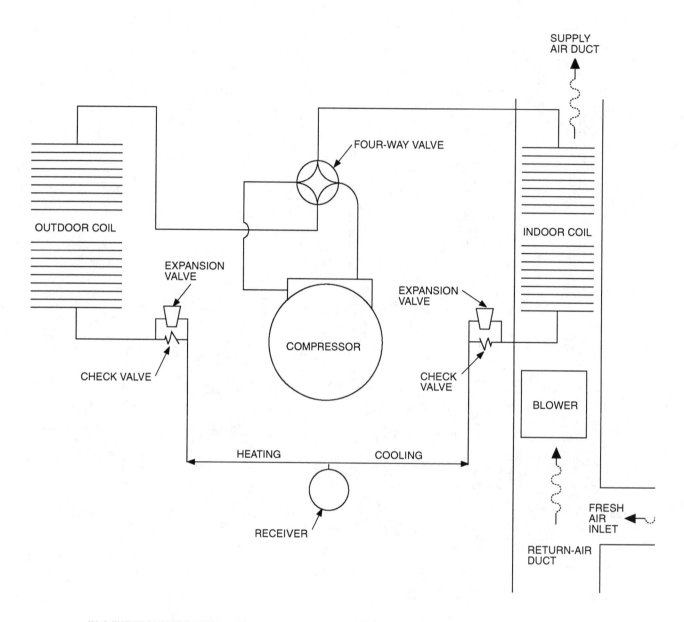

SUPPLY
AIR DUCT

FOUR-WAY VALVE

OUTDOOR COIL

INDOOR COIL

EXPANSION
VALVE

EXPANSION
VALVE

COMPRESSOR

CHECK VALVE

CHECK
VALVE

BLOWER

HEATING

COOLING

FRESH
AIR
INLET

RECEIVER

RETURN-AIR
DUCT

**IN A "HEAT PUMP" SYSTEM, REFRIGERANT FLOW IS REVERSED BY MEANS OF A FOUR-WAY VALVE**

**FIGURE 11-17**

*(Continued from page 134)*

densate overflow, a watertight pan of corrosion-resistant metal must be installed beneath the cooling coil or unit to catch the overflow condensate that might result from a clogged condensate drain, or one pan with standing overflow and a separate drain may be provided in lieu of the second drain pan. The additional pan or standing overflow must be provided with a drain pipe $^3/_4$-inch (19 mm) nominal pipe size, discharging at a point which can be readily observed. Additional requirements for condensate piping are detailed in Section 310. Disposal of condensate wastes and the point of discharge of the condensate wastes are covered by the Plumbing Code.

Some manufacturers have provided built-in secondary condensate drains within the equipment. In this case, the secondary drain pan required by this section may be omitted.

The requirement for an overflow drain depends on the determination by the jurisdiction that damage may result from overflow of condensate. Although the code is not specific as to what constitutes damage, it is commonly agreed on that wetting and drying of wood structural members and gypsum board are regarded as justification for requiring a redundant drain system. However, damage to ceiling tiles would not require this precaution, unless there is a possibility of damage to computer equipment or other types of electrical equipment that may be located below the tiles. In general, condensate draining onto a concrete floor is not regarded as causing damage.

It should be noted that for the same reason that UBC Section 1506.3 prohibits roof drains and overflow drains from being connected within the building, tying the overflow drain to the primary drain should not be allowed, and the drain and overflow should drain separately to approved locations.

The overflow drain should discharge to a point which can be readily observed. The following locations may be accepted: over a window or door; over a bathtub, shower or wash basin; or to floor sink or floor drain.

## SECTION 1106 — REFRIGERATION MACHINERY ROOMS

**1106.1 When Required.** Refrigeration machinery rooms serve to contain accidental releases of refrigerant vapors which could endanger the life safety or health of occupants. Refrigerant vapors are generally denser than air and tend to displace the oxygen in the air from the floor upward. Whether the vapors are toxic or not, their release can cause asphyxiation. Thus, if the quantity that could be accidentally released per 1,000 cubic feet (28.3 m³) of occupied space exceeds the quantity permitted by Table 11-A, a machinery room such as illustrated in Figure 11-18 is required as a life-safety measure.

**Item 4.** A system containing any quantity of A2, B1 or B2 refrigerants requires enclosure in a refrigeration machinery room. Readers should note that Table 11-A does not include any A2 refrigerants, although ANSI/ASHRAE Standard 34 does include at least two so categorized.

**1106.1.1 Equipment in refrigeration machinery rooms.** Refrigeration machinery rooms must house all refrigerant-containing portions of the system other than the piping and evaporators permitted in refrigerated process and storage areas; pressure-relief devices, Section 1116; discharge piping from pressure-relief devices, Section 1117; and cooling towers regulated under Section 1125.

**1106.4 Refrigerant-vapor Alarms.** The F mark in the margin indicates that the provisions are to be maintained under the IFCI code change procedures; otherwise, the provision is similar to the requirement in the 1994 UMC. Refrigeration machinery rooms must be equipped with refrigerant vapor detectors located in an area where the vapors from a leak are likely to collect. Notice in Table 11-A, Column 9 contains the specific gravity of the vapors with respect to air. With the exception of ammonia, listed refrigerant vapors are more dense than air, and hence, would tend to collect at the low point of the machinery room floor. This characteristic indicates that the point of sampling for detection should be at or just above floor level. It also indicates that as vapors escape, exposed personnel may soon find themselves immersed in a sea of vapor. The section also specifies the concentration at which alarms shall activate. Note that alarms are required to provide both audible and visual alarms.

**1106.5 Separation.** Machinery rooms are required to be separated from other portions of the building and sealed to inhibit the passage of refrigerant vapors.

**1106.6 Combustion Air and Return Air.** Machinery rooms may not be used as a source of combustion air or return air. This requirement prohibits inclusion of boilers or other fuel-burning appliances in a machinery room, a restriction contained in earlier editions of the UMC but frequently overlooked. The conversion of refrigerating equipment to the new refrigerants is likely to create questions and resistance by owners when it is discovered that Section 104 is construed to require separation between refrigeration machinery rooms and boilers and other fuel-burning appliances.

**1106.7 Special Requirements.** The provisions of the section were amended in the 1997 edition by the addition of Exception 3, which is highly debatable as providing equivalent life safety. The decision was based instead on financial hardship to owners of nonconforming installations.

## SECTION 1107 — REFRIGERATION MACHINERY ROOM VENTILATION

In Sections 1107.5, 1107.6 and 1107.7, the descending F margin indicates that the provisions are to be maintained under the IFCI code change procedures; otherwise, the provision is similar to the requirement in the 1994 UMC. The section was extensively revised in the 1994 edition primarily by requiring a mechanical ventilation system whereas the 1991 edition permitted an alternate gravity ventilation system. The criteria for routine ventilation is 0.5 cfm (152 L/s•m²) per gross square foot (m²) of ma-

*(Continued on page 145)*

NO OPEN FLAMES OR DEVICES HAVING SURFACE TEMPERATURE EXCEEDING 800°F (427°C) EXCEPT ROOM USED EXCLUSIVELY FOR DIRECT-FIRED ABSORPTION EQUIPMENT. SECTION 1106.7

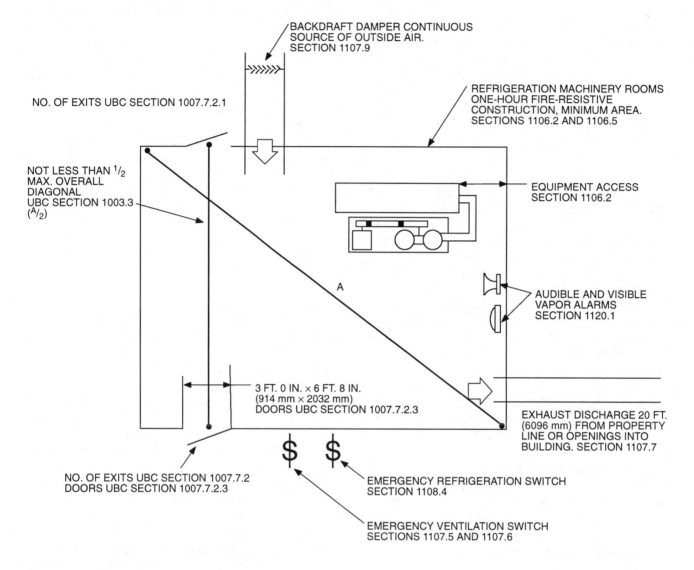

NO DIRECT OPENING TO ANY AREA HAVING OPEN FLAME SPARK PRODUCER OR SURFACE OVER 800°F (427°C) SECTION 1106

REFRIGERATION MACHINERY ROOM REQUIRED WHEN
(1) QUANTITY OF REFRIGERANT EXCEEDS TABLE 11-A AMOUNT
(2) GROUP A1 SYSTEM HAS AGGREGATE COMPRESSOR HORSEPOWER EXCEEDING 100 HP
(3) GROUP A2, B1 OR B2 REFRIGERANTS ARE EMPLOYED
(4) DIRECT-FIRED ABSORPTION UNITS OTHER THAN THOSE EMPLOYING LITHIUM BROMIDE WITH WATER AS THE REFRIGERANT

EXCEPTION:
    MACHINERY ROOM NOT REQUIRED IN REFRIGERATED PROCESSING OR STORAGE SPACES. SECTION 1104.3

NUMBER OF EXITS: ROOMS EXCEEDING 1,000 SQUARE FEET REQUIRE TWO EXITS. UBC SECTION 1007.7.2.

**REFRIGERATION MACHINERY ROOMS**
(Reference UMC Section 1106)

**FIGURE 11-18**

*(Continued from page 143)*

chinery room area to remove heat rejected into the room atmosphere. The ventilation system must further limit the internal temperature of the machinery room to 104°F (40°C) and also provide an emergency purge of escaping refrigerant having a capacity of

$$Q = 100\sqrt{G}$$
$$\text{For } \mathbf{SI} : Q = 70\sqrt{G}$$

**WHERE:**

*G* is the refrigerant mass in the largest system in pounds (kg) and *Q* is the airflow rate in cfm (L/s).

The emergency purging system is required to be both automatically and manually controlled. The ventilation system requires one or more makeup-air inlets opening directly to the exterior.

## SECTION 1108 — REFRIGERATION MACHINERY ROOM EQUIPMENT AND CONTROLS

**1108.1 General.** Equipment, ducts, piping, vents and devices which are essential to refrigeration processes may be placed in the machinery room. Other piping, ducts, plenums, wiring and equipment unrelated to the refrigeration processes should not traverse or pass through a machinery room.

Equipment essential to refrigeration processes often include, but are not necessarily limited to, the following:

1. Refrigeration compressors.

2. Condensing units.

3. Pumps, associated piping and automatic control valves for refrigerant, condenser water, and brine or chilled water.

4. Refrigeration control devices and panels.

5. Machinery room ventilation equipment (see Section 1107).

6. Cooling towers or portions thereof (see Part II of this chapter).

7. Refrigerant receivers and accumulators.

8. Refrigerant vapor-detection and alarm systems (see Section 1106).

9. Machinery room fire sprinkler system exclusive of its shutoff valves.

10. Machinery room lighting and service receptacles.

11. Motor control centers and electrical panels for machinery room systems.

**1108.2 Electrical.** Refrigeration machinery rooms are not classified as hazardous locations except that fans employed for the emergency purge of A2 and B2 refrigerants must meet the requirements of a Class 1, Division 1 hazardous location as specified by the Electrical Code.

**1108.3 Storage.** Storage of materials in a refrigeration machinery room is regulated by the Fire Code.

**1108.4 Emergency Control.** A readily accessible identified single-emergency refrigeration control switch of the break-glass type must be provided to shut off all electrically energized equipment in a machinery room except the mechanical exhaust ventilation system. This switch must be located at a point outside of the required opening to the machinery room and be labeled "Emergency Refrigeration Switch" in letters at least $1^{1}/_{4}$ inches high (32 mm) complying with UMC Standard 11-2. In addition to the manual emergency shutoff, an automatically activated emergency shutoff is required when the concentration of refrigerant vapor in the machinery room exceeds 25 percent of the lower flammable limit.

## SECTION 1109 — REFRIGERANT PIPING, CONTAINERS AND VALVES

All materials used in the construction and installation of refrigerating systems must be suitable for the refrigerant, refrigerant oil or brine in the system, and materials or equipment must be compatible.

Copper and brass piping, fittings, containers, valves and related parts must be approved for such use. (See *Refrigeration Piping* in the list of reference standards in Chapter 16.

Systems installed with iron and steel refrigerant piping must be approved. Piping more than 2-inch (51 mm) iron pipe size must be electric-resistance-welded or seamless pipe.

Brass pipe, copper pipe and copper tubing must be approved.

## SECTION 1110 — ERECTION OF REFRIGERANT PIPING

Piping and tubing must be installed so as to prevent extensive vibration and strains at joints and connections.

All piping and tubing is required to be securely fastened to a permanent support within 6 feet (1829 mm) following the first bend from the compressor and within 2 feet (610 mm) of every other bend or angle. Piping and tubing must be supported at points not more than 15 feet (4572 mm) apart.

Refrigerant piping and tubing must be installed so that it is not subject to damage from an external source.

Refrigerant piping and joints connected and installed in the field must be exposed for visual inspection and accepted by the building official before being covered or enclosed. This requirement does not apply to soft annealed copper tubing enclosed in a rigid piping, conduit, molding or raceway when no fittings or joints are concealed within.

Iron or steel refrigerant piping placed underground must be protected with an approved coating to inhibit corrosion.

Iron or steel pipe joints are required to be threaded, flanged or welded. Threaded joints must be of an approved type (see *Pipe Threads* in Recognized Standards in Chapter 16, Part III, of the UMC). Exposed threads must be tinned or otherwise coated to inhibit corrosion.

Welds must be of an approved type (see *Refrigeration Piping* in Recognized Standards in Chapter 16, Part III, of the UMC).

Copper or brass pipe of iron pipe size must be threaded, flanged or brazed.

Tubing joints and connections must be flared, lapped or swaged and brazed.

## SECTION 1111 — REFRIGERANT CONTROL VALVES

**1111.1  Location.** Stop valves are required in refrigerant piping to facilitate removal and repair of refrigeration machinery with minor or no loss of the refrigeration. A new UMC Standard 11-2 provides for identification of piping and valves.

**1111.2  Support.** When the valves are installed in refrigerant lines of copper tubing $^3/_4$ inch (19 mm) or less in outside diameter, they must be securely supported independently of the tubing or piping.

**1111.3  Access.** Stop valves must be readily accessible.

**1111.4  Identification.** A valve chart protected behind glass must be installed near the principal entrance to the machinery room.

## SECTION 1112 — PRESSURE-LIMITING DEVICES

**1112.1  When Required.** A pressure-limiting device is required to be installed on systems operating above atmospheric pressure.

> **EXCEPTION:** Listed systems having a charge mass less than 22 pounds (10 kg) contained in a factory-sealed enclosure.

**1112.3  Connection.** Stop or shutoff valves are not to be placed between any pressure-limiting device and the compressor it serves.

## SECTION 1113 — PRESSURE-RELIEF DEVICES

Positive-displacement-type compressors must be equipped with a pressure-relief valve by the manufacturer.

Pressure-relief valves must be connected to the refrigerant discharge side of the compressor it serves, between such compressor and any stop valve.

Pressure-relief valves may, on other than positive displacement compressors, discharge into the low-pressure side of the refrigeration system it serves or discharge to the outside of the building. A pressure-relief device that discharges from the high-pressure side of the refrigerating system into the low-pressure side must be of a type that is not appreciably affected by back pressure.

Stop or shut-off valves must not be installed between a pressure-relief valve and the compressor it serves.

A required pressure-relief valve terminating outdoors must discharge at least 15 feet (4572 mm) above adjoining ground and 20 feet (6096 mm) from any window, ventilation opening or exit from a building.

A pressure vessel more than 6 inches (152 mm) in diameter which may be shut off by valves from other parts of the system must be equipped with a pressure-relief device or devices.

## SECTION 1114 — PRESSURE-RELIEF DEVICE SETTINGS

**1114.1  Pressure-relief Valve Setting.** Except as provided for in this section, pressure-relief devices must be set to function at a pressure not exceeding the design pressure for the portion of the system to which it is connected and for the type of refrigerant in the container.

**1114.2  Rupture Member Setting.** Rupture members used in series with or in lieu of a relief valve must protect at a pressure not exceeding design pressure.

## SECTION 1116 — OVER-PRESSURE PROTECTION

**1116.5  Discharge Capacity.** The minimum required rated discharge capacity of the relief device or fusible plug for a refrigerant-containing vessel must be determined by the following:

$$C = f \times D \times L$$

**WHERE:**

$C$ = Minimum required air discharge capacity of the relief device in psi (kPa).

$D$ = Outside diameter of the vessel in feet (millimeters).

$L$ = Outside length of the vessel in feet (millimeters).

$f$ = Factor depending on kind of refrigerant as follows:

| Kind of Refrigerant | Value of $f$ |
| --- | --- |
| Ammonia | 0.5 |
| R-12, R-22 and R-500 | 1.6 |
| R-502 | 2.2 |
| All other refrigerants | 1.0 |

Figure 11-19 illustrates the location of pressure-relief devices in a refrigeration system.

## SECTION 1117 — DISCHARGE PIPING

The discharge pipe from a pressure-relief device must not be smaller than the outlet of the valve it serves. Discharge pipes from more than one device may be run to a common header provided its area is not less than the sum of the areas of the discharge pipes served. When discharge piping exceeds 50 feet (15 240 mm) in length, it must be increased one pipe size.

## SECTION 1118 — SPECIAL DISCHARGE REQUIREMENTS

**1118.2 Design Requirements.** The F mark in the margin indicates that the provisions are to be maintained under the IFCI code change procedures; otherwise, the provision is similar to the requirement in the 1994 UMC.

*(Continued on page 148)*

EXAMPLE OF SYSTEM OPERATING ABOVE ATMOSPHERIC PRESSURE (SEE **NOTE 3**)

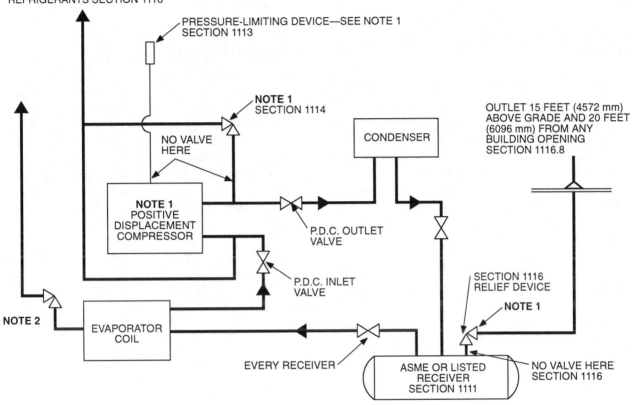

**SYMBOLS & ABBREVIATIONS:**

—PRESSURE RELIEF DEVICE

—STOP VALVE

P.D.C.  —POSITIVE DISPLACEMENT COMPRESSOR

ASME  —AMERICAN SOCIETY OF MECHANICAL ENGINEERS

**NOTE 1:** PDC must be provided with pressure-relief device by manufacturer.

**NOTE 2:** Evaporators within 18 inches (457 mm) of heating elements or coils must have a pressure-relief device.

**NOTE 3:** Pressure-limiting device required on systems operating above atmospheric pressure.

**FIGURE 11-19**

## SECTION 1119 — AMMONIA DISCHARGE

The F mark in the margin indicates that the provisions are to be maintained under the IFCI code change procedures; otherwise, the provision is similar to the requirement in the 1994 UMC.

## SECTION 1120 — DETECTION AND ALARM SYSTEMS

The F in the margin indicates that the provisions are to be maintained under the IFCI code change procedures; otherwise, the provision is similar to the requirement in the 1994 UMC.

## SECTION 1121 — EQUIPMENT IDENTIFICATION

In addition to labels already required elsewhere, condensers, receivers, absorbers, accumulators and similar pieces of equipment of more than 3 cubic feet (85 L) in gross volume must be equipped with a permanent label listing the type of refrigerant in the vessel.

Figure 11-20 illustrates typical refrigeration labeling. UMC Standard 11-2 contains identification requirements for systems and components. Legends must be sized as required for 6-inch (152 mm) pipe, that is, in $1\frac{1}{4}$-inch-high (32 mm) letters.

The main emergency control switch as required by Section 1108 must have a permanent label reading "Emergency Refrigeration Switch."

Exhaust ventilation systems required by Section 1107 must have a permanent label reading "Emergency Ventilation Switch."

In refrigeration machinery rooms, and for every direct refrigerating system of more than 10 horsepower (35 kW), there must be a permanent sign within 10 feet (3048 mm) of the compressor giving the following information:

1. Name of the contractor installing the equipment.

2. Kind of refrigerant in the system.

3. Amount of refrigerant in the system.

Required pressure-relief devices must be labeled to comply with Section 1115.1.

## SECTION 1122 — TESTING OF REFRIGERATION EQUIPMENT

**1122.1 Factory Tests.** Factory-assembled refrigerant-containing parts of units must be tested by the manufacturer at the design pressures for the high and low sides, except that units with a design pressure of 15 psi (103 kPa) or less must be tested at 1.33 times the design pressure.

**1122.2 Field Tests.** Refrigerant-containing portions of a field-assembled refrigerating system which is intended to operate at a pressure in excess of atmospheric pressure must be tested at a pressure not less than the pressure shown in Table 11-D for the kind of refrigerant in that system.

The test pressure must be at least equal to the lowest of the pressure in Table 11-D or the setting of the pressure-relief devices installed in the high and low sides of the systems, respectively.

*(Continued on page 150)*

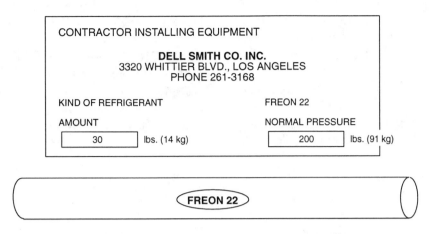

CONTRACTOR INSTALLING EQUIPMENT

**DELL SMITH CO. INC.**
3320 WHITTIER BLVD., LOS ANGELES
PHONE 261-3168

KIND OF REFRIGERANT                  FREON 22

AMOUNT                               NORMAL PRESSURE

30        lbs. (14 kg)               200        lbs. (91 kg)

FREON 22

ONE LABEL REQUIRED ON EACH 30 FEET (9144 mm) OF PIPING

## MAIN-DISCONNECT

# EMERGENCY-REFRIGERATION SWITCH

**EMERGENCY-REFRIGERATION SWITCH**

**FIGURE 11-20**

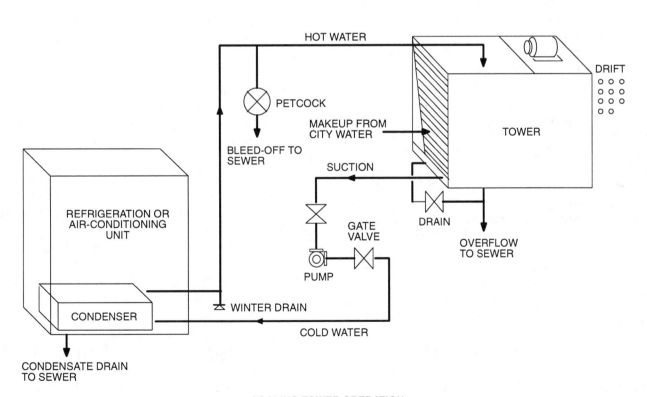

**COOLING TOWER OPERATION**

**FIGURE 11-21**

These test requirements do not apply to:

1. Safety devices, pressure gages, compressors and control mechanisms which have been factory tested.

2. Pressure vessels constructed in accordance with approved standards.

The Fire Code contains additional tests of emergency devices and systems.

**1122.3  Test Medium.** Refrigerating systems must not be tested with oxygen, flammable or combustible gases or gas mixtures.

**1122.5  Brine Systems.** Brine-piping systems must be tested at a pressure 1.5 times the design pressure.

## SECTION 1124 — STORAGE OF REFRIGERANTS AND REFRIGERANT OILS

Refrigerants and refrigerant oils not charged into a refrigeration system are stored in accordance with the requirements of the Fire Code.

## Part II—Cooling Towers

## SECTION 1125 — COOLING TOWERS, EVAPORATIVE CONDENSERS AND FLUID COOLERS

**1125.1  General.** Cooling towers are devices used to cool water which flows through a refrigerant condenser. Heat from the circulating water is transferred to the air by the evaporation of a portion of the circulating water. Water-cooled condensers are commonly used with large air-conditioning systems and certain commercial and industrial processes. See Figure 11-21.

Cooling towers are often constructed of a metal fiberglass reinforced plastic or wood structure with a waterproof sump at the bottom and water-spray nozzles at the top. Heat from the water is transferred to the air by evaporation as the water either flows or falls over the louvers or slats, which are made of wood, metal or plastics.

As drops of water fall or flow from the top of the tower to the sump at the bottom, some water evaporates. Latent heat is extracted from the water, causing a further cooling effect, reducing the temperature of the water. A water supply and float valve are usually located in the sump to replace the water lost due to wind, evaporation and other causes. Water is pumped from the bottom of the sump through a heat exchanger and recirculated to the top of the cooling tower.

Evaporative condensers perform essentially the same function as a cooling tower in a single piece of equipment; that is, they extract heat from compressed refrigerant gases by transferring the heat energy to water vapor which is then ejected to the atmosphere, usually by a fan. Cooling hot refrigerant gases facilitates a phase change in the refrigerant from a vapor to a liquid.

Water treatment is often required in cooling towers to reduce scale deposits in the circulating system. Care must be taken to avoid backflow from a cooling tower into a potable water system because water in cooling towers is often treated with chemicals.

When located on a roof, cooling towers must comply with the requirements for roof structures as specified in the Building Code.

**1125.4  Drainage.** Cooling towers and evaporative condensers which are equipped with positive water discharge to prevent excessive alkalinity build-up and used for water-cooled condensing units or absorption units should discharge their waste water into an approved disposal system. "Approved" means a system or location acceptable to the jurisdiction. The inspector should verify that the waste water is not excessively alkaline or laden with corrosive chemicals if the sanitary drain system is used as the point of disposal. It is most important that cross-connection control practices be rigorously enforced on cooling towers. Algaecides and corrosion-inhibiting chemicals used in cooling towers can be very toxic. Therefore, makeup water and other connections of potable water to the cooling tower should be closely checked for required air gaps or other suitable approved backflow-prevention devices.

**1125.5  Chemical Treatment Systems.** If chemicals which present a contact hazard to personnel are utilized, emergency eye-wash and shower facilities must be provided at the site.

**1125.6  Location.** Discharge plumes from cooling towers, evaporative condensers and fluid coolers must be maintained at least 5 feet (1524 mm) above or 20 feet (6096 mm) laterally from ventilation air inlet into buildings.

**1125.7  Electrical.** Fans must be provided with vibration detector switches to shut down out-of-balance wheels. Lightning protection is required for roof-top-mounted equipment.

**1125.8  Refrigerants and Hazadous Fluids.** Equipment containing refrigerants in a closed-cycle system must be installed as required in Part I of the chapter. Other combustible, flammable or hazardous fluids must comply with the Fire Code.

**Table 11-A.** The line entry for R-123 raises the permissible exposure limit from 10 ppm to 30 ppm based on Dupont data and supported by ANSI/ASHRAE Standard 34.

The line entry for R-500 reduces the permissible pounds from 16 to 12 based on ANSI/ASHRAE Standard 34.

The line entry for R-744 reduces the PEL from 10,000 to 5,000 based on ANSI/ASHRAE Standard 34.

**Table 11-E.** The size of condensate drains may be for one unit or a combination of units, or as recommended by the manufacturer. Drain capacity is based on slope of 1 unit vertical in 96 units horizontal (1% slope), with drains running three-quarters full:

| Outside Air—20 Percent | | Room Air—80 Percent | |
|---|---|---|---|
| DB | WB | DB | WB |
| 90°F | 73°F | 75°F | 62.5°F |
| (32.2°C) | (23.7°C) | (23.8°C) | (16.9°C) |

Condensate drain sizing for other slopes or other conditions shall be approved by the building official.

# Chapter 12
# HYDRONICS

Chapter 12's contents were moved from Appendix B by Code Change M6-95-1. This chapter has been one of the most widely neglected chapters in the UMC. The last code change to this chapter occurred when polybutylene piping material, in Standard Dimension Ratio 11 (SDR-11) 1985, was added for use in hot water panel heating applications where the pressure is less than 100 psi at (689 kPa) 180°F (82°C) or less than 80 psi (552 kPa) at 200°F (93°C). No other significant changes have been proposed in the intervening twelve years.

# Chapter 13
# FUEL-GAS PIPING

## SECTION 1301 — GENERAL

This chapter governs the installation of fuel-gas piping in or in connection with a building or within the property lines of a parcel of real estate. It does not apply to service piping as defined in Section 221. Service piping is that portion of the fuel-gas piping between the street gas main and the building gas piping system inlet and is installed by and is under the control of the serving gas utility. Usually this means the fuel-gas piping between the street main and the gas meter outlet.

## SECTION 1302 — PERMIT

This section requires that owners comply with Chapter 1, Administration, and specifically Section 112 by submitting plans, obtaining at minimum, a rough piping inspection and a final piping inspection. Usually when the final inspection reveals that the piping system complies, the building official authorizes fuel gas to be served to the premises.

## SECTION 1307 — AUTHORITY TO RENDER GAS SERVICE

The serving gas supplier is often a public utility duly franchised to distribute fuel gas in a certain area. A few suppliers are municipally owned, but the most common arrangement is for a privately owned company to provide fuel-gas services within a jurisdiction. Such companies are franchised (usually by the state) and are not code enforcement agencies. The utilities operate under rules (a charter) approved by the state public utilities commission. As with building departments, one of their principal concerns is fire and public safety. Where the first connection (turn on) is made, all unused openings in the piping system must be capped or plugged with threaded fittings to prevent escape of the fuel gas. Occasionally, an inexpert house owner will attempt to plug an opening with a cork, rubber stopper or a wooden plug. Such makeshift arrangements should always be corrected prior to approval of the system.

## SECTION 1308 — AUTHORITY TO DISCONNECT

Because of the fire- and life-safety hazards inherent in noncompliant gas appliances or piping, either the serving gas supplier of the building official is authorized to disconnect a defective fuel-gas installation. Again, it is emphasized that a serving fuel-gas supplier is acting to enforce the corporate rules, not the fuel gas code. Only the building official is authorized to enforce the fuel gas code in a specific jurisdiction. It often happens that a duly franchised utility will attempt to minimize the stigma of enforcing their rules by telling the customer "it's the code."

All unsafe fuel-gas distribution systems should be tagged to show by whom and why a system was disconnected.

## SECTION 1311 — MATERIAL FOR GAS PIPING

The UMC recognizes the use of corrugated stainless steel tubing (CSST) complying with ANSI/AGA LC1 in interior applications. Such CSST should not be buried or used in exterior applications. Each listed system is proprietary, so the building official should obtain the manufacturer's installation instructions for the specific system to be employed. However, since all proprietary systems provide an adapter fitting for joining with threaded steel pipe, it becomes possible to interconnect various proprietary systems by the use of a steel pipe nipple. The practice is not recommended, but it is well to recognize that it may be done.

## SECTION 1312 — INSTALLATION OF GAS PIPING

**1312.1 Joints.** The reference to the definition of a pipeline welder in Section 218 has been replaced by a reference to an approved qualified welder as defined in Section 203 in the first errata.

**1312.3 Piping through Foundation Walls.** This section was added to the 1997 edition to provide protection of gas piping penetrating foundation walls.

**1312.4 Aboveground Piping Outside.** This section was amended to recognize exterior fuel-gas piping that requires protection from damage.

**1312.7 Electrical Isolation of Fuel Gas Piping.** Code change M1313-951 adds a requirement for electrical isolation of underground gas piping from the house piping system. The isolation fitting is to prevent stray electrical currents on the underground system from affecting house piping. The listed isolation fitting required is unavailable, so local approval of the fitting will be required. Although the proponent testified that the requirement comes from the *National Fuel Gas Code* (NFGC), a reference search of the NFGC failed to identify the source of the requirement in the *National Fuel Gas Code*, NFPA 54/ANSI Z223.

## SECTION 1313 — APPLIANCE FUEL CONNECTORS

This section requires that fuel gas connectors shall have a diameter not less than the inlet connection to the appliance by rigid pipe as specified in Section 1311.1. This is followed by a series of eight exceptions. Exception 4 provides connector sizing criteria based on Table 13-B-1 or 13-B-2 as applicable. Table 13-B-2 is for use with listed metal appliance (fuel gas) connectors where the gas pressure is less than 8-inch water column (1990 Pa); Figure 13-1 shows the size-making code utilized by AGA. Figure 13-2 illustrates the difference between a flexible and a semirigid fuel gas connector.

Exception 2 was modified by adding the words "or casing" after "appliance housing" to clarify that only rigid steel pipe may pass through an appliance casing. The rationale was that vibration of the appliance casing could produce chafing of a soft metallic fuel gas connector eventually leading to leaks in the connector.

## SECTION 1320 — FUEL-GAS EQUIPMENT AND INSTALLATIONS IN MANUFACTURED OR MOBILE HOME OR RECREATIONAL VEHICLE PARKS

Section 1321 was revised in its entirety in the 1997 edition by Code Change M1321-95-1 to expand the coverage regulating fuel-gas piping systems from that provided in the 1994 code by adding coverage for manufactured homes and recreational vehicles in parks.

GAS CONNECTOR VALVES

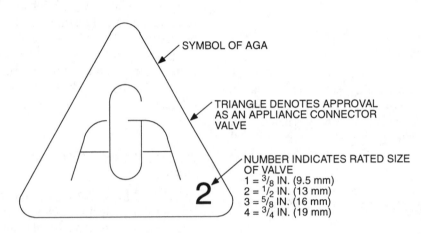

SYMBOL OF AGA

TRIANGLE DENOTES APPROVAL AS AN APPLIANCE CONNECTOR VALVE

NUMBER INDICATES RATED SIZE OF VALVE
1 = $^3/_8$ IN. (9.5 mm)
2 = $^1/_2$ IN. (13 mm)
3 = $^5/_8$ IN. (16 mm)
4 = $^3/_4$ IN. (19 mm)

**NOTE:** When factory installed with an approved connector, the triangle is omitted on the valve.

**FIGURE 13-1**

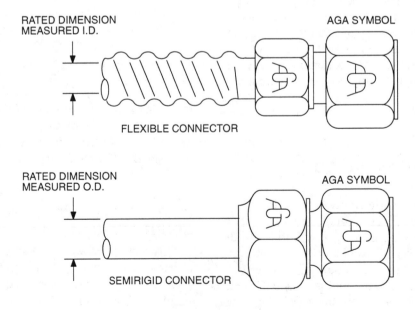

RATED DIMENSION MEASURED I.D.

AGA SYMBOL

FLEXIBLE CONNECTOR

RATED DIMENSION MEASURED O.D.

AGA SYMBOL

SEMIRIGID CONNECTOR

**FIGURE 13-2**

# Chapter 14
# SPECIAL PIPING AND STORAGE SYSTEMS

## SECTION 1401 — OIL-BURNING APPLIANCES

The standard recognized in Part III of Chapter 16 is Tank, Piping and Valves for Oil-Burning Appliances, Chapters 2 and 3 of NFPA 31-1978 entitled *Standard for the Installation of Oil-Burning Equipment*.

The title of Chapter 14 was Process Piping in the 1994 code. It was originally intended to establish correlation between the use and occupancy requirements in fabrication areas in a Group H, Division 6 or 7 Occupancy, and the requirements for piping or tubing that conveys liquid or gases that are used directly in research, laboratory or production processes and which are not regulated under either the Plumbing Code or the Mechanical Code. The end product of such activities is production of semiconductors that are intrinsically nonhazardous. UBC Section 307.11, Group H, Division 6 Occupancies, indicates that the life-safety hazards the code intended to protect against are the various manufacturing processes involved in fabricating semiconductors. The 1997 UBC has dropped the Group H, Division 7 Occupancy designation.

The definitions in 1994 UMC Section 1402 have been relocated to Chapter 2 in the 1997 edition. Otherwise, the 1994 provisions from the appendix appear unchanged in the 1997 code.

# Chapter 15
# SOLAR SYSTEMS

There are no mandatory requirements in Chapter 15. That is, Section 1501, Heat Source, is retained in Appendix B and hence remains as an option to be adopted as required.